Lifelong Learning and the New Educational Order

Second revised edition

John Field

Trentham Books

Stoke on Trent, UK and Sterling, USA

Trentham Books Limited
Westview House   22883 Quicksilver Drive
734 London Road   Sterling
Oakhill   VA 20166-2012
Stoke on Trent   USA
Staffordshire
England ST4 5NP

First published 2006

British Library Cataloguing-in-Publication Data
A catalogue record for this book is available from the
British Library

ISBN-13: 978-1-85856-346-6
ISBN-10: 1-85856-346-1

Designed and typeset by Trentham Print Design Ltd,
Chester and printed in Great Britain by Cromwell Press Ltd,
Trowbridge.

Contents

Acknowledgements

Many of the ideas in this book are not my own, originating and being developed in discussions with friends and colleagues. I owe particular thanks to Peter Alheit, John Berkeley, Joan Broader, Loraine Blaxter, Frank Coffield, Tom Collins, Kathryn Ecclestone, Richard Edwards, Martha Friedenthal-Haase, Christina Hughes, Ewart Keep, Klaus Künzel, Mieczyslaw Malewski, Barbara Merrill, Russell Moseley, Kaori Okumoto, Mike Osborne, Rosemary Preston, Michael Strain, Malcolm Tight and Ming-Lieh Wu. I have learned over many years from discussions with Julie Allan, Chris Duke, Tom Schuller and Alan Tuckett. Earlier versions of the argument were presented at seminars and conferences in a number of European countries, as well as Malaysia and Taiwan; the central lines of thought were aired during an inaugural lecture at the University of Warwick. I am grateful to comments from other participants, who have forced me to rethink my own ideas, and to the organisers for allowing me to rabbit on at their expense. For reasons which seem good enough to me, I sent the revised text for this edition to Trentham almost a year later than planned; my publishers have demonstrated the patience of secular saints.

Finally, let me acknowledge a rather significant debt to John Eggleston, who died shortly after the first edition appeared. In 1999, I bumped into John in a launch at a bookshop, and we spoke about the difficulty I was experiencing in turning my inaugural lecture into an article. John grinned over his glass of red wine and offered a solution to my problem: instead of shortening the paper for a journal, why not enlarge it into a book; and if a book, then he would like first refusal for Trentham. Among John's many other qualities, I always greatly admired his principled opportunism; you have the result in your hands.

Preface

L ifelong learning is a beautifully simple idea. It is obvious that people learn throughout their lives. From our earliest attempts to walk and talk, our capacity to adapt and learn extends through a remarkable variety of new abilities and knowledge, and it can be almost as unconscious as breathing. And while learning clearly has some connection with what goes on in schools and colleges, it is not limited to the planned instruction that these great institutions deliver. On the contrary: a lot of what is learned at school, though it may be very significant, has little or nothing to do with the official syllabus. So, since everybody knows how to learn, and most people seem to do it pretty effectively throughout their lives, why take up anyone's time with a book on the subject?

One reason is simply that so much time, effort and resources are being devoted to promoting the idea of lifelong learning as a solution to society's current ills. Since the first edition of this book appeared in 2000, we have seen a steady flow of official documents and policy statements on the subject, as well as a stream of programmes and materials that are intended to support learning activities throughout the lifespan. There are strong signs that this combined flood of official pronouncements and learning programmes is matched by growing evidence of a broad and general acceptance that a one-off dose of school and college will not serve to get you through life's many challenges and opportunities. And since 2000, we have also seen the publication of much scholarly research and critique on lifelong learning. While much of the research comes from Europe and Australasia, there has also been a growing contribution from other parts of the globe, plus a smaller body of work that is genuinely transnational in character. In preparing the second edition of this book, then, I have had no difficulty in finding new policy approaches, new bodies of evidence, and new and sometimes stimulating critiques.

Although so much is new in the second edition, I have kept the opening paragraph unchanged. I have certainly rewritten large sections of the book, partly in the light of new evidence, and partly in response to the lively debate that has gone on over lifelong learning since the first edition appeared in 2000. But my underlying argument is more or less the same, reflecting my long-standing concerns with the political economy of adult learning. A number of these concerns are personal. As someone who has experienced cheerfully the benefits of a second chance for adults (both I and my sister entered university as mature students), and then found work in the field of adult learning in the late 1970s, I am an unashamed advocate of lifelong learning. I think it is, by and large, a good thing. We need to do more of it, we need to make it much easier than it currently is, we need to look again at schools in the light of adult aspirations, and we need to value it much more. I think it really is that simple.

Yet I also see problems and difficulties. The first is definitional: isn't 'lifelong learning' rather a loose and all-encompassing term, stretching way too far to have much purchase on reality? Of course it is. By emphasising learning rather than education or teaching, the phrase does indeed draw attention to something that all of us do; often without even knowing that we are doing it, we learn new facts, skills, ideas and emotional capacities simply by virtue of enrolling with that permanently instructive institution, the University of Life. We learn from dialogue with friends and family, workmates and strangers; we learn by trying new things out, or looking over someone else's shoulder; we learn by watching television and reading books; we learn by browsing through record catalogues or surfing the internet; we learn by thinking and reflecting. Whether this learning is trivial or significant is a secondary issue. In this broad meaning of the term, you cannot stop yourself from being a lifelong learner. The phrase covers pretty much everything – and rightly so.

But lifelong learning is also a way of thinking about and structuring our society's approach to education. In this narrower sense, lifelong learning has been very fashionable in recent years, particularly among policy-makers.While I am delighted to see greater political interest in learning across the lifespan, this should also put us on our guard. In his foreword to the 1998 English white paper on lifelong learning, the Secretary of State for Education and Employment wrote movingly of the human development and growth that can arise from an open, enquiring, reflective approach to learning at any age:

To cope with rapid change and the challenge of the information and communication age, we must ensure that people can return to learning throughout their lives. We cannot rely on a small elite, no matter how highly educated or highly paid. Instead, we need the creativity, enterprise and scholarship of all our people. As well as securing our economic future, learning has a wider contribution. It helps make ours a civilised society, develops the spiritual side of our lives and promotes active citizenship. Learning enables people to play a full part in their community. It strengthens the family, the neighbourhood and consequently the nation. It helps us fulfil our potential and opens doors to a love of music, art and literature. That is why we value learning for its own sake as well as for the equality of opportunity it brings. (DfEE, 1998a, 7)

Such breadth is breathtakingly imaginative. Yet when subjected to closer inspection, much of the policy interest in lifelong learning has in fact been preoccupied with a rather narrower agenda, namely the development of a more productive and efficient workforce. In Britain and most other advanced nations, lifelong learning policies are mostly driven by a desire to raise the nation's economic competitiveness and improve its standard of living, defined in largely material terms. For evidence to support this argument, I refer you to the first two chapters of this book.

Sometimes, lifelong learning has been used by policy makers as little more than a modish repackaging of rather conventional policies for post-16 education and training, with little that is new or innovative. This tendency to wrap up existing practice in a more colourful phrase can also be seen in the rush by providers to claim their adherence to lifelong learning: annual reports, prospectuses, adult education brochures, and even professorial titles have all been subjected to this rebranding. And researchers have not been immune from these trends: many studies of adult learning have been published that refer to lifelong learning in the title, without much sign that the authors have reframed their focus and analysis in ways that reflect an important new conceptual framework. The educational result is a kind of linguistic hyperinflation, in which the term is constantly devalued, to the point where it might become intellectually worthless.

If this is such a loose expression, and so open to abuse, why keep it? I think there are at least four reasons for continuing to speak and write about lifelong learning. First, it is important to retain the aspirations that it embodies. The ability to learn continually throughout the lifespan is no less than a precondition for exercising

3

reasoned choices about our lives. As I argue here, we have no choice about the fact that we are faced throughout our lives with a multitude of choices. Yet much of our education and training system is still geared to the assumption that we face major choices only at easily defined points, most of them in the first phases of our lifespan – when we change school, leave school, enter university, embark on our first job, leave home, get married, start a family or retire, for instance. These may or may not be significant turning points in our lives, but they are no longer arranged in such a simple linear sequence as they once were, and in many learning lives such turning points are experienced repeatedly, in a variety of different sequences.

Given the constancy of change and readjustment in our life span, and even more the constant talk of change and flexibility, an ability to acquire new skills, ideas and aptitudes is not going to emancipate and empower on its own – but it is an absolute precondition. We see this reflected in individuals' behaviour, which is increasingly reflexive and conditional. There has been a silent explosion in informal and self-directed learning, sparked off by the frictions that people experience as a result of continuing transformations in their lives and their identities.

One central theme of this book is that the silent explosion in lifelong learning is that this is only partly driven by economic changes. If we are to understand the directions in which people channel their learning activities, we need to attend to the changing cultural, social and political circumstances in which people create meaning and experience transformation, not just the technological or organisational changes that they face in working life. In so far as the silent explosion is fuelled by economic factors, I suggest that consumption is as important as production in determining the way in which people are deciding to acquire new skills and capacities. But much of this takes place outside of the economic domain entirely; social and cultural forces are also increasingly important in determining the ways in which people behave as lifelong learners. If this analysis is accurate, the implications for the entire education and training system – and not solely the post-16 sectors – are tremendous.

My second reason for holding on to the concept of lifelong learning is a belief that, whatever the weaknesses and confusions of current policy, something new is under way. Lifelong learning is not a myth, a mish-mash, a fashion or a discourse. Or rather, it is not just any or all of those things, though even if it were it should still command some attention. At least two levels of analysis are required. One, conventionally enough, is the level at which we make sense of policy: we need to understand critically what policy-makers are doing, why they are doing it, how they are doing it, whom they involve, and with what consequences. Policy in turn needs to be understood both as a political process at system level, and also at the level of institutions and sub-systems.

Policy, though, is only part of the story. Lifelong learning as an expression has taken off partly because it points to patterns of behaviour that are now very widespread indeed. Everyone seems to have noticed that something new is afoot in the contemporary world. Journalists, managers and cultural critics routinely talk of the information society or the knowledge economy. In more exalted language, two of Europe's most respected social scientists, Anthony Giddens and Ulrich Beck, have made what they call 'reflexivity' a central part of their thinking: for both, late modernity is characterised by the requirement placed upon individuals and institutions to reflect upon what they know in order to make their choices about who they are and how they behave (Giddens, 1991; Beck, 1992). In short, continual learning has become a key defining characteristic of modernity – or, if you prefer, late modernity, post-modernity or hyper-modernity. Particularly in the first chapter, I explore further the relationship between this sociological concern with reflexivity and the general explosion of informal and self-directed learning that is undertaken by individuals in the course of their daily lives. Lifelong learning is what many of us do, more or less consciously, in order to pursue our everyday goals; the fact that we may not see it as learning is an important but second order issue.

Third, lifelong learning matters because it is now a mechanism for exclusion and control. As well as empowering people, it also creates new and powerful inequalities. This is a basic consequence of two key shifts: the move towards a knowledge-based economy and the general development of what we might, following Beck and Giddens, call reflexive individualisation. Both trends are presented in detail later in the book. In outline, I argue that in a knowledge-based economy, those who have the lowest levels of skill and the weakest capacity for constant updating are less and less likely to find paid employment, particularly of a sustainable and reasonably secure type. At the same time, trends towards reflexive individualisation mean that access to social support mechanisms – from immediate social relationships to welfare systems – is constantly being weakened or made conditional. Among other consequences, these tendencies are being expressed in a somewhat authoritarian and coercive discourse of training and development: those who will not upgrade their skills, it seems, do not deserve support from the rest of us. If anything, the period since the first edition appeared in 2000 has only served to provide further evidence of this broad tendency for lifelong learning to serve as the basis for what is largely accepted as legitimate inequality, and this worries me.

Fourth and last, the concept of lifelong learning is worth keeping because its linguistic reach can help provide a kind of intellectual forum, in which a variety of people with different perspectives and interests can engage in shared debate over something that matters. Language often divides: the use of unnecessarily convoluted jargon, for example, has precisely the function of excluding the uneducated plebs. This is not a complaint about the use of complex concepts, which can be very useful when they have a highly specialised meaning which helps us to understand the world around us. Readers will find that I use theories of reflexive modernisation in the book, for example, and I also quote a number of authors whose work is sometimes dense and intricate. My point is rather different, and it concerns the possibilities of democratic dialogue about the key challenges in people's lives. And this has presented me with the challenge of presenting a range of evidence and ideas, some of which are in truth complex, in what I hope is an accessible way.

Lifelong learning is a topic that interests a range of people, from sociologists and philosophers to pianists and plumbers, but it does not affect them all in precisely the same ways. As a kind of 'forum concept', it can allow for a vigorous debate between researchers, practitioners, the policy community and indeed adult learners, in which problems are identified and solutions proposed from a range of different disciplinary and professional and personal perspectives. Does this involve intellectual compromises? Of course it does – but these are nothing compared to the weasel concessions of conscious academic isolationism. Opportunities for researchers to make a difference are rare; we should take them when we can.

In its substance, the book is something of an extended essay. While some of it is drawn from my own research, large parts draw on the work of other scholars, or consider the ideas and experiences of policy-makers and professionals in the field. After a brief discussion of the key concepts and approaches used in the analysis, the first chapter considers the silent explosion in every day informal learning, and argues that our late modern world has effectively created a learning society, in that a refusal to acquire new ideas and skills is simply no longer an option. Perhaps to a fault, we will no longer tolerate the idea of doing things simply because this is how they were done in the past. More familiar territory, in the form of work-related learning, forms the core of the second chapter. I take a somewhat qualified view of the knowledge economy; we should remind ourselves that many people are still employed in routine and physically demanding labour, largely unaffected by the economic and technical changes of recent decades.

Similarly, I believe that some recent accounts of globalisation are wildly exaggerated. Much of the stress upon lifelong learning's value for economic growth seems to me misplaced. At best, it further heats up the process of linguistic hyperinflation. It makes more sense, I argue, to identify the ways in which ideas, information and skills are communicated between individuals and firms, and then build on these rather than directing the education and training system towards the short-term needs of employers. Those who lack skills and may be on the margins of the workforce form the central concern of the third chapter, which explores the impact of lifelong learning upon social inequality and exclusion. In the fourth chapter, I review the implications of my analysis for the education and training system. Most of the existing debate understands lifelong learning as the concern of post-school institutions and sub-sectors, and much of this chapter covers ground that is familiar to specialists. But attention here is also extended to the school and family as core sites for the generation of 'learning dispositions': that is to say, where we learn to learn – or, conversely, may learn how to resist the imposition of new skills and ideas. My interest includes the nature of the contract between institutionally-provided learning and the wide variety of informal everyday learning that is undertaken by individuals; my argument is that tendencies towards reflexive individualism suggest that publicly-funded provider institutions face considerable challenges if they are to retain anything of their present position. Partly for reasons of equity, and partly for reasons of public good – particularly for environmental reasons – I believe that they should rise constructively to these challenges.

The winds of change, it seems to me, are blowing in a favourable direction. One small sign of the level of interest in this subject is the fact that the book is appearing in its second edition. My central arguments remain unchanged, but I have reconsidered some issues in the light of subsequent developments. In what remains a fast-moving field of policy and practice, the world has moved on since the first edition was written, on the eve of the present millennium. Some practices, which seemed exciting or important in the 1990s, seem to have exhausted their potential rather more rapidly than I had anticipated, while others continue to show promise and generate enthusiasm among professionals and learners alike. Policy likewise has continued to evolve from the heady days of the late 1990s. Britain's New Labour government was one of those who embraced lifelong learning in the mid-1990s, and here as elsewhere there has been ample opportunity to put new policies to the test of time.

And my colleagues in the academic community have been busy studying and writing about lifelong learning; this includes an impressive number of research students. While I have benefitted from some of the theoretical literature in revising the book, I have also been struck by the increasing volume and quality of empirical evidence appearing in recent years. After completing a series of empirical studies of social capital and adult learning, I have also acquired new interests and insights, and have drawn on these in the second edition. This growing body of empirical and theoretical research in itself reflects growing interest – and ability – of scholars in this area, but it is also a consequence of decisions to allocate resources to researching lifelong learning. All these developments seem to me grounds for optimism about the future, at least for the foreseeable future.

1

Lifelong learning:
a design for the future?

Lifelong learning – that is, the recognition that learning may stretch out across a lifetime – is the new educational reality. All around, politicians and others are repeatedly warning that knowledge is the most important source of future advantage. In this case, politicians are simply restating what virtually everyone believes: one European Union study showed that in every country, an overwhelming majority saw lifelong learning as important for all citizens, and not only for the young or even those in their middle years (Centre européenne pour la développement de la formation professionelle 2003, 5-7). The human brain is taken to constitute a new 'grey capital' to be set alongside the more familiar resources of land, labour and finance. Human capital, uniquely, is a resource that anyone may use and renew, entirely sustainably, throughout each individual's lifespan. May use and renew – and at the same time, must use and renew.

Knowledge is highly marketable, though it is not always clear whether it is being sold as commodity or brand image. So faddish is the talk about a knowledge society that Laurence Prusack felt obliged to introduce a collection of papers from the Organisation for Economic Co-operation and Development with the blunt question:

> Is it yet another one of the multitudinous management enthusiasms that seem to come and go with the frequency of some random natural phenomena? We don't think so ... there is no sustainable advantage other than what a firm knows, how it can utilise what it knows, and how fast it can learn something new! (Prusack, 1998, ix).

Some American corporations have appointed a Vice President for Intellectual Capital, others a Chief Knowledge Officer. And what holds true for firms also holds true, it seems, for nations. Plucking one example from a multitude on offer, one government advisory committee recently claimed that Britain suffers a significant competitive disadvantages by 'failing to utilise the full potential of our whole workforce' (DfEE 2000, 6). In all the advanced nations, business has successfully lobbied government to extend the scope of copyright protection and patentability; the most advanced knowledge economies – particularly the USA, of course – have pursued intellectual property protection globally, through agreements and institutions such as the World International Property Organisation. The learning age, then, is characterised not simply by the need for good, old-fashioned investment in skills and knowledge, but by the primacy of knowledge – and this now applies not to a small minority of skilled workers or specialised professionals but to 'our whole workforce'.

Much of this policy imperative has become commonplace. Conventionally, the new stress on knowledge is seen as the more or less natural outcome of the dramatic economic and technological changes that have overwhelmed the entire world system since the 1960s. It is certainly true that we have seen the convergence of a series of scientific and technological innovations to constitute a new technological paradigm. While virtually every area of human life has been affected, the most dramatic of these innovations have occurred in microelectronics: the inventions of the transistor (1947), the integrated circuit (1957), the planar process (1959) and the microprocessor (1971) were in turn applied together to revolutionise information processing, and were further enhanced and extended by such fundamental innovations as laser technology, superconductors, optical fibre and renewable energy sources; in turn, they made possible further innovation in fields with such far-flung ramifications as biotechnology (Castells, 1989, 12). What these changes have in common, Castells believes, is that they have revolutionised humanity's ability to manipulate information and to apply the results across a wide range of human activity.

These are dramatic changes. They have profoundly influenced most people's lives, and they have reshaped the environment in which industry and services function. By underpinning a process of constant innovation and change, their consequences for our learning needs are indeed profound and far-reaching. And they are not the only factors involved in the shift towards lifelong learning – and may even not be the most important ones. As well as these large scale and somewhat abstract economic and technological changes, we also face a whole series of intimate and often small scale demands for change and adaptability, rooted as much in our daily lives as in the global ebb and flow of government, economy and science. Yet public policy tends to be driven, globally, by largely economic concerns: competitiveness, rather than citizenship, is the primary focus for policy.

Lifelong learning: a global policy consensus

During the 1990s, lifelong learning emerged onto the policy scene with the suddenness of a new fashion. In a slightly different formulation (lifelong education), the idea was widely touted in the early 1970s, and it briefly won a degree of political favour. Although the debate over lifelong education had some influence on government behaviour, particularly in Sweden, its main power base lay in the relatively innocuous world of intergovernmental think tanks such as UNESCO and the OECD (Knoll, 1998). It then re-emerged in the labyrinthine policy corridors of the European Commission, where it formed one of the cornerstones of Jacques Delors' white paper on competitiveness and economic growth (Commission of the European Communities (CEC, 1994). When the Commission subsequently declared 1996 to be the European Year of Lifelong Learning, the idea rapidly re-entered the mainstream political vocabulary, but with an intriguing linguistic shift: rather than lifelong education, as in the 1970s, all the talk was now of lifelong learning.

Britain offers an instructive example of the speed with which this process occurred. In 1997, the incoming Labour government appointed Dr Kim Howells as the country's first Minister of Lifelong Learning. In the following year, separate Green Papers outlined proposals for Wales, Scotland and England, followed by a White Paper (*Learning to Succeed*) for post-16 education and training in England. An Advisory Group for Continuing Education and Lifelong Learning, created in early 1998, produced two wide-ranging reports on future policy developments (Fryer, 1998; Fryer, 1999). A series of policy initiatives then followed, some of them designed to lift levels of demand for learning among adults – especially among people who had few if any formal qualifications from previous training and education – and some of them intended to refashion the supply of educational and training opportunities to adults (Taylor, 2005).

Britain was hardly alone in this development. As well as organising its Year of Lifelong Learning, the European Commission published

11

its own white paper on education and training subtitled 'Towards a Learning Society' (CEC, 1995). Five years later, at its Lisbon meeting, the European Council set the EU the ten-year target of becoming 'the most competitive and dynamic knowledge-based society in the world'; among the first steps taken by the European Commission was the publication of a *Memorandum on Lifelong Learning* (CEC, 2000). In its mid-term review of the Lisbon strategy, the European summit – now enlarged to 25 member states – placed the main emphasis for achieving these goals on knowledge, innovation and human capital (Jones, 2005, 253). Elsewhere, Taiwan had already adopted lifelong learning as the core of its Five Year Plan for the Development and Improvement of Adult Education, which was adopted in 1996 following debates at the Seventh National Con- ference on Education in 1994 (Wu, 2000, 106-9). While the EU was marking its European Year of Lifelong Learning, UNESCO asked Jacques Delors to chair a commission on education and training, whose report elaborated on the arguments that its chair had already outlined while President of the European Commission (Delors, 1996). Lifelong learning policy papers have also appeared from the Dutch, German, Norwegian, Finnish and Irish governments (Ministry of Culture, Education and Science, 1998; Department of Education and Science, 1998; Dohmen, 1996; Dohmen, 1998). The phrase lifelong learning has become – not only in Europe but in several nations – a convenient political shorthand for the modernis- ing of education and training systems.

How did this happen? A number of writers have traced the genesis of the concept back to the intellectual ferment of the late 1960s, which perhaps influenced educational thinking more than any other area of public policy (Boshier, 1998; Knoll, 1998; Okumoto, 2004; Wu, 2000). Like many 1960s ideas, it drew both on the radical thinking of the student movement and on the post-industrial rhetoric of future- gazers like Alvin Toffler, whose apocalyptic warnings of 'mass dis- orientation' posed a direct challenge to educational planners. No doubt the early slowing down of the relatively high economic growth rates of the post-war decades also had something to do with the re- thinking of educational priorities and institutions.

But discussions of lifelong learning predated the upsurge of interest in the late 1960s and early 1970s. The idea itself can be traced back to the intellectual ferment that followed the end of World War One; influenced by the active debate over the extension of citizenship rights to women and to working class men, as well as by such inter- national developments as the Bolshevik Revolution in Russia, an official committee in Britain argued in 1919 that

> Adult education must not be regarded as a luxury for a few excep-
> tional persons here and there, nor as a thing which concerns only a
> short span of early adulthood, but it is a permanent national neces-
> sity, an inseparable aspect of citizenship, and therefore should be
> both universal and lifelong. (Adult Education Committee of the
> Ministry of Reconstruction, 1919, 5)

Subsequently, one of the committee's officials, Basil Yeaxlee of the
Young Men's Christian Association, spoke of the growing demand for
'education as a lifelong process' (Yeaxlee, 1920, 25). However, the
1919 report was rapidly overtaken by events; while it represented a
broadly liberal consensus on citizenship, in the climate of economic
crisis combined with labour unrest, this vision was not especially
attractive either to organised labour or to an increasingly conservative middle class. And although the education and training of
adults were an increasingly important focus for policy and provision, they remained somewhat on the margins of a system whose
main purpose remained the socialisation of the young. Only in the
early 1970s did the idea really start to penetrate the starched world
of educational policy-making.

The debates of the 1970s were both far-reaching and, in the long
term, influential. Characteristically, the debates over lifelong learning tended to be the preserve of educational specialists meeting in
the framework of intergovernmental bodies such as the United
Nations Educational, Social and Cultural Organisation (UNESCO)
and the Organisation for Economic Co-operation and Development
(OECD). UNESCO in particular fostered a global debate, leading to
the 1972 publication of *Learning to Be*, the report of an international
committee of experts chaired by Edgar Faure, a former French Prime
Minister and Minister of Education (Faure, 1972). As a public state-
ment on the principles of lifelong education – more rarely, at this
stage, lifelong learning – the Faure report was a turning point. Its
essential humanistic concern was with achieving the 'fulfilment of
man' through flexible organisation of the different stages of education, through widening access to higher levels of education, through
recognition of informal and non-formal as well as formal learning,
and through what were then new curricular concerns such as health
education, cultural education and environmental education.
Education, in UNESCO's view, should last the whole life for all
individuals and not just be tacked on to school or university for a
privileged or specialised few. A broad and visionary manifesto, in
Joachim Knoll's words, *Learning to Be* served to 'initiate an
optimistic phase of international educational policy and reform,

and also as the beginning of the debate over lifelong education'
(Knoll, 1998, 38; emphasis in original; see also Borg and Mayo, 2005,
259-60).

OECD's contribution was couched more in terms of human capital
thinking, albeit laced with more than a few dashes of radical
humanism. In a series of studies, OECD tried to develop policy
instruments for what it called 'recurrent education', the aim of which
was to provide governments with practical ways of realising lifelong
education (OECD, 1973). Typical of these instruments was the pro-
posal for paid educational leave (PEL), to sit alongside statutory
entitlements for paid holidays (the German and French terms for
PEL translate pretty much as education holidays). PEL, it was
argued, would promote a learning culture for all, helping to promote
both increased competitiveness and greater social equality (OECD,
1973). Legislation on PEL was subsequently introduced in Sweden
and in several of the German Länder, and a similar approach was
adopted in France in the form of the 1971 law on continuing education. These initiatives were, moreover, watched closely and with
some sympathy elsewhere. In practice, the experience took somewhat different directions from those anticipated, not least in the
relatively low numbers of participants compared with the total of
those who were legally eligible, and in the drift away from continued
training and education towards short, consumer-oriented activities
such as study tours that were allegedly light on the study side
(Nuissl, 1988). PEL was born at a time when the OECD's member
states were toying with the idea of industrial democracy as a way of
integrating trade unions into an industrial order that was embarking
on a process of technologically-induced adaptation and change.
After the large-scale labour unrest of the late sixties and early seven-
ties came to an end, and unemployment figures started to rise, talk
of industrial democracy faded, and PEL lost much of its impetus
(Field, 1988).

Other than PEL, concrete policy developments were relatively rare.
Adult educators found legitimation in the new concept and its es-
pousal in such reputable quarters (Gustavsson, 1995, 90). And
indeed some nations – notably Sweden – expanded their expenditure on adult education. In Britain, the Russell Committee was
appointed to advise the government on its policies for adult education; while rather uninspiring in its recommendations, the committee did support the creation of a small number of new agencies
to promote particular types of provision such as basic literacy teaching and residential adult education (Department of Education and

Science, 1973). Yet taken together the cumulative impact of the early debate was muffled and diffuse.

It is not that there was any lack of specific policy proposals to supplement the work of OECD and UNESCO. In terms of practical developments, though, relatively little was achieved as a direct outcome of the debate over lifelong education. In Britain, a new Adult Literacy Resources Agency was created, initially as a unit within the National Institute for Adult Education in England and Wales, and a parallel agency was established in Scotland; a new residential adult college was opened, in Barnsley (though this owed more to the support of the South Yorkshire local authorities than to interest on the part of national government); there were some relatively small scale initiatives in fields such as guidance and multi-cultural education. And that was about it. The early debate over life-long education was rapidly overtaken by events, and in particular by the onset of the 1973 oil crisis which precipitated a decade or more of rising unemployment levels in the West, along with a drift away from the consensus around the post-1945 welfare settlement. In Britain, James Callaghan's minority Labour administration was plagued by industrial unrest as well as by rising youth unemploy-ment. Its educational priorities were broadly reflected in Callaghan's 1976 speech at Ruskin College, which called for schools to pay greater attention to the preparation of young people for the world of work. Nor was adult education exempt from these pressures, parti-cularly as the experience of unemployment started to spread from young people to the adult workforce (McGivney and Sims, 1986) at a time when local authorities found themselves under pressure to re-duce spending on non-statutory services. The broadly humanistic ideals that had inspired Faure and his followers were replaced by what the government's left-wing critics called 'the new vocationa-lism'.

For much of the 1980s, the international and intergovernmental bodies found relatively little to say on the topic. Tackling unemploy-ment replaced earlier preoccupations as the central task for adult education and training. However, they returned to it in the 1990s with renewed vigour, with key policy texts appearing from the Euro-pean Commission (CEC, 1995), OECD (OECD, 1996), UNESCO (Delors, 1996) and the Group of Eight industrial nations (Group of Eight, 1999). There is little need to summarise these papers in detail, as in essence they all said much the same.

The European Commission's white paper on education and training blended the visionary with the practical. Coming as it did towards

the end of the Delors presidency of the commission, its main function was to propose ways of bringing education and training in line
with the requirements of the single European market, whose com-
pletion in 1992 in many ways marked the high point of the Euro-
peanisation process. The Commission's diagnosis was simplicity
itself: the European Union was faced by the threats and opportunities of globalisation, information technology and the application of science. If they were going to stand up to Asia and the USA,
the EU's member states had to pool some of their sovereignty and
resources, in education and training as in other policy areas; this
would also help develop a sense of European citizenship and foster
social inclusion. The central role of lifelong learning had already
been flagged in the commission's 1994 White Paper on competitiveness:

> Preparation for life in tomorrow's world cannot be satisfied by a
> once-and-for-all acquisition of knowledge and know-how ... All
> measures must therefore necessarily be based on the concept of
> developing, generalising and systematising lifelong learning and
> continuing training (CEC, 1994, 16, 136).

The subsequent education and training white paper offered the
same message, as did UNESCO's 1996 report.

Prepared during the build-up to its 1997 world conference on
education, the UNESCO report was drafted by an international
commission chaired by Jacques Delors, the recently-retired president of the European Commission. Its strong emphasis on the role
of non-governmental organisations (NGOs) in promoting lifelong
learning – an angle that is common to a wide range of UNESCO
policy discussions – set it apart from both the OECD and EU positions (Delors 1996). Otherwise, despite an occasional radicalism of
language, it said little in substance that was new or different.

With regard to its influence, OECD stands somewhere between the
EU's policy institutions and UNESCO. Its function is concerned
almost entirely with the critique and development of policy in
various areas, primarily but not exclusively relating to the effects of
these policies on the global economy. Since its membership consists
of the world's wealthier nations (chiefly but not exclusively Western),
since its main audience consists of relatively senior policy-makers,
and since much of its work results in inter-ministerial debates, the
OECD has influence, if not – as does the EU – direct power.

Throughout the 1980s and 1990s, the OECD pursued the goal of
supporting governments in 'encouraging macro-economic

stabilisation, structural adjustment and the globalisation of production and distribution', while secondarily paying attention to the preservation of 'social cohesion' (Miller, 1997, 24). It was in this context that OECD convened its 1996 meeting of education ministers under the title of 'Lifelong Learning for All'. Once more, an emphasis on lifelong learning was justified by reference to global competitive pressures and the changes being wrought by science and the new teachnologies. However, OECD went somewhat further in its interests than either UNESCO or the EU. Taking lifelong learning to mean 'the continuation of conscious learning throughout the lifespan', OECD emphasised that this must embrace learning undertaken 'informally at work, by talking to others, by watching television and playing games, and through virtually every other form of human activity' (OECD, 1996, 89). This was reflected in the weight attached by OECD to the building of links between informal learning and the formal education and training system.

Certainly among the intergovernmental agencies, then, the policy consensus in favour of lifelong learning is virtually unanimous. National governments too, certainly among the more prosperous nations, have generally moved in much the same direction. Lifelong learning has even featured, positively, in Anthony Giddens' attempt to provide a theoretical backdrop for the entry of 'Third Way' politics onto the stage of European social democracy (Giddens 1998). If lifelong learning is so widely regarded both as desirable and as a legitimate focus for government intervention, we may well ask the question: what is actually happening?

The changing course of life and the new learning challenges

It is common to complain that lifelong learning is little but 'human resource development (HRD) in drag' (Boshier, 1998, 4). And certainly it is true that so far as policy making is concerned, the debate has been largely driven by economic preoccupations. Significantly, some of the leading proponents of lifelong learning have come in recent years from such temples of human capital thinking as the Organisation for Economic Co-operation and Development (OECD) and the European Commission, where lifelong learning is regarded primarily as a source of competitive advantage. Marred by its narrow vocationalism, this dominant policy-led definition of lifelong learning has rightly been criticised by those who seek a more humanistic approach. Moreover, as I argue later, it underestimates the extraordinary level of change in areas of life other than the economic. Social

17

transformation processes have arguably been at least as rapid and far-reaching in recent years as economic change, with highly significant consequences for learning. Some have gone further still, such as Peter Alheit who pointedly asks whether it is 'ultimately our own life *programme* that has changed – the biographical construc- tions that *reflexive modernity* ... compels us to adopt?' (Alheit 1999, 66). We might add that while policy debate has tended to focus largely on the economic dimensions of lifelong learning, most academic and theoretical debate has presented lifelong learning overwhelmingly as emancipatory; this pattern, Bagnall rightly notes, is something that most of the academic critics of lifelong learning have managed to overlook (Bagnall, 2005).

Accepting these important qualifications, we cannot help but con- clude that the transformation of work in modern society has been profound. The implications for education and training – potential as well as actual – are far-reaching. The very meaning of work itself is changing. First, most people spend much less time on it than they used to, creating time that has to be used in other ways (and which often calls on us to exercise a degree of choice). In the nineteenth century, work took up most of the waking day, every day but Sunday; by 1906, it is estimated that the average working year took up some 2,900 hours; this had fallen by 1946 to 2,440 hours; by 1988 it had dropped to 1,800 hours (Hall, 1999, 427). This shift was uneven in its impact, of course, and nowhere more so than in respect of gender. While male workers have over the long run spent less and less of their time on their paid work, the reverse has been true for most women, who usually have to combine paid work with other tasks (often associated with caring responsibilities).

Secondly, occupations are becoming less stable and predictable. Some individuals are thrown out of their occupation by redundancy or closure, while others constantly opt to switch careers, and yet others work sporadically or on a part-time basis for parts of their working lives (Arthur *et al*, 1999, 29-37). Inevitably, work is losing some of its central role in determining one's identity. After the indus- trial revolution swept through the Western world, people's jobs be- came bound up centrally with who they were. At the time, many social commentators thought that this was itself emancipating. They contrasted the inherited status of feudalism, where identity was ascribed at birth, with the 'achieved status' of industrial capital- ism, where occupation determined one's position in the social hier- archy. This was predominantly a male phenomenon but not exclu- sively so; the domestic servant's status could be stamped powerfully on the self-image of women who worked 'below stairs', for example.

This profound association between job and identity was not limited to the individual subject. It also came to dominate much of Western European and Australasian politics, as organised labour – political parties, trade unions, co-operatives – came to stand for the collective interests of the working class as a whole. In much of Europe, there were also distinctive political parties representing farmers (such as the Danish Venstre), as well as parties whose supporters came chiefly from the middle class. Now, however, it is no longer a surprise for car workers to vote conservative (or in some countries, for the radical right) and lawyers or estate agents to vote for parties of the left, while increasing numbers of citizens from all social backgrounds do not bother to vote at all.

It is not that work has lost its role as both an external marker and a source of self-identity. On the contrary, it remains a significant force in both respects. But many people now spend more of their lifetime out of the labour force than in it, and not just because they spend ever longer periods in the initial education system and then retire at an earlier age than in the past. Average life expectancies are still growing, even though they have increased considerably over the past century. In Britain, for example, average life expectancies rose by around 30 years during the twentieth century. But work is increasingly accompanied by a plurality of competing sources of identity.

For many people, identity may draw on group qualities such as generation, gender and ethnicity, as well as on largely self-selected sources of identity such as life-style. For it is not only work that has destroyed the predictability of life's critical stages. Marriage is not necessarily a once-for-all, linear stage; the family may be more of a convoy, made up of children from several different pairs – or, increasingly in Europe, no children at all – than a nest; friendships similarly may be strung out over time and space as a result of individual mobility (Pahl and Spencer, 1997). For the first time in history people in the developed world spend more of their lives as the offspring of parents who are still living than as the parents of young children, who we are now likely to see growing into mature and even retired adults themselves. Even those who retain a single partner and conventional career are faced with 'risk situations' which demand that they think about and weigh up alternatives, with no certainty that they are making the correct decision (Beck, 1992).

All of us face constant discontinuities in our life course. And we face them in ways that often seem to leave us relying largely on our own resources. Social changes have eroded the traditional social networks from which earlier generations might have taken support and comfort; in their place are networks that are more open, fluid and ephemeral – and also more unpredictable and unreliable. Social changes have also reduced the relevance of older role models, so that we rarely make choices by identifying what someone like our fathers or mothers might have done, but must instead consider a plethora of alternative models of behaviour – some of them ex-perienced only fleetingly and at a distance, through television or a newspaper. We face a multitude of daily challenges, and they come in such fresh and varied forms that our life needs seem to corres-pond ever less closely to a set of standardised, ready-made and formulaic solutions. Often the options seem almost endless. A host of 'authorities' are competing for our attention, and anyway expert advice is often contradictory and later turns out to be wrong. In these circumstances, as sociologist Anthony Giddens has put it, 'self-identity becomes a reflexively organised endeavour ... which con-sists in the sustaining of coherent, yet continuously revised, bio-graphical narratives' (Giddens, 1991, 5).

This process can be readily illustrated with reference to theories about the life cycle. In 1976, Gail Sheehy published a best-seller called *Passages*, with the revealing subtitle: 'predictable crises of adult life' (Sheehy, 1976). In this book, which topped the paperback list in both the USA and Britain, she outlined the different stages of the life cycle, along with the characteristic challenges and oppor-tunities that went with each stage. Drawing upon the work of researchers in the field of social psychology, Sheehy interviewed 115 adults with a view to establishing whether there were common patterns in the ways adult personalities developed and changed over time; she was particularly interested in identifying moments of predictable crisis for couples. Examples included the move into the adult world that occurred with marriage, home-building and con-solidation of a career goal; then followed the search for stability as career progressed, children went to school and both partners re-appraised the relationship (leading to possible separation and even remarriage); and so forth. Perhaps this picture was already a little out of date when Sheehy was writing, but its international reception showed that it touched a nerve: people saw themselves in her arche-types, and they wanted to see whether they could learn from her diagnosis in ways that might help them plan their own lives.

By the 1990s, this picture of the world had lost much of its magnetic power. Twenty years after *Passages*, Sheehy wrote a new book trying to show the ways in which boundaries between age and life stage had become jumbled up and stretched out and pluralised, so that there was no saying when any individual might expect to find a job, get married, have children, build a career, and retire – or even whether they did these things at all (Sheehy, 1996). Despite the best efforts of Sheehy and her publishers, this book by no means reached the international best seller status of its predecessor.

Why has Sheehy's approach lost so much appeal? The answer is that, far from being a sequence of 'predictable crises', individual bio-graphies are increasingly diverse and heterogeneous (Alheit, 1992, 186-8). The phases of adult life have started to overlap and stretch: entrance to the labour market is no longer the fate of an entire cohort of (generally male) school leavers, but is stretched out by ever-lengthening periods of 'stopping on' at school, college or university, which in turn are frequently combined with part-time and even full-time employment. Family life, if never quite as simple as some claimed, is considerably more complex, and individual trajectories through different family forms and arrangements are much more pluralistic and varied. Relations of authority have also changed, within even the most traditional families. Not only has patriarchy come under a sustained challenge, but popular teen and child-oriented media and children's advocacy bodies alike explicitly 'encourage children to take a more active role in shaping the con-ditions and possibilities of making a satisfactory life in their own family' (Strain, 2000). At quite another stage of the lifespan, retire-ment no longer occurs for all at the same age, but can be 'early' or can be delayed; what is certain is that many people spend a greater proportion of their lives in retirement, not least because people now live longer. Biography no longer revolves around work in the way it once did, especially for men. Some even argue that individuals must now construct their own biography; even the meaning they attach to it is increasingly self-generated. It is in this context that Peter Alheit has written of *Bastelbiografie* – the do-it-yourself biography (Alheit, 1994).

Sheehy's fate was particularly resonant for the field of education. Much of the theory of adult education, largely developed in the United States by Malcolm Knowles and others, drew heavily upon life cycle theory. Knowles, for example, developed his account of andragogy through a stage-based analysis of the adult life course (Knowles, 1983). Designed as a way of helping adult educators to develop the 'art and science of teaching adults', the concept of andragogy was enormously influential as a way of conceptualising what it was that distinguished adult education from the education of children (or pedagogy, in Knowles' terms). The breakdown of a straightforward chronological, stage-based model of the life course in turn undermined the dominant conceptual frameworks that had shaped the discourse and assumptions of Western adult education professionals.

Little wonder, then, that adult educators have responded with ambivalence to the growing policy clamour over lifelong learning. On the one hand, lifelong learning appears as a gallant prince, set to rescue the adult education Cinderella from a long life of neglect on the margins of education policy. The grounds for enthusiasm have been well summed up by an eminent and highly experienced Northern Ireland adult educator:

> Sometimes an idea comes along and, even before it has been understood, it communicates an excitement, a sense that it can help us see the world in a different way. Lifelong learning has been like that ... Suddenly, we're fashionable. (Nolan, 1999, 4)

On the other hand, the lifelong learning debate appears to threaten the existing adult education structures, not only because it is so clearly dominated by economic and vocational concerns, but also because it celebrates and promotes a fragmented and distributed view of learning. If we all learn all the time, then responsibility for promoting learning lies not with a small group of readily identifiable specialists but with a vast range of people who might at some time shape the environments in which adults undertake their learning (Edwards, 1997). As the Scottish Health Education Board has recognised in the case of health promoters, many of those who support adult learning may not even be aware that they are doing so, and certainly do not regard this as their primary function (HEBS, 1997). If Knowles' concept of andragogy provided a comforting theoretical underpinning for the idea of a specialised adult education profession, the idea of lifelong learning shatters the role of supporting learners into a thousand fragments.

Education and the learning society

What does all this mean for the future of the education and training system? Today's system is, after all, the product of the Enlightenment – that cluster of processes of urbanisation, industrialisation and intellectual discovery that hit large parts of Europe and North America in the late eighteenth and early nineteenth centuries. Yet today this arrangement looks remarkably similar in its basic framework across virtually the entire world (Adick, 1992), and can be seen as an enduring keystone of modernity. Jürgen Habermas appears to take great pleasure in pointing out that in attacking the intellectual inheritance of the Enlightenment, even the post-modernists invariably use the very procedures of logic and debate that have been characteristic of modern thought ever since (Habermas, 1985). It might also be said that the postmodernists are postmodernists because of their socialisation in the educational institutions of modernity, where they are now more or less happily employed. Yet while the potential of modernity is far from being exhausted, the very achievements of modernity are placing the existing education and training system under enormous pressure. Three key factors in particular appear to be driving the desire for change: the ever-increasing speed with which knowledge is applied to practice; the ever-greater capacity of new technologies to process and transmit information; and the powerful impact of globalising tendencies.

The first point of reference in the contemporary debate is the increased economic and social importance of knowledge. So significant are scientific, technological and other information and ideas in the contemporary world that some believe that we have left behind the industrial and agricultural phases of our history, and now live in 'the knowledge society'. Manuel Castells, one of the most eloquent exponents of this approach, prefers to speak of 'the informational society', whose key distinguishing characteristic is, he believes, 'that here knowledge intervenes upon knowledge itself in order to generate higher productivity' (Castells, 1989, 10). In a parallel development, researchers have also elaborated new theories of learning, which emphasise that it is not simply a passive absorption of information, but rather an active process in which people construct knowledge and understanding, usually in cooperation with others who may not themselves be teachers. Learning is, then, increasingly seen as a participatory process, involving continuing reworkings of meaning and knowledge (Lave and Wenger, 1991; Jarvis et al, 1998; Felstead et al, 2004). It is in this broader conceptual sense that terms such as knowledge society, information society or learning society really do have some degree of analytical purchase. If these terms are accurate descriptions of reality, then we stand on the threshold of a new set of social arrangements.

It is vital not to be overwhelmed by rhetoric. Just what these terms mean is not always clear, and their usage varies quite considerably. Some commentators, such as Ronald Barnett, speak of the 'knowledge society' as being confined to the 'post-industrial' societies of the West, who have abandoned manufacturing to the developing countries (who in turn are also investing heavily in human capital). In language that reminds the reader of the Marxist distinction between (economic) base and (ideological) superstructure, Barnett suggests that 'Knowledge has become so important to modern society that, if it has not yet become the base itself, it is at least definitely integrated with it' (Barnett, 1990, 67). For Castells, on the other hand, knowledge has become a powerful force of internationalisation, affecting all nations (albeit unevenly) and drawing them into an interlocking, networked flow of information and production (Castells, 1989, 126-45).

The supposed primacy of knowledge has itself become something of a fashionable concept. Among other practical consequences, it has spawned the sub-discipline of knowledge management – which, ultimately, might be viewed as an attempt to ensure that an organisation is able to exploit the entire potential range of information, skills and ideas held by its individual members. In practice, the field of knowledge management has come to be dominated largely by IT systems experts, and in particular with the introduction of new interactive tools such as groupware and intranets. But it is also attracting growing attention from human resources professionals (Scarbrough, 1999, 68), as well as from policy-makers and their advisers (Social Exclusion Unit, 2000).

Moreover, the dominance of knowledge is not without contradictions. Most obvious is the proliferation of sources of expertise, and an accompanying (and partly related) decline in lay deference towards experts. Both tendencies are made visible in television's enthusiasm for audience discussion programmes in which 'ordinary people' – usually represented by the host – can hold experts to account (Livingstone and Lunt, 1991). 'The Weakest Link' offers a rather complicated example of this: Anne Robinson, the UK host of what has now become a global quiz show, became infamous for her rudeness to competitors who got the answers wrong. Was she mocking ordinary people who simply got something wrong? Or was she rather representing ordinary people's frustration at the complacency of people who thought it clever to be dumb?

For policy-makers seeking to develop effective strategies for competition in the knowledge economy, such concerns are marginal. Drawing a contrast with the investments in plant and machinery that inspired the industrial revolution, one recent UK policy paper asserted that

> The information and knowledge-based revolution of the twenty-first century will be built on a very different foundation – investment in the intellect and creativity of people ... We will succeed by transforming inventions into new wealth, just as we did a hundred years ago. But unlike then, everyone must have the opportunity to innovate and gain rewards – not just in research laboratories. (DfEE, 1998a, 9-10).

The unskilled, unqualified and uneducated, it seems, are not only likely to face diminishing opportunities themselves; they also become a millstone, holding back the application of knowledge and preventing the educated and creative majority from enjoying to the full the accessible fruits of the knowledge society.

If the first reference point is the new role of knowledge in general, the second is the remarkable impact of new information and communications technologies (ICTs). It is not simply that the technologies themselves have evolved rapidly which is so momentous, nor even the multitude of uses to which they may be put, but also the extent to which convergence between different technologies has multiplied their consequences and proliferated new applications. One obvious example is the convergence between telephony, broadcasting and internet systems, which has in turn transformed a range of business processes as well as introducing new domestic entertainment media and communications systems. This poses stark questions about who has ready access to the new ICTs and who has at best only restricted and partial access: citizenship of the information society is conditional upon the availability of the technologies.

Training and education are directly affected by the pace of change in ICTs, since many of the new technologies have been adapted to support learning activities. But the more important consequences of the new ICTs arise from their impact on other areas of life. In particular, their application in industry and services is driving much of the new agenda for lifelong learning. Across the world, governments and corporations are fearful that innovations arising from new applications of the new technologies will leave them stranded, while competitors race ahead. For governments, the solution is blindingly obvious. Hardly a single policy paper emerges from the European Commission on education and training that does not refer to the need to build a European information society, frequently buttressing the argument by warning of a real or future crisis for European society (Field, 1998, 174-82). Once more, the implications for education and training are generally held to be dramatic.

Some enthusiasts believe that the new technologies are inherently liberating. As one enthusiast said about the internet: 'Here suddenly was a medium where the readers could be writers, the kids could be as smart as the suits, boundaries crossed readily, hierarchies challenged, new collaborations formed. Such nice people too' (Wilcox, 1998). More commonly, though, the new ICTs are viewed with some concern. In its report on the 'information society', the European Commission warned that 'The information society represents the most fundamental change in our time, with enormous opportunities for society as a whole but with risks for individuals and regions' (CEC, 1996a, 28).

Part of the Commission's concern arose from a powerful sense of backwardness in comparison with Japan and the USA, and part from an opportunistic recognition that talk of crisis is a good way of persuading member states to support European policies. There were also internal worries about the effects of ICTs in displacing not only manual labour but also some white collar and professional occupations. In 1996, a European Commission working party noted that 'in many countries' the introduction of new ICTs was 'widening traditional zones of job-insecurity to include the middle classes' (Information Society Forum, 1996, 19). Again, the logical consequences were straightforward:

> The pace of change is becoming so fast that people can only adapt if the Information Society becomes the 'Lifelong Learning Society'. In order to build and maintain competitive economic advantages, skills and talents must be constantly reshaped to meet the changing needs of the work place, wherever that is. (Information Society Forum, 1996, 2)

Once again, this thesis is so widely accepted as to be almost commonplace.

Globalisation is the third factor to feature in the conventional discourse of lifelong learning. Largely seen as an economic process, globalisation is conventionally presented as a twin process of cross-border corporate expansion and intensifying global competition, in which the world's trading and manufacturing activities are woven increasingly closer together (Ritzer, 2000). In 1995, the World Bank estimated that the combined sales of foreign affiliates of multinational corporations exceeded the total of all world imports (World Bank, 1995). In Vincent Cable's summary, it can be seen as 'economic integration' across national borders, bringing with it important political consequences in the form of the diminishing power of the nation-state (Cable, 1995). This, though, turns out on closer inspection to be a somewhat crude and short-sighted approach.

While the central globalising tendencies do include important economic forces, their impact should not be exaggerated. Analysing a range of long-term indicators, Linda Weiss has suggested that in many respects the world economy is less fully integrated than it was in the late nineteenth or early twentieth centuries (Weiss, 1997). Moreover, many of the phenomena that are often seen as aspects of globalisation are in fact the result of deliberate policies aimed at de-regulating markets. Perhaps it might be better to follow Giddens in speaking of 'globalising tendencies' rather than of fully-fledged globalisation. But in seeking a more balanced view, it is important to remember that governments (and electors) may face stark challenges as a result of decisions taken in corporate headquarters that involve choices as between a range of national options. BMW's unhappy disentanglement from ownership of the Rover Group in early 2000 provoked widespread anger in Birmingham. Equally indicative, though, was the decision of Nissan a year earlier to concentrate its down-sizing strategy on achieving sizeable job reductions, not in its operations in Sunderland or Mexico, but back in Japan. In both cases, the relevant national governments were seen to be relatively powerless to respond.

But globalisation is not just an economic process. The conventional view of globalisation risks overstating the economic dimension, and understating the force of globalising tendencies in the social and cultural spheres. Giddens has stressed the role of instantaneous global communication and mass transportation in transforming – if unevenly – large tracts of daily life (Giddens, 1994, 4). Global diasporas emerge, such as the world-wide community of people of Irish descent, nurtured by broadcasting, popular music, the internet and cheap flights. Global diasporas are often presented as racial constructs (for example, 'the Celts'). However, they are really defined – and self-defined – in cultural terms (ranging from the modern notion of Celticism itself to such commercial products as 'Riverdance', for instance). Information technologies have played an important role in helping to construct these culturally-based networks, for example through genealogical websites.

Taste, habits and beliefs are all uprooted from their locale and exhibited to a global audience; but equally, what Giddens calls 'communities of taste, habit and belief' are detached from a specific location, and even from the confines of the nation state; local contexts then have to be reconsidered and perhaps defended or altered in the light of these processes (Giddens, 1994, 81). This is not the same as arguing that the world is becoming a more homogeneous place – though perhaps it is. Rather, at certain levels, it seems that cultural and social patterns are being actively reordered in response to, and as part of, globalising tendencies.

Globalising tendencies are also actively promoting an interest in lifelong learning. For one thing, lifelong learning is widely regarded as a defence against global competitors. As a leading management thinker predicted in 1994:

> The unskilled living in the first world are going to have to compete with the unskilled living in the third world, head to head without the help of having access to more natural resources, more capital, more technology and more complementary skilled workers with which to work ... In the economy ahead, there is only one source of sustainable competitive advantage – skills. Everything else is available to everyone on a more or less equal access basis. (Thurow, 1994, 51-2)

Though in less gung-ho language, a similar analysis was sketched out in a joint report from European university rectors and the major West European business forum:

> Globalisation means that many jobs that do not add much value are exported to poorer and cheaper countries ... The only way for rich countries to stay rich in the long term is to have people who are more productive – which often means that they are better educated. (Cochinaux and de Woot, 1995, 22)

Secondly, lifelong learning has been presented as a means of embracing globalisation. To become a global citizen, one must acquire new skills – linguistic, interpersonal, cultural – and attitudes (Wilterdink, 1993).

In practice, this may not be as convincing a solution as it first appears. It assumes that nations elsewhere do not opt for a similar strategy, yet the pace of growth and development in educational attainment throughout much of Asia (Reynolds, 1995) suggests that skills are no more a sustainable source of competitive advantage than are abundant coal reserves. And while it is true that capital, unskilled labour and many raw materials are now virtually ubiquitous, the same is increasingly true of highly skilled labour. Knowledge has always been footloose, but the information revolution means that explicit and codified forms of knowledge can be more easily and rapidly diffused than almost any other commodity. Information mobility is at the cutting edge of globalising tendencies. But this has not (yet) reduced the policy appeal of lifelong learning as a solution to the apparent threats and opportunities of the knowledge economy, the information revolution, and far-reaching globalisation.

Policy – missing, presumed dead?

At the level of general commitment, policy endorsement of lifelong learning is virtually universal. When we turn to policy development and implementation, the picture is more patchy. In this field, a favourably policy climate has paradoxically failed to generate much that is new or innovative in terms of specific policy measures. Moreover, in so far as policy developments have evolved into deliverable measures, these have almost universally focused on one single area: interventions designed to improve the skills and flexibility of the workforce.

The first paradox is the existence of a large gap between policy rhetoric and resourcing commitments. Several writers have noted this, as though with surprise. British commentators tend to assume that this is a little local difficulty: Thatcher was famous for cutting public spending, and New Labour for standing by the Conservatives' spending limits. Things must surely be better elsewhere? But they are not. Having identified the revolutionary implications of lifelong learning, governments – other than Japan, discussed in greater detail below – have done relatively little. Moreover, as we have already seen, a similar lack of policy action followed the initial debate over lifelong education in the early 1970s, so it should not come as an entire surprise that something similar followed the debate of the 1990s. Where governments have increased spending on some types of adult learning – usually work-related or basic skills – they have tended at the same time to reduce spending on other types of learning – usually non-vocational or liberal adult education. In the UK, for instance, we can witness what at first might seem a remarkable paradox: from the moment at which government actively embraced concepts of lifelong learning, participation in liberal adult education fell steadily as resources were switched towards other priority areas (Fitzgerald *et al*, 2004, 14).

The lack of immediate policy direction is indeed striking (Rubenson, 1999), as is its consistency over time. Reviewing experience in the OECD member states, a team of specialists concluded in one of several national surveys of education policy conducted in the late 1980s and early 1990s that there has been 'much reference to the ideal of lifelong learning and the importance of second-chance education ... but, as in nearly all other countries, there is no evidence of any concerted effort to render it a reality' (OECD, 1991, 33). Half a decade on, in a survey of international policy undertaken for the fifth UNESCO world conference on adult education, Ursula Giere and Mishe Piet concluded:

> Everywhere in the world statements identify adult education as a key to the survival of humankind in the 21st century, attributing adult education with the magic to contribute positively to education for all ... and yet, almost everywhere in the world, adult education is a widely neglected and feeble part of the official educational scene. (Giere and Piet, 1997, 3-4)

Seven years later, the UNESCO Institute of Education concluded that a shift in terminology, from adult education to adult learning, had not yet succeeded in widening the perspectives of the main stakeholders:

> In many countries, adult learning is considered equivalent to acquiring literacy skills. In others, it is confined to vocational education. Learning as the key principle underlying development processes, whether in the areas of active citizenship, health or environment, still needs to be recognised and incorporated in theory and practice. (UNESCO Institute for Education, 2004, 133)

Within the heart of the EU, a recently retired civil servant concluded that specific policy measures to promote the Lisbon agenda through lifelong learning had been 'somewhat disappointing' (Jones, 2005, 253). It is almost as though governments have noticed that they face a considerable policy challenge, but are reduced to rebranding and posturing when it comes to developing specific measures.

Others have noted that even where there has been action, it has tended to concentrate almost exclusively upon work-related education and training. In my judgement, Carmel Borg and Peter Mayo go rather too far in describing the European Commission's *Memorandum* as 'a neo-liberal inspired set of guidelines' (Borg and Mayo, 2005, 272). Yet although the Commission continues to reflect a characteristically European concern with a middle way, balancing social cohesion with the search for competitive advantage against Asia and the USA, Borg and Mayo rightly note that the road to achieving this goal is largely through the modernisation of vocational training systems, and this has also been true of most of the advanced nations. Again, Japan is a partial exception. Elsewhere, policy-makers have tended to concentrate on microprocessors rather than intimate relationships or even cultural change, at least in their approach to public policy. The director of the UNESCO Institute for Education, for instance, has warned of the imbalance between 'the many areas of activity where there is a need for a more active, informed and competent citizenry' on the one hand and the 'economic element' that dominates current continuing education policy initiatives on the other (Bélanger, 1999, 187).

Much has been promised in the public domain, but most of the action has taken place within the private domain, by individual actors and by enterprises. What achievements there have been in public policy have mainly fallen within the vocational domain. Was this simply a result of political bad faith or lack of political will, as so many claim (Baptiste, 1999, 95; Boshier, 1998, 9; Collins, 1998, 45; West, 1998, 555)?

One school of thought argues that this policy sterility is inherent in the concept of lifelong learning. Bernt Gustavsson, for example, suggests that while the term itself is 'used as a vision', it tends to be 'rather empty of content', with no clue as to how it may be 'transformed into practice' (Gustavsson, 1995, 92). And indeed, one difficulty lies in the nature of the issue itself. It is not governments that will produce more learning among more people, but citizens. This is an issue which requires citizens to act. For governments, this presents obvious difficulties. Rather than government doing things directly, it is required to persuade citizens to change their ways. Lifelong learning is far from being the only such issue; many others are driven by civil society including public health, environmental action, racial tolerance and tackling crime. And in the process of shifting away from service delivery or legislation to offering guidance and trying to steer citizens' behaviour, government has had to change its own ways of working.

Lifelong learning is one of several policy areas where there is a new balance of responsibilities between individuals, employers and state. Of course, unlike schooling or conventional higher education, adult learning has never been solely or even mainly a public responsibility. Apart from anything else, many of the most important providers have always been non-governmental bodies. Indeed, much of the modern adult education system is inherited from nineteenth century social movements that were created partly to challenge the state of their time, like the Swedish temperance movement or the British trades unions. Similarly, many of the costs have always been paid by individuals or employers; the public contribution has always been relatively small. But even if adult education and training were widely seen as Cinderella services, by the 1950s they were acknowledged as part of the family of public provision that had been established through the social settlements of the late nineteenth and mid twentieth centuries. And although there has not been a single, dramatic blow to the adult-learning Cinderella – despite occasional attempts to axe spending levels – there has been a steady, incremental change in her status.

No longer Cinderella of the public sector, adult learning now has so many suitors that she has – to pursue the metaphor – become rather promiscuous. Certainly, adult training is now a major industry in its own right. In the USA, it is estimated that the training market is currently worth over $60 billion a year. Part of this growth has taken place with little reference to the public sector of provision; many of the corporate players are powerful actors in their own right. Motorola, for example, has its own 'university' which operates at a range of levels deemed appropriate for the company's employees. Motorola University was said in 1998 to have some 1,000 academic staff with centres in 49 countries and classes in 24 languages. William Wiggenhorn, president of the Motorola University, estimated that around 10 per cent of his staff came from existing universities, but thought that university lecturers were generally 'too boring' to hold an audience and wanted to 'do their own thing' rather than what the company required (*EUCEN News*, June, 1999, 9).

This explosion has also powered changes in the public sector. In conventional universities, the demand for MBA (Masters in Business Administration) courses has continued rising inexorably since the 1950s, despite the hefty premium charged by universities to students or their employers. Moreover, despite constant warnings that the market is saturated, this demand-led growth has taken place among both individuals and employers. On a smaller scale, we have seen similar growth in the demand for other forms of adult learning from individuals; as was frequently pointed out in the UK when government was considering the introduction of tuition fees for undergraduates, the adult students of the Open University had always paid privately for their studies. By 1999, when the private fee system was well-established, the Labour minister for higher education was urging universities to treat their students as 'customers' (*Times Higher Education Supplement*, 1 October 1999).

If learning is a business, government itself is in flux. In a reflexive world, the idea of an all-powerful providing state is attractive neither to politicians, bureaucrats nor citizens. It is not simply that the modern state machinery has become too expensive, although this is frequently a charge levelled by fiscal conservatives. Robert Reich, Secretary of Labor for the first four years of the Clinton adminis-tration, has attributed the failure of policy in this area to a com-bination of Treasury caution and business lobbying. Instead of approving Reich's proposals for human capital tax credits and job training programmes for unemployed youngsters, Reich's cabinet colleagues opted for public deficit reduction combined with subsidies to corporate America (Reich, 1997). Yet this insider view, though it offers highly significant insights into the power and in-fluence of the Treasury and the Federal Reserve in determining macro-economic policy, only tells part of the story. High levels of public spending are a relatively small problem in the post-scarcity societies of the Western world, and it is notable that the govern-ments which most vigorously advocated the principle of fiscal con-servatism ended up, like the Reagan and Thatcher administrations, spending just as much as ever (Castells, 1989, 28).

The principle of state provision has in recent years run up against three blockages. First, there are increasing numbers who can either supplement or opt out of state-provided benefits. In areas such as housing, pensions, health and even education, citizens who have provided for their own needs – or think they have – are rarely happy when it comes to spending their taxes on citizens who have chosen – as they see it – to spend their own money elsewhere. Second, universal and direct state provision can serve as an unintended bureaucratic block on society's capacity for learning and innovation. The trick, as Castells has put it, is 'to be able to steer a complex society without suffocating it' (Castells, 1989, 18). Third, public servants do not always want to serve. As Sharon Wright has shown in the case of active labour market policies, many of the new policy instruments require front-line civil servants – so-called 'street level bureaucrats' – to treat service users as customers; yet public service sector workers are already struggling to cope, and adapt their conception of their job accordingly. Her study of Job Centre workers in Scotland showed that staff were adept at reducing the strains imposed by active labour market policies, while making sure that they visibly complied with the performance targets imposed upon them from above (Wright, 2001).

During the 1980s, a number of Western governments experimented with new forms of governance. Seeking to introduce private sector management, governments explored privatisation, market-testing, purchaser-provider splits, disaggregation of separate activities, and closeness to the customer. At the same time, new methods of public management were developed for those services that remained within the public sector: hands-on professional management, decentralised authority, service-level standards, and target-related funding. Efforts were made too not simply to provide services but to engage with the private and voluntary sectors through catalytic partnerships. Finally, and continuing into the new century, there has been a new preoccupation with bringing together the different arms of government (and corporate decision-making) at a number of different levels, including the transnational, to function as a coherent network – the so-called 'joined-up government' approach.

Taken together, this transformation of the public sector 'involves 'less government' (or less rowing) but 'more governance' (or more steering)' (Rhodes, 1996, 655). It also implies 'learning government' which can adapt policy and structures in line with evidence of what works and what does not, and which therefore has the capacity to manage its knowledge resources effectively (Social Exclusion Unit, 2000). This process has taken a different shape in different countries and at different times. In Britain there was more emphasis on privatisation in the 1980s, for instance, and a stronger interest in social partnerships after the 1997 change of government, while Sweden and the Netherlands have witnessed shifts in policy focus away from social partnership towards individualism (Fejes, 2005). The general thrust, though, has been broadly similar in a wide range of countries.

The new public management is not without its problems, however. With the move towards a contract culture, voluntary organisations are being confronted with a series of control mechanisms as government seeks to ensure accountability for public spending; there is a greater emphasis upon the identification of 'approved providers' and the specification of government-approved quality standards. By adopting the language of partnership, policy-makers clearly hope to make this change more palatable. Further, the discourse of partnership frequently cloaks a profound inequality between the so-called partners, with the voluntary sector coming a poor third after government and business (Geddes, 1997). Voluntary organisations find themselves competing against one another – and against the private sector – for contracts, and this can destabilise relations within the voluntary sector and unsettle previously harmonious relationships between voluntary bodies and local government (Commission on the Future of the Voluntary Sector, 1996, 53). The language of markets and competition is, moreover, in tension with the trust, interdependence and stability required for effective network building, as is shown by the failure of Training and Enterprise Councils in Britain to steer the training system in ways that overcame existing deficits (Rhodes, 1996, 664). Finally, the entire approach risks rejection by public opinion. Ralf Dahrendorf has ridiculed 'Third Way' social democracy for its belief that government should 'no longer pay for things, but tell people what to do' (Dahrendorf, 1999, 27). This implies a long-term commitment to partnership; yet most political pressures are relatively short-term.

For all its shortcomings, the new public management has particular relevance for lifelong learning. Lifelong learning is precisely the sort of problem that persuaded governments that the old ways of working were not enough. As in a number of other policy areas, such as public health or environmental protection or enterprise promotion, government alone can deliver very little. According to a German report published to support the European Year of Lifelong Learning, participation in a more open, learning-network society requires that

> learners themselves will have to chose and combine learning processes and strike the right balance between available routes of learn-ing in a way that meets their specific needs. In other words, they will be largely responsible for directing their learning themselves. (Dohmen, 1996, 35)

Individual behaviour and attitudes are at the heart of the new approach – and this at a time when values of autonomy and independence are deeply embedded in our culture. In so far as lifelong learning is consistent with these values, we can expect individuals to respond positively; equally, where lifelong learning is perceived as a dissonant experience, we can expect individuals to respond with a radical scepticism.

One example of this is the problem of 'soft' objectives. Governments have to win people over by articulating a vision and seeking to change people's culture and values, and unlike income levels or types of qualification these are not easily measured. In its White Paper on post-16 education and training, the British New Labour government proclaimed 'Our vision of the Learning Age is to build a new culture of learning and aspiration' (DfEE, 1999b, 13). Two and a half years into office, the government noted the problem of 'insufficient demand' as central, and identified as a key goal that of 'driving up demand' (DfEE, 1999b, 55-6). It had designed a number of reforms with this aim in mind, including tax incentives for vocational training, the creation of a national system of individual learning accounts, the launch of a national helpline (Learndirect), and the inclusion of a major promotional function in the early plans for the University for Industry (UfI). But all these are designed to stimulate demand from individuals rather than change the culture of society. By contrast, initiatives such as the Adult and Community Learning Fund (ACLF) and Union Learning Fund were allocated relatively small sums, partly because of the difficulties faced by government of establishing whether the results offered value for money.

Nor is it easy to define precisely how government might accurately measure the success of its own strategies. Specific indicators are lacking even in such relatively well-defined areas as the measurement of skills and competence (Tuijnman, 2003), let alone in measuring the achievement of broad and ambitious goals such as 'lifelong learning for all'. Cultural change is inherently insusceptible to easy quantitative measurement, so that it is impossible for finance ministries to determine whether or not this is an efficient investment of government funds. Soft objectives also lay government open to the charge of throwing money away; unpleasant it may be to say so, but community development projects occasionally show a tendency to fall victim to fraud and abuse (see for example Northern Ireland Audit Office, 1995 and 1996). But in the absence of agreed and standardised outcome measures, the only alternative appears to be restrictive and heavy-handed regulation, stifling the very process of change that policies have been designed to foster.

Further, lifelong learning policies usually involve a partnership between state and civil society. In principle, partnership working is seen as a way of engaging a range of stakeholders in pursuing a common objective. In this way, government seeks to leverage change across a wider range and more effectively than it could do on its own. In particular it seeks to obtain 'buy in' from such important actors as the private sector and the voluntary sector, as well as from the education and training sector itself (Jones, 2005). But partners invariably have their own aspirations and demands, which can in turn not only influence their decision to join a partnership but also shape their behaviour within it. At one extreme, arms-length arrangements can provide a cloak for fraud and abuse, a climate within which a shady fringe grows on the margins of the training industry. The most spectacular example of this in recent years is surely the unfortunate case of Individual Learning Accounts in the UK, where lurid tales of bogus courses and fictional learners came to overshadow some remarkable stories of individual success (House of Commons Select Committee on Education and Skills, 2002). More commonly, everyday tendencies towards goal distortion are the inevitable consequence of governance through partnership, which is based upon a search for compromise and consensus. Again, the risk is that government will seek to maintain control through rules and procedures which are at odds with precisely the climate of trust and reciprocal confidence that enables partnerships to thrive (Avis, 2002).

Lifelong learning, then, is an inherently difficult area for government. Perhaps these intrinsic obstacles help explain why it is that general policy so rarely leads to innovative measures. It may also explain why it is that, when governments do act, they restrict themselves to the area of vocational training. Firstly, this area has considerable legitimacy, and is therefore 'safe' in political terms. Particularly in respect of training for unemployed people, this is a long-established area of direct intervention. It is associated with wealth-creation and living standards, and state training subsidies are usually welcomed by employers. Secondly, it represents a relatively easy field for non-regulatory types of intervention. Much responsibility for implementation and delivery will rest with relatively low-status and local actors (FE colleges, employment offices, and so on); partners can be won over through incentive funding; and the prospect exists of hard short-term targets (such as jobs found, qualifications gained, or people trained). Thirdly, finance ministries are usually favourable to this type of public spending (this is an extremely important quality for policy-makers). As a glance at the World Bank's website will confirm, finance ministries the world over share a faith in the human capital approach to human resource planning (http://www.worldbank.org). Investments and returns are priced in a way that seems largely impossible for such new, intangible areas as social capital, cultural change, or citizenship. Vocational training is, then, the one area where governments feel impelled to act; and even here, they choose relatively familiar and uncontroversial measures.

But this is not all. The general policy banner of lifelong learning cloaks a second arena for action where governments appear to feel comfortable: initial education. In Britain, for example, the New Labour government's green paper on lifelong learning was used to launch a substantial expansion in initial higher education, aimed at drawing in new types of younger student following two-year vocational programmes (DfEE, 1998a). In the Netherlands, the supposedly 'new' public spending on lifelong learning was largely allocated to such measures as the lowering of the age of compulsory education to four, the provision of guidance and counselling to secondary school drop-outs, and the in-service training of teachers (Ministry of Culture, Education and Science, 1998).

This pattern seems to be virtually universal. Only Japan appears to be an exception, with a considerable record of activity since the mid-1980s (Trivellato, 1996; Thomas, Takamichi and Shuichi, 1997; Okumoto, 2004). Partly in response to a series of reports on UNESCO's concept of lifelong learning, the Japanese government started debating lifelong education in the early 1970s, seeing in it a possible solution to the rigidities and 'examination hell' of 'credential society' (or gakureki shakai – see Okumoto 2004, 100-2). Unusually among the industrial nations, Japanese policy makers persisted in examining the potential of lifelong education as a mechanism for liberalisation of the system, with a major report on the topic from the Central Council for Education in 1981; Okumoto also shows that Japanese policy makers also hoped that a shift towards 'self-learning' would help them cut or at least control public spending (Okumoto, 2004, 103; 116). Subsequently the Japanese government established a Lifelong Learning Bureau within the ministry of education, governed by a Lifelong Learning Council dominated by non-educational agencies and ministries. In 1990, the Japanese government passed a Law Concerning the Development of Mechanisms and Measures for Promoting Lifelong Learning, again based on an inter-ministerial approach (with the powerful Ministry for International Trade and Industry – MITI – playing a particularly important role). This was followed by the creation of an advisory body for lifelong learning, which published a series of recommendations for measures to be adopted by universities, schools, local authorities and other bodies, leading to a substantial amount of activity, particularly at local and regional level. Further activity continued through the 1990s, with continuing impetus arising from the 1991 bursting of the so-called 'bubble economy' and increasing concerns over the social and cultural side-effects of what was otherwise judged an extremely successful education system (Okumoto, 2004, 198-203). In contrast to Europe, many new initiatives in Japan were directed, not solely or even primarily at expanding continuing vocational education and training, but at promoting opportunities for individual and community based lifelong learning.

How can we explain these differences between the Japanese and the European approaches? In her pioneering doctoral dissertation, Kaori Okumoto (2004) compared British and Japanese policy approaches to lifelong learning against the background of recent social and economic history. She points to the way in which Japanese policies have been concerned with community building and social reconstruction, while British policies have been concerned with economic competitiveness and growth. According to Okumoto, each nation is responding to different policy challenges: in Japan, the major challenge is perceived to be social isolation and the break-down of traditional community structures, associated with the stresses of a competitive and rigid academic examinations system. My own view is that these differences are possibly not so great as she suggests. While there are differences in policy emphasis, this book argues that many of the economically advanced nations face similar challenges. These include the economic and cultural consequences of globalisation; the prospects of steady demographic change with falling birth rates and increasing longevity; and the decline of tradi-tional forms of civic participation and family structure. I suggest that contemporary patterns of lifelong learning also reflect funda-mental changes in the norms and values people espouse. Access to information and knowledge has itself become one of the causes of changing norms and values, in a process that some contemporary sociologists describe as 'reflexive modernisation'. Japan is also clearly facing similar economic challenges to Europe, though its proximity to the emerging economic powerhouse of China means that the challenges and the opportunities of globalisation can take different forms. Nevertheless, despite these fundamental social and economic similarities, the two approaches do differ, and Okumoto further argues, convincingly, that the different approaches taken have influenced the legitimacy and adaptability of lifelong learning in the two countries.

Is Japan a model? Certainly, the new policy measures have been characterised by their comprehensiveness and breadth. Flower arranging classes were promoted alongside access to the new tech-nologies, older adults were at least as much a focus as were em-ployees or jobseekers. However, as I have suggested, it would be wrong to overestimate the degree of Japanese exceptionalism. In at least four respects, the Japanese policy debate shows marked similarities with discussions on the opposite side of the globe.

First, to some extent the legislation and activity were partly a re-branding of well-established patterns of what in Japan was known as social education and in the English-speaking world might be called liberal adult education. While the level, status, funding and coverage of social education were all increased (at a time when many Western nations were planning cuts in their equivalent programmes), there was no radical new departure from existing practice.

Second, the government did have a number of priorities which had been chosen for their economic relevance. The first of these was the hope of creating a cultural climate where individuals would take increasing responsibility for their own development, rather than continuing to rely on their employer to provide lifelong learning along with a lifelong job. MITI has a strong, direct influence over education policy, particularly through its representation on the key policy bodies. Further, in a parallel development, MITI created its own lifelong learning office in 1990 to promote developments in Japanese industry. The second was that Japanese politicians were articulating their own discourse of crisis around competitiveness, focusing particularly upon the alleged lack of creativity of the workforce, which was attributed largely to the formalistic rote learning needed to succeed in a credential society. Reforms in the initial education system proving difficult, they therefore saw lifelong learning as a chance to promote creativity later on. And there was also a distinctively Japanese concern with the psychological damage created by the once-for-all pressures of examinations.

Third, the new system provided an opportunity to modernise social education through the application of the new technologies, thus familiarising the wider population (particularly older adults) with the merits of computing and the internet, not simply as part of the curriculum but also by developing highly sophisticated systems of online information and advice that could be accessed by adults through local learning centres (*kominkans*) and also through schools and universities.

Finally, there is a distinctly conservative overtone to much of the discussion around learning as a means of building community. Japanese culture and traditions are much emphasised, as is the moral value of the Japanese family. All are presented as bulwarks against the 'new desolation' of liberal individualism (Okumoto, 2004, 210-14). At the same time, as in Europe, there has been growing interest in creating a virtuous cycle of lifelong learning and civic engagement. While it is always possible that policy makers are hoping to cut public spending by encouraging both volunteering and lifelong learning, the public debate has focused much more strongly on community building and the promotion of democratic participation (Okumoto, 2004, 219-26). None of this is to minimise the significance of the Japanese lifelong learning legislation and its consequences, but rather to stress a number of important similarities with developments elsewhere. Otherwise, lifelong learning suffers not so much from policy neglect as from bafflement in the face of uncertainty, immeasurability and risk.

A global agenda

Globalisation too has helped change both the behaviour and power of the nation state. Lifelong learning, like public sector reform, has taken a roughly similar shape across nations. Globalisation has, it seems, helped strengthen the nation state, in that governments 'learn' from each other, and seek – usually selectively and not always successfully – to transfer effective policies from one context to another. Lifelong learning exemplifies this process: the language, and some specific policy measures have been adopted by several nations.

But globalisation can also reduce the scope of national sovereignty. Whether capital actually moves around the globe any more smoothly than in earlier times is a matter of debate (Beck, 1997). From a policy perspective, what matters is that political leaders appear to believe that capital is now relatively footloose, and that multinational corporations in particular are able to switch resources and investments from one country to another in search of reduced costs and higher productivity. Indeed, the flightiness of capital has become one of the most frequently-used justifications for the adoption of lifelong learning. This development has been fastest, as we have seen, with intergovernmental policy bodies – and not only with think-tanks or discussion fora like OECD and UNESCO, but also with decision-taking bodies with real policy bite, like the European Commission.

In a variety of ways, then, globalising tendencies appear to be promoting a degree of convergence around the lifelong learning agenda. This, though, may be a somewhat superficial analysis, since the degree of convergence is far from being total. Some themes are common, such as the widespread adoption of active labour market policies; the UK government's New Deal programme for training the unemployed is a good example of this trend. Apparently influenced by similar programmes in North America (Gardiner, 1997), the UK's adoption of the New Deal reflected broader thinking across the EU, as is shown by the European Commission's repeated calls since the early 1990s for active labour market policies to be adopted in the struggle against unemployment (CEC, 1994, CEC, 1998a, CEC, 1999;

CEC, 2003). In turn, this can be traced to earlier debates across Europe over the future of the welfare state in a post-scarcity world, yet where governments also had little faith in their capacity to stimulate demand for labour and were therefore drawn to policies which increased the supply, flexibility and mobility of labour (Rosanvallon, 1995). Rhetorically, moreover, policy makers often seem to treat lifelong learning as an almost magical solution to our present ills: much of the debate, Mark Murphy has rightly said, sounds triumphalist in tone (Murphy, 2001, 20).

Globalising tendencies can, therefore, both increase and reduce the power of the nation state. It is sometimes hard to demonstrate this, since each nation state has a vested interest in telling its citizens that its sovereignty is intact, even where – as in the EU – a number of states have agreed to place constraints on their individual sovereignty in order to maximise their joint powers on the global stage. Thus to judge by the British government's information service, the New Deal was nothing to do with the EU. On the contrary, it was Britain which was influencing and leading the rest of Europe. An official press release greeted the adoption by the Council of Social Affairs Ministers of a common position favouring active labour market policies as a 'European New Deal', quoting the Secretary of State for Education and Employment as claiming the agreement as 'a sign of the success of the Social Affairs Council – under the British Presidency – replacing the old agenda by putting jobs, skills and employability at the heart of Europe' (DfEE Release, 4 June 1998). In fact, the agreement had originated under the German Presidency in 1996, and was finalised under the Dutch Presidency in 1997; most of the 'old agenda' had been replaced while the British Labour Party was still in opposition. Indeed, once in power the Labour government drew heavily upon the European Structural Funds to finance the New Deal. The question of sovereignty, in a period of powerful globalising tendencies, is a complex one, and the statements of the central actors themselves have to be taken with a large pinch of salt.

But there is another way in which lifelong learning can be seen as part of a global agenda. George Orwell once wrote that something could be true even though the *Daily Mail* said it was true. Given my scepticism over policy rhetoric, I should therefore say that I entirely agree with the consensus in one respect: human creativity and ingenuity is indeed a renewable resource. The globalisation of economic activity and political decision-making has helped create a new and challenging series of global disorders. Involuntary population movements and inter-ethnic conflicts, the failures of international aid and support for vulnerable peoples and nations, and above all the difficulties of environmental degradation and resource depletion all demand responses that transcend boundaries. Are they particularly to do with lifelong learning? I think so, not least because all – if in different ways – represent important learning challenges. Environmental problems and solutions are a good example, since this is an area in which governments have no answers that are independent of the attitudes and behaviours of individual citizens. Neither can we take solutions, ready-made, from expert knowledge, as the experts tend to disagree on both the causes and the answers. The knowledge economy, and reflexive individualism, are at the heart of both the problems and the solutions. If lifelong learning has no part to play in this of all areas, we might as well forget it.

Lifelong learning will not go away. Given the important roles of fashion and novelty in loosening the bonds of tradition, I confidently expect the terminology to change. But while the term may be replaced, the disparate bundle of concerns and challenges that have been given the label are so deeply-rooted in contemporary economic tendencies, social processes and cultural patterns that there is no prospect of their disappearing. Yet as we have seen, the likelihood of legislative and governmental resolution is negligible. Indeed, given the tendency of lifelong learning towards fragmentation and diffusion, even the search for alternative models of governance – partnership, sub-contracting, devolution into the workplace – are likely to generate as many unintended as intended consequences. In the following chapters, I examine the ways in which this vibrant, diffuse and indeed revolutionary agenda is shaping our lives in a number of different settings: among individuals, their families and their communities; in the workplace; and in relations between rich and poor, powerful and powerless, included and excluded. In each of these dimensions, lifelong learning stands in an ambiguous position: partly emancipation, partly coercion, but always present and always influential.

2
The silent explosion

Why has lifelong learning detonated such widespread interest? Is it any more than the latest educational fad, laced with a strong dose of political expediency? Or is there real substance to it? There are several plausible answers to these questions, and most have at least some basis in reality. Policy-makers are likely to say that lifelong learning is vital because it represents an achievable strategy for competing in a fast-moving world market place, or that it represents a sensible way of tackling social inequality. In many European countries, policy makers may believe that it can combine both of these goals (Fryer, 1998). Informed observers of a more cynical bent might see lifelong learning as the most recent way in which the adult education profession has tried to improve its status (Gustavsson, 1995, 90), or in which government has tried to shift responsibility for funding and planning away from the state and onto learners themselves (Coffield, 1999). But I do not believe that it is possible to understand the persistence and appeal of the lifelong learning agenda without recognising the fundamental, underlying shift in the behaviour of ordinary citizens, who increasingly regard the day-to-day practice of adult learning as routine, perhaps so routine that they give it little explicit attention.

Most people already inhabit a learning society. Virtually every citizen has become a 'permanently learning subject, throughout their whole life' (Dumazadier, 1995, 249). This is not just in the loosest sense of lifelong learning, which is simply recognition of unavoidable biological fact: we learn as we breathe, all the time, without giving it any thought. This can easily become a trivial observation, a sideshow to the real action. What is striking is the extraordinary explosion in intended, reflexive learning throughout the life span. Virtually no one behaves as though they feel that, by 18 or 21 years of age, they know pretty much everything they need to know, and anyway are unlikely to change greatly in the future. Rather, we all behave as though we have untapped inner potential, are capable of extraordinary transformations, and both can and should pick up new skills and knowledge as and when we want and need to.

Exploding in silence: the impact of a learning society

The idea of a learning society has itself been widely debated in recent years. It has been around since the 1970s, when the Swedish civil servant and academic Torsten Husén published a collection of essays under that title (Husén, 1974). Husén contended that the school was no longer as influential a force as it had once been. Rather than receiving new information about the wider world chiefly from teachers, school pupils now had access to a wide range of knowledge drawn from magazines, film, television and foreign travel. Husén argued that, in reacting to these changes, schools had to concentrate on their main task of teaching young people how to learn. The term was revived in the mid-1990s, partly as a result of the Economic and Social Research Council's decision in 1994 to launch a programme of studies under the umbrella label of 'The Learning Society' (Field and Schuller, 1999). But by this time the language of the learning society had become widely adopted as part of a wider discourse of political modernisation. It featured in the title of the European Commission's 1995 white paper on education and training (CEC, 1995) as well as in the thinking of the incoming Labour Government in Britain in 1997 (Fryer, 1998). The idea had moved beyond Husén's original formulation, to embrace a range of proposals for restructuring and modernising the education and training systems.

Usually, these propositions have been presented as a plan for the future. Conventionally, the idea of a learning society is of something that remains a distant goal. Usually it is depicted as a utopia, desirable but not yet achieved. More rarely, it is seen as a dystopia, a coercive state of permanent instruction and control. In either case, the learning society is somewhere in the more or less remote future. It follows that the primary task of scholars and policy makers is therefore to design structures and foster cultures that will nurture the yet-to-be-born utopia – or, conversely, help us better to resist the impending dystopia. Both perspectives have something to commend them, and both are equally wrong. My argument is that the learning society is already here: we live in it, here and now, and it already displays both the positive and negative features that mark the utopian and dystopian visions.

The learning society has a relatively brief history. Its core idea is the plasticity of the human adult: however much has been invested in initial schooling, the belief is central that untapped potential is the norm rather than the exception. Thomas Hardy's *Jude the Obscure* was written at a time when entry to university as an adult remained unusual (it was published in 1895). Hardy's novel turns on the fact that the autodidactic mason is denied access by a university with no interest whatever in his intellectual abilities. Of course, this was also the period when the ancient English and Scottish universities started offering extra-mural classes to an adult audience; the ill-fated stone mason is himself described as attending an adult class at one stage in the novel. Yet such classes were largely seen as compensatory, an opportunity for 'working men' (and increasingly women) to taste the heady brew of science and liberal arts as presented by the best minds of the day. Even early psychoanalysts assumed that the adult personality was more or less fixed, a product of early childhood. It seems as though the widespread recognition (or invention?) of adult plasticity dates from the first two decades of the twentieth century, and particularly from the period after the First World War (Field, 1996).

Total war frequently turns the world upside down. During the conflict of 1914-1918, large numbers of men and women were mobilised for wartime duties that required them to learn a range of new skills. Whereas soldiers in the past had largely acquired their military skills by rote learning, new methods were demanded in the circumstances of the 1914-1918 conflict. To take one small but telling example: women munitions workers were trained and set to skilled work, apparently successfully, in a fraction of the time that was traditionally spent in apprenticeship systems. In Britain, immediately following the war, the Ministry of Labour was charged with retraining veterans for civilian life. By the early 1920s, not only did the Ministry have a training department, as did the US War Department (with all that this implied for policy developments) but there was also an evolving science of adult learning, largely based on the experience of the war and its immediate aftermath. This is to focus only on one field of change, and by comparison with the Bolshevik Revolution, with its aim of creating Socialist Man, or the sudden expansion of citizenship rights, it is rather a limited one.

After 1918, there could be no serious doubt about the capacity of adults to acquire, very quickly, a wide range of new skills and knowledge. Later – notably in the 1960s – this recognition was extended steadily to encompass the emotions and personal identity as well. But by then, belief in the 'plasticity' of adult competences was well established: capacities for learning were demonstrably large in adult life, as well as in childhood. This keystone of the learning society was therefore in place by the early 1920s, and was well-entrenched by the 1950s.

But is this the same as arguing that we are already in a learning society? At first sight, the suggestion might seem preposterous. Across the world, adult education remains as neglected an area of public spending as it has ever been. Universities and colleges are notably unwilling to deal with adult learners other than on their own, very restricted terms. Large parts of the adult population remain functionally illiterate, even in the comfortable Western nations. Surely these are signs that we are far from being a learning society? And indeed, in the utopian sense in which the term is usually used, this is a powerful objection. But this is not how I understand the term. A learning society is not necessarily either a pleasant, an efficient nor an egalitarian place; on the contrary, it may well generate even more deeply-rooted inequalities than we have yet seen, it may place its citizens under renewed stress and pressure, and it may involve the creation of forms of instruction that have little or no impact upon human productivity and creativity. Its key features are surely that the majority of its citizens have become 'permanently learning subjects', and that their performance as adult learners is at least in part responsible for determining their life chances. By these standards, our learning society is already well-entrenched, and the challenge now is to adapt it so that it fits our needs more closely.

Learning subjects and subject learners

Much of the debate around lifelong learning slides readily into hype. Further, the apparent linguistic shift, away from 'lifelong education' to 'lifelong learning', includes quite a bit of re-badging, and the term 'learning' can encompass a variety of different meanings (Felstead *et al*, 2004). What, then, is the evidence? Three key indicators are surely that adults routinely take part in organised learning throughout their lifespan; that the post-school system is populated by adults as well as by younger people; and that non-formal learning permeates daily life and is valued. On this basis, the evidence is unambiguous. The learning society is indeed here around us.

The first indicator of a learning society is that most people continue to take part in organised learning activities throughout their adult lives. The evidence for this is somewhat mixed, but overall it suggests that the volume and level of recorded participation in formal adult learning are increasing, not just in Britain but in the USA and across Western Europe. The sharpest rises seem to have been in North America. In Canada the proportion of adults involved in organised learning rose between the mid-1980s and the mid-1990s from 20 per cent to 38 per cent (Livingstone, 1999, 167). In the USA, an estimated 90 million adults took part in adult education activities in 1999, giving an estimated participation rate of 46 per cent of the adult population; this represented a rise of about a third since 1991 (Westat and Creighton, 2000, 2). But the shift in Europe has been almost equally dramatic. In Finland, for example, participation in organised adult learning rose by 28 per cent between 1972 and 1995 (Tuomisto, 1998, 158). In the Netherlands, participation rose from around 15 per cent in the 1960s to 20 per cent in the 1980s and approaching 38 per cent in the mid-90s (van der Kamp, 1997). The UK government claimed optimistically in 1995 that 'Adult participation in further and higher education has grown by about 60 per cent in the last ten years, although many of these adults are under 25' (DfEE, 1995, 8). Rather more cautiously, surveys conducted by the National Institute of Adult Continuing Education (NIACE) in Britain appeared to show a 'slight rise in overall participation between 1990 and 1996'; more tentatively, it looked as though the 1990 level was itself higher than that found in a 1980 survey (Sargant *et al*, 1997, 21). More recent findings from NIACE suggest that while the growth has been sustained, participation in the UK remained more or less stable between 1996 and 2005 (Aldridge and Tuckett, 2005. A government survey, using slightly different methods, reports a small overall rise in learning between 1997 and 2002 (Fitzgerald *et al*, 2003, 13). According to the authors, participation in non-vocational learning fell markedly during this five year period, but it was balanced our by growth in self-directed learning and vocational learning (Fitzgerald *et al*, 2003, 14). On balance then, UK survey data suggest a sustained rise in participation between the 1960s and 1990s, with the gain being maintained subsequently.

It should be said right away that these trends are not as clear-cut as the statistics might suggest. Firstly, they all refer primarily to registrations on formal adult education and training programmes. As a result, it is extremely difficult to determine at any one time whether participation in adult learning – broadly defined – is rising or falling. Reviewing British survey data, Malcolm Tight noted that although each investigation offered a reasonably clear-cut definition of formal education and training activities, it also sought to include various types of informal learning. As the different surveys then used differing definitions of informal learning, the results cannot be compared with any confidence (Tight, 1998a). Thus the authors of the 1997 government-sponsored national adult learning survey, comparing their own findings with those produced by other studies in the 1990s, conclude that most of the differences arose from varia-tions in methodology, in particular the phrasing of key questions that defined learning (Beinart and Smith, 1998, 36-7). Since Tight's overview, the UK government carried out a follow-up survey in 1999, using the same definitions as in 1997, revisiting a sample of respon-dents from the earlier study (La Valle and Finch, 1999). Subsequently it carried out a similar follow up sample survey of respondents to its 2001 national adult learning survey (Snape *et al*, 2004). Where reasonably similar questions have been used in British studies, the findings generally suggest a small and steady rise in the proportion of adults taking part in learning of some kind.

Moreover, within the context of an overall rise in participation, not all groups have fared equally. Recent NIACE surveys show a marked fall in participation since the mid-1990s among those aged over 55 (Sargant and Tuckett, 1999; Aldridge and Tuckett, 2005). Similarly, a long-term study of adult learning in South Wales suggests that, particularly for men, there has been a marked drop in participation in adult learning, associated with the decline of heavy industries such as coal-mining, and the related collapse of trade unionism and working class political engagement (Gorard *et al*, 1999a). Further-more, there has been sharper growth in some forms of learning than in others. In Finland, much of the rise in participation has been due to increases in work-related learning; learning for personal develop-ment grew by a relatively small amount (Tuomisto, 1998, 159). Yet despite the unevenness, there is little doubt about the overall trend: in nearly all countries where reasonably reliable and comparable data exist, the period between the 1960s and the 1990s witnessed a substantial expansion of participation in organised adult education and training.

The second indicator of a learning society is that the post-school education system recruits primarily on the basis of learning need or demand rather than chronological age. In the UK, most further education colleges now teach a mainly adult clientele, and adults account for around half of all university undergraduates. As you might expect, adults tend to be found in different areas of the institutions from school-leavers, and most of those who teach adults believe that mature students remain somewhat marginal to the institution's sense of what it is basically about. Yet again, the underlying trend is clear enough. Major institutions that used to be full of young people, learning from older teachers, are now much more mixed.

This trend is now well-established. By the mid-1980s, the further education colleges in England had overtaken local authority adult education centres as providers of education and training for adults. In spite of their origins as technical training institutes, concentrating largely on day release programmes for young apprentices, FE colleges by the 1970s had become a second chance route for school-leavers, as well as playing a growing role in the new training programmes for young unemployed people. Their role as adult education providers, if less visible to commentators at the time, was equally dramatic (Field, 1991). Recruitment of adults became even more attractive to colleges in the deregulated competitive environment that followed removal from local authority control in 1992, not least because the new funding regime meant that resources followed student numbers (provided that they were enrolled on prescribed types of programme). By the late 1990s, adults were a clear majority of the English FE college population; some 80 per cent of students on publicly-funded courses were aged 19 and over (Unwin, 1999).

Similar patterns are visible in the higher education system. As it emerged from the expansionary programmes of the 1960s, the higher education system in Europe was primarily designed for a population of full-time young students, entering more or less directly from school. In some countries (notably Sweden and the UK), an expansion in capacity during the 1970s and 1980s was accompanied by a deliberate targeting of growth on mature entrants, so that by the 1990s a considerable proportion of entrants were aged 21 or over at the time of starting their studies. This was an extremely patchy process. In Ireland, for example, fewer than 6 per cent of higher education entrants were adults in the late 1990s, and in Belgium the figure was only 2 per cent. In 1998, the Irish government asked universities to review their admissions policies with a view to increasing the number of adult entrants (Department of Education and Science, 1998). There are also sizeable disparities between institutions, with the largest numbers of adults usually being found in the least prestigious universities and between subjects, with adults confined largely to the social sciences and humanities (Merrill and Collins, 1999). While it is premature even in the UK to speak of 'the adult university' (Bourgeois *et al*, 1999), there has been a steady erosion of age-based patterns of exclusion across most European societies.

One result is that adults are now either a substantial minority, or in some cases a majority, in institutions not originally designed for adults. Rather, they were intended almost exclusively for asymmetrical or 'top down' teaching to a relatively young audience who could be expected to carry out their studies along a fairly predictable track, and to use their qualifications for initial entry into their career. University students since 1945 offer an instructive example: it is not only that most could be expected to devote most of their waking time to being students (not necessarily the same thing as studying for most of their waking time), but that their primary identity – who they felt they were – was as students. Those who ran the higher education system assumed that their students stood in an asymmetrical relationship to the teaching staff. Indeed, one of the issues at stake in the student upheavals of the late 1960s was the fact that the university stood formally in *loco parentis* ('in place of the parent') and was entitled to regulate its students' private behaviour. For many students today, work, learning, family and other commitments are interwoven. A thirty-year-old woman with a young family, or a police officer who studies on a part-time basis, is unlikely to define their identity primarily as that of 'student', nor are they likely to regard their lecturers as somewhere between unchallengeable founts of wisdom or superannuated bores. One result is that many adults in higher education have never felt like 'real' students (Merrill, 1999). Similar changes in further education student populations mean that many colleges in England, and some universities, are now effectively adult education and training institutes.

But far from reinventing themselves to meet the needs of their new constituencies, universities and colleges have made relatively minor incremental adjustments. In the case of the further education sector, Lorna Unwin has argued that the changes have been sufficient for FE colleges to have lost their distinctive character but without finding a new firm identity to help them engage more securely with their environment in the future (Unwin, 1999). In higher education, traditional entry qualifications are usually reinforced by those institutions and programmes where entry is most competitive, so that adults are funnelled into low status areas which inevitably produce a lower pay-off in terms of final career outcomes (Merrill, 1999), while adult recruitment strategies may derive more from a desire to protect institutional funding than from capacity to deliver (FEFC, 1999). Programme flexibility is severely limited, and would-be learners face significant constraints on choice, such as timing and availability (Blaxter and Tight, 1994). In her study of women entering care courses in the early 1980s, Skeggs found that 'The decision to go on a caring course is not so much a positive decision as an attempt to find something within constricting cultural and financial limits which they will be able to do and be good at' (Skeggs, 1997, 58). In the British case, it should also be said that in recent years, provision geared to adults has frequently been disrupted by sudden and often significant changes resulting from funding regime adjustments. Finally, attitudes among employers and others often mean that, even on acquiring a new qualification, adults are at a disadvantage when it comes to finding appropriate employment (Purcell and Hogarth, 1999).

In short, the weakening of age-based entry criteria has transformed the student population in some central traditionally youth-oriented institutions. However, it has yet to transform large areas of institutional practice. A number of unintended consequences appear to have resulted from this mismatch, including a *de facto* funnelling of adult learners into those institutions and areas where demand is weakest among traditional students, compounding the labour market disadvantages facing adults as a result of age-based prejudice, or specific prejudice against those groups who are least likely to have gained qualifications at a younger age.

The third indicator concerns opportunities for, and the value placed upon, non-formal learning. Conventionally, non-formal learning occupies a middle position between learning that is an incidental by-product of other activities (informal learning) and intentional instruction (formal learning). Though in practice our learning does not take place in ways that fall neatly into such clear cut categories, the issue is whether there is sufficient recognition of non-formal learning to indicate that constant learning is now believed to be 'normal' and even valuable. In principle, it could conceivably be true that recorded participation in formal education and training is rising, while the incidence of non-formal and self-directed learning is declining or its content is discounted as trivial or second rate.

It is certainly true that some important changes have taken place in the field of non-formal learning, as in other forms of social and economic life. Surely there is evidence of much decline, as we can see in the slow bleeding away of members from the Women's Institute (WI), the steady professionalisation of the Workers' Educational Association (WEA) and the apparent disappearance of the proletarian autodidacts celebrated during the 1970s by the radical scholars of History Workshop. Indeed, during the 1980s, History Workshop itself became less of a learning movement and more of a publishing agency. As for the autodidacts, one long-term study of adult learning patterns in South Wales over the past century has shown a secular decline in much informal learning, particularly among working class men, as a result of the diminishing significance of trade unions, chapel and left-wing political parties (Gorard *et al,*1999a). Individual spending on reading is declining, falling by 11 per cent between 1971 and 1996 (Henry, 1999, 284), though part of this at least is attributable to a relative decline in the prices of paperbacks. But it is wrong to see in these developments the death of non-formal learning.

Informal learning permeates the life world, often absorbed so fully into daily routines and habits that people do not think of it separately as learning but just as a relatively unquestioned activity they choose to pursue. Studies of informal learning in North America since the early 1970s show consistently that, despite the huge growth in formal education and training, adults generally continue to devote far larger amounts of time – and possibly increasingly so – on informal learning projects (Livingstone, 1999, 169-70).

What is new, though, is that much informal learning no longer takes the old forms. Rather, it is increasingly accompanied by new forms of adult learning, many of which are related to consumption and leisure, and not just work (the issue of informal learning in work is discussed in the next Chapter). While these are diverse and encompass a wide range of forms, they differ from more established forms of non-formal learning in that they are more highly individualised, more privatised and more ephemeral. In this, they differ substantially from the non-formal education offered by bodies such as the WEA or WI. Such bodies were created to pursue a clearly identified social purpose on behalf of a broader movement, and they provided courses in clearly organised bodies of knowledge. Thus the WEA specifically aimed to create a bridge between the universities – relatively few in number at the time of its creation in 1903 – and the labour movement whose members were increasingly taking on the rights, and responsibilities, of citizenship. At a time of urbanisation and extension of the franchise, the WI brought together women in rural areas to discuss and learn about matters of common interest to women. These were movements of collective self-improvement and enlightenment, based broadly around collective identities, and pursuing agendas of social change. And while there was a broad range of more or less specialised adult education bodies, they shared a relatively cohesive identity in comparison with the dispersed field of contemporary adult learning.

The new adult education not only takes new forms, it also pursues new purposes. Where the WEA and its equivalents elsewhere saw popular enlightenment as the key to social change, the new adult education allows participants to work actively on their identities and renegotiate their place in a complex world. The new adult learning is markedly less 'collectivist' than the type of informal and non-formal learning associated with industrial working class movements of the nineteenth and early twentieth centuries. While such movements may well have helped improve the individual life chances of their most active members, their underlying purpose – and the source of their status as *movements* – was to advance the common interests of the oppressed, and strengthen their struggle against their oppressors. The new adult learning, by contrast, could be described as a highly individualised form of adult learning. It is also characterised by a highly complex but interdependent relationship with consumer culture.

Typical of the new adult education are such activities as residential short courses, study tours, fitness centres, sports clubs, heritage centres, self-help therapy manuals, management gurus, electronic networks and self-instructional videos. The outburst of book clubs and reading circles in the western world is a case in point. In her detailed study of reading groups in Houston, Texas, Elizabeth Long convincingly argues that the members – mostly women, it should be noted – are not solely meeting to share ideas about the books that they have read together. They are also actively using the process of reading and discussion to create meaning, to 'articulate and even discover who they are: their values, their aspirations and their stance towards the dilemmas of the world' (Long, 2003, 145). Rather than building collective organisations, the participants in the new adult learning are more likely to pursue their own autonomy and assert their own individual position in the hierarchies that matter to them.

If the new adult learning is about struggle, then, it is often focused on a struggle with oneself. As an example, much of the new non-formal learning is concerned with empowering individuals to take charge of their own bodies. Pierre Bourdieu is among a number of commentators who have pointed to the importance of the body as a symbolic expression of identity, invested in as a form of cultural capital (Bourdieu, 1984). In a study of young working-class women who entered care courses in the early 1980s, Beverley Skeggs found that by the late 1980s and early 1990s a number of her interviewees had become anxious about their bodies; noting that the more obvious differences of physique between classes have now more or less disappeared, Skeggs concluded that the women's investment in body shape and tone served as an increasingly important way of demonstrating a capacity for 'care of the self for the self' (Skeggs, 1997, 83-4). Body shape, among adults and perhaps especially among women, has become a signal of capacity for investing in one's symbolic capital, a sign that one still has hopes of 'improving'. Neglect of the body, translated into obesity, will harm promotion prospects, while active abuse, for example through overuse of alcohol or narcotics, may well lead to formal or informal disciplinary measures.

Particularly in a more open and fluid society, we might expect to see a concern with the body as typical of those social milieus and age groupings who are most insecure and vulnerable in their (perhaps newly-acquired) status. The state of the fitness industry is, therefore, a good guide to the health of the learning society. Books, videos and clubs help people to work on their own body, its appearance and its contribution to their overall sense of well-being. In the late 1990s, it was estimated that around 10 per cent of American adults and 5 per cent of Britons belonged to at least one private health and fitness club (Daneshku, 1998, 17; Henderson, 1999, 1). According to the Fitness Industry Association, over three and a half million Britons belonged to a private club by 2005 – double the number of members five years previously (Box and Waples, 2005, 5). Moreover, by this time a smaller but growing number had installed private gyms in their own homes, thereby avoiding the embarrassment of exposing a less than perfect body to the gaze of strangers.

Partly because these are mostly private ventures, relying on customer loyalty and word-of-mouth for their income, gym organisers pay great attention to learner expectations. If you join a fitness club, you are likely to find that it is managed so that you can learn and exercise new techniques with others like yourself, and perhaps even with those who have similar body shape to yours. While gender may well be one important factor – with separate classes for men and women – there is some evidence that age or generation may well be more significant. Certainly one German study has found that attitudes toward beauty and body varied far more by age than by gender or other factors such as occupation, with most people start-ing to worry less about their appearance at some time during their fifties (Kluge *et al*, 1999). But this study does not really distinguish chronological age from generational attributes, and this could be important if attitudes towards the body are influenced more by generation than by age, as seems likely. Just as teenagers of the 1960s have become today's jeans-wearing grannies and granddads, so it seems likely that health club membership, anorexia and bulimia will characterise the generation of grandparents of the 2050s.

Fitness curricula demonstrate a curious mixture of individualism and community. Your first session may be devoted to the analysis of your personal level of fitness at present, followed by the design of a personal fitness plan. Staff are encouraged to establish a strongly egalitarian rapport with learners, minimising the social distance be-tween them, and perhaps flattering rather than challenging. As one interviewee put it:

> [Trainer's first name] was terrifically friendly from the word go, you can be cynical about it if you want but she really did make me feel that the personal plan was for me, that she'd done it specially for me ... she said that I had the ideal body for it, and my attitude, that was just right for it as well. (Female interviewee, Northampton, 18 June 1998)

Another woman drew an explicit contrast between her experience and that of the groups who attended public adult education fitness courses:

> You build up a relationship with your personal trainer, you start day one and you both build it from there. You get to know each other. It's very, very individualised and it's about *your* fitness and your own goals and it's lifelong. I don't think evening classes are like that, really, are they? (Female interviewee, London, 7 July 1998)

Tuition and support, then, are designed and delivered with the aim of appearing to learners to be both flexible and personalised, but also to present quite a different experience from that conventionally associated with the relations between 'teacher' and 'taught'. Yet despite the individualistic ethos of much fitness training, parti-cipants are in fact engaging in a common project, and because drop-out levels are extremely high, staff seek to encourage a high level of bonding and identification with the club. The participants dress in much the same branded sportswear – some fitness clubs even adopt semi-military discipline, encouraging learners to attend in camouflaged sportswear (Brockmann, 1999). This, then, is a paradoxical form of individualisation, combined as it is with a degree of uniformity and sociability (Bauman, 1998, 30).

Yet the fitness industry also typifies the contradictions of the learning society. While functioning as adult teachers, workers in the industry may find themselves described alternatively as trainers, consultants, advisers or leaders; subjectively, only where their classes are run by an adult education service are the staff likely to see themselves as explicitly having any connection with adult learning. The industry's growth has generated a welter of qualifications and courses, many of them in the further education sector, others in the larger chain firms such as Living Well, founded as a subsidiary of the Stakis hotels and casinos group, subsequently taken over by Ladbroke. Yet in much of the industry pay levels are reportedly low and insiders say that career prospects are poor (Henderson, 1999, 1). Fitness centre staff, particularly when working directly with the public, are almost invariably youthful; according to the owner of an Edinburgh-based fitness consultancy, they also have to 'look healthy, be full of life and be enthusiastic at all times' (Henderson, 1999, 1). In this, the industry mirrors wider trends in the growth of 'aesthetic labour' and 'emotional labour', which are explored in the following chapter.

Much of the new adult learning is concerned with appearances: the 'enterprising self' (Fenwick, 2003) has to look and act the part. A visible neglect of either the body or the mind can spell death for the managerial career. The successful manager is careful not only to grapple with the latest gurus but to be seen and known to be familiar with their thinking, but effortlessly, as a matter of routine, rather than through any extraordinary feat of autodidacticism. At the same time, any competition between managers will be won by whoever is the first to be heard denouncing this or that influential trend-setter as a notorious has-been, provided that the denunciation is plausible. There has been a steady growth in the number of management fads since 1945, accelerating rapidly from about 1990 to become a veritable industry. Moreover this expansion has taken place even though many of the managerial panaceas have turned out to be actively harmful when put into practice, rather than beneficial. Perhaps it is true, as has been suggested, that the whole phenomenon is best understood as providing a legitimation for managers' 'political strategies for mobilising resources and enrolling people toward a particular objective' (Knights and McCabe, 2003, 46). While part of the explanation lies on the supply side, for example, the vested interest of consultants and gurus in in-built obsolescence, the extraordinarily uncritical way in which gurus are received is largely due to the display value of their products to the managers who consume them so sycophantically (Ramsay, 1996, 155-67). Yet guru knowledge contains an in-built tendency to intellectual obsolescence; combined with the context-bound nature of much management and entrepreneurial know-how, the struggle to keep ahead brings with it the anxieties and tensions of what Tara Fenwick calls 'fluid knowledge' (Fenwick, 2003, 176).

The new nonformal adult learning is a form of active consumption. It enables individuals to work on their body, their identity, and their relationships. Rather than struggling against the oppression of another class or nation, the new adult learners are struggling with themselves and their intimate relationships. Much of the provision has grown, rapidly and so far largely unregulated, whether in the commercial sector or around the alternative economy of therapies, dietary regimes and self-administered complementary treatment. This is not to say that it has no social purpose whatever; even at the subjective level, participation in such adult learning may be emancipatory or be felt as emancipatory. Courses in complementary medicine may make you feel more independent of the health professionals, for example; fitness training may liberate you from the constraints of your existing body shape; relationship counselling may help you find the 'real me' that has been hidden in an unsatisfactory marriage. Even adult educators must demonstrate that they are enterprising subjects, taking risks and demonstrating their adaptability, their capacity to duck and weave and adjust to new trends. Indeed, as Fenwick shows, some adult educators are abandoning an increasingly neglected public sector to find new roles for themselves in the new nonformal adult learning, balancing their new-found freedoms and autonomy with the anxieties of continuous change and all the tensions of fluid knowledge (Fenwick, 2003). And certainly this type of learning is contributing to significant social change (Giddens, 1994). Nevertheless, much of the new non-formal learning is seen by learners as part of an extended project of personal development or self-realisation. It is one among many trends that are contributing to, and shaped by, the wider processes of individualisation.

Fashion and the individual

How seriously are we to take these phenomena? Are they simply fads, the result of a hyperbolic sales pitch on the supply side and neurotic insecurity on the demand side? If so, they can be disregarded by any serious student of lifelong learning, or even lamented as a sign of the degradation that lifelong learning has wrought on a once-vigorous culture of enlightened self-improvement. Or is there something more substantial going on?

Take the example of self-help texts. Such texts are part of a wider cultural milieu – a world of books, magazines, television programmes, counselling, newspaper articles and training activities that are closely interwoven with the encounters and discourses of everyday life. Their scale has become increasingly significant. It was estimated recently, for example, that more than one third of adult Britons regularly reads at least one lifestyle magazine (Hancock and Tyler, 2004, 621). Moreover, the best-selling forms of self-help texts tend to focus on what Hancock and Tyler (2004, 623) call 'broad issues of 'being' – intimate relations, the body, impression management and style – rather than hobbies and skills, finding readers particularly among the young (defined socially and culturally rather than chronologically, ranging from 'tweenies' to 'silver surfers') and comparatively affluent. They are marked by constant change: reiki has displaced crystal therapy, Atkins the high fibre diet, Nordic walking challenged indoor fitness regimes, and all in turn will give way to something newer still. Celebrity endorsements attract attention to the new and signal the death of the old, yet celebrity too has a short use-by date, and must either reinvent itself constantly – as Kylie and Madonna have done – or sink into the by waters of supermarket opening ceremonies.

This remarkable phenomenon has attracted attention from a variety of social scientists as well as journalists. Giddens, for example, has famously used self-help texts to undergird his theory of institutionalised reflexivity as a key dimension of everyday life in late modernity (Giddens, 1991). Other social scientists have seen self-help literature as part of the colonisation of the life world, the McDonaldisation of everyday life through controlled, managed, bureaucratic routines (Hancock and Tyler, 2004). For both sets of commentators, the management of the self is a hallmark of contemporary social change. Yet until recently, the self-help phenomenon has commanded little interest from professionals and scholars concerned with lifelong learning.

The sole exception to date, published since the first edition of this book, is a study of the construction of learner identities in self-help texts, among other contexts (Chappell, Rhodes, Solomon, Tennant and Yates, 2003). Rather, many educationalists and researchers have dismissed self-help publishing and reading as a lightweight and superficial activity, with no real implications for education and training. Academic critiques are almost invariably dismissive and even sneering. One group has referred disparagingly to 'fast capitalist texts' (Lankshear *et al*, 1997, 83), while Paul Lichterman, in his account of popular psychology in the USA, describes this material as representing what he calls 'thin culture':

> Educated, middle-class readers approach self-help psychology books ambivalently. They participate in a culture of popular psychology reading that allows them to simultaneously trust and discount books, all the while maintaining an open-minded, experimental attitude towards new titles as they appear. The ambivalence stems in part from readers' recognition of the books as commodities, and in part from relations with other points of reference which readers juggle together with their self-help reading as they improvise ways of coping with personal troubles. (Lichterman, 1992, 427)

Lichterman's point, though, is more substantial than his terminology initially suggests: it is not that these texts are negligible, but that they express and enable a certain disposition towards the self.

The texts themselves come, and they go. Gail Sheehy's work has already been referred to as an example. It is one of many self-help texts that have had their day, duly replaced by others which in their turn will be eclipsed. And that is precisely the point: modishness and ephemerality are important because they allow their consumers to feel themselves pioneers, to demonstrate their ability to experiment, to pick and choose among the variety of solutions on offer. This behaviour is far from thoughtless or irrational; it is the very stuff of the contemporary learning society.

In-built ephemerality, novelty for its own sake, the search for sheer pleasure – these consumerist dispositions can also be found right across the sphere of adult learning. Is the new informal learning rather superficial? For sure, there is an increased risk that individuals may be tempted to 'discard convention' for the sake of it, simply in order to appear to be 'up for it'. Rather than discarding established modes of behaving and thinking by making a rational choice, the temptation is to throw away all the old role models and standards in a completely unreflexive manner (Jansen and van der Veen, 1992). The late Christopher Lasch spoke of the 'banality of pseudo-self-awareness', complaining that contemporary advertising 'educates' the masses into an unappeasable appetite not only for goods but for new experiences and personal fulfilment' (Lasch, 1980, 137). More recently, Frank Furedi has described such phenomena as parent education and counselling as evidence of a learned helplessness (Furedi, 1997, 91). For Furedi, we live in a climate of fear, where individuals turn to counselling or education as a form of insurance. But does this make the new adult learning intrinsically superficial? We might reply that the formal educational system offers equally superficial knowledge in the face of many everyday challenges: how has school or university helped us learn to cope with the death of a loved one, the birth of a child, or the break-up of a marriage? Yet even this seems to miss the point.

Much of the new adult learning is designed to enable learners to deal with intangibles and uncertainties. In a relatively fluid and open society, the fact that learning – and its public performance – can often provide only temporary reassurance seems to be an acceptable price to pay in return for the confidence to go into social spaces with no other compass. As Skeggs has pointed out, cultural capital is 'difficult to access and use when one is not accustomed to it, when it is not part of the background and dispositions which are used to define oneself' (Skeggs, 1997, 90). When the value of cultural capital can fluctuate rapidly, a lightweight approach to learning makes a great deal of sense. And the readers of self-help texts are themselves active participants in this process; it is hardly a challenge for those with sufficient confidence or experience to respond with ambivalence, cynicism or outright rejection to the messages of mastery of the self (Hancock and Tyler, 2004, 637).

Fashion is also driven by commercial pressures. The new adult education has grown almost entirely on a commercial basis, even among not-for-profit agencies who want to attract people interested in environmental or social issues. Earthwatch, an environmental organisation which recruits fee-paying volunteers for working vacations on field-based projects, saw its membership increase on average by over 20 per cent a year between 1971 and 1991 (Cherfas, 1992). By 2000, with funding from the government's Adult and Community Learning Fund, Earthwatch had developed a number of environmental field projects for adults from disadvantaged groups. However, their capacity to widen their reach in this way rested primarily on the steady stream of income from learners able to pay quite substantial sums to take part in residential field work.

Similarly, the fitness industry has grown up mainly in the private sector. Britain's private sector fitness industry is now worth over £1 billion a year. In the public sector, many institutions have chosen to increase their commercial income, as a way of providing a cushion against the vagaries of state funding regimes – ironically so, given that it is the commercial market place that has traditionally been seen as insecure, and the pre-new-public-management state as guaranteeing a degree of continuity. Once active in the market place, any provider must not only keep abreast of current trends but must be seen to do so. A reputation for concentrating on outmoded programmes can be the kiss of death. New subjects appear, take the entire adult education world by storm, then vanish with barely a trace. Recent examples include women's self-defence, djembe drumming, line dancing and tai chi, all of which started out as somewhat controversial and even avant-garde topics, became apparently firm favourites, eventually lost much of their popularity, and were then scorned as ludicrously old-fashioned. Pressures to stay ahead of the game, and provide courses on the latest hot topic, are therefore as powerful for the public sector as for its commercial competitors.

Can this new fashion-conscious adult learning really be called individualistic, and if so in what sense? Is it not simply the instinctive, visceral movement of a herd – or a flock of sheep? Is anything deeper going on than simple modishness? Certainly there is a growing emphasis in curriculum thinking on the individual needs and responsibilities of the learner. In a 'knowledge society', passive forms of learning are no longer enough; rather, 'learners must become proactive and more autonomous' (CEC, 1998b, 9). Indeed this form of learning is self-directed in two senses. And, typically, the resources that support this type of learning lend themselves to use by individuals who do their studying alone. Self-help texts routinely reach the bestseller lists: one relationship self-help text, John Gray's *Men are from Mars, Women are from Venus,* reached UK sales well above the half-million mark (*Sunday Times*, 11 October, 1998).

Much of the new learning takes place in the home, often involving the different generations, and is supported by resources you get while you are doing your shopping. The immediate family is an important site for the new adult learning. It meshes in with the wider shift towards home-based entertainment, mirrored by the growth in such phenomena as interactive home-based technologies or the explosion of the heritage industry. Overall spending on sight-seeing, for example, nearly trebled in the period between 1971 and 1996 (Henry, 1999, 284). Again, this forms an important part of wider changes in social behaviour. Summarising the findings of a Henley Centre study of time use patterns, Alan Tomlinson has written that the general pattern

... is clear enough. After early adulthood more and more people spend more and more of their spare time in and around the house. Televisions, gardens, home improvements, home screenings, home entertaining. These constitute the core elements in a consumer culture which develops the home as self-governed leisure centre. (Tomlinson, 1986, 47)

If you want to bone up on Turkey before your family holiday, get yourself in shape, or improve your golf, then buy a video or CD-ROM, or simply go online.

A great deal of hype surrounds the educational use of the new technologies. Usually, they are presented completely uncritically as a terrific boon, something that will make education and training accessible to all. And perhaps this is true. The new technologies are often already comfortable and familiar parts of our homes, leisure, shopping, or workplace. Educational and leisure subjects now take up around 5 per cent of video shelf space in Virgin megastores. In France, a substantial software industry has emerged to re-engineer products for the local market, so that Microsoft's best-selling *Encarta* encyclopaedia, with its 30,000 entries, acquired some 2,500 new entries, and lost such irrelevancies as the entries for US vice presidents and English cities (Latrive, 1997). These materials are available for all to buy on every high street, through the internet, in every shopping centre, in railway stations and in airports. Internet access to information and learning programmes is expanding exponentially; according to one estimate, the projected value of the pay-per-view market would rise to £6 billion by 2008, with distance learning taking a growing share (Vision Consultancy Group, 1999).

Most of the resources you can buy in the high street are not all that new – audio tapes, self-help books, and video tapes are hardly revolutionary. Even the newer technologies like the internet and interactive TV are relatively simple to use. And most of them dovetail neatly into our daily lives. More cars on the road means more time spent driving (or sitting in traffic), so that drivers start to use their CD players to learn a new language or bone up on their meetings skills. More DVD players in our homes mean that more people can record educational programmes or play instructional DVDs. More networked households or workplaces mean that people can explore the informational boundaries of the internet, to an extent which has employers divided between those who want to stop their employees surfing during working hours and those who are delighted that their staff are acquiring new know-how. But the very familiarity of these resources brings its own penalties. Because we have grown accustomed to their use for entertainment, we tend to view educational materials as though their main purpose was pleasurable. Often this is a minor challenge to producers: in the 1970s and 1980s, for instance, the comedian John Cleese developed a highly lucrative and popular sideline by turning out serio-comic management videos. But the viewer's expectations still place limits on what the new resources can deliver effectively.

As an illustration, take the attention span of TV viewers. We know that the MTV rock station was surprised when its researchers discovered that the average viewer watched their programmes for around two and a half minutes before switching channel; the company had assumed that the average viewing span was closer to ten minutes (Front Row, 1999). If this behaviour were replicated among adult learners viewing screen-based learning materials, producers might have to impart information in very short bursts if they are to retain attention. In itself, this isn't too great a challenge – but it does mean that any topic which requires sustained exposition and concentrated attention is probably not well suited to screen-based media. It may also mean that even those topics which can be dealt with in short bursts will have to be presented without assuming that the viewer has any sense of context, since they may or may not watch the previous and following short bursts. These are serious limitations on any form of planned instruction.

An increasing focus on the home also implies an increasing emphasis on the family. However, the family too has changed. Families are much smaller, children are treated as consumer goods and simultaneously seen as possessing rights, and there is a powerful idealisation of youth in western cultures. Sometimes children teach adults, much more often they teach each other. Some have argued that we can now identify something called 'inverse socialisation' – that is, children are occasionally able to induct adults into the mysterious ways of modern existence (Cochinaux and de Woot, 1995, 27). The most obvious example is the new information and communications technologies, where from a comparatively early stage, competence appears to decline with chronological age. Once more, though, the role of family and friendship networks appears to be critical.

Similarly, the popularity of complementary therapies – which by 1995 were on offer in well over a third of general practices – is reported to be due to the time that therapists give each patient, the way in which the therapy relates to the 'whole person', and the patient's desire to take a degree of control over their own health

(Vaughan, 1999, 20). In British industry in 1999, it was estimated that around 700 employers offered voluntary counselling to employees. For many, this service was part of a package that was sub-contracted from a health-care provider (MacEarlean, 1999, 9). While the employers concerned were perhaps more worried about productivity and performance levels than about facilitating self-realisation among their workforce, they felt obliged to undertake the latter in order to promote the former. This too is a way of individualising responsibility for any problems – it is individual employees who need a boost to their self-identity – and of pathologising the problem itself: low performance is deemed evidence of a faulty personality.

From the perspective of an older type of adult education dedicated to enlightenment, social improvement and the support of social movements, this individualism represents an abandonment of social purpose. But the type of social movement that gave rise to social purpose adult education has itself changed. Trade union meetings are attended by a tiny minority of members; the Christian churches are almost empty; even environmental or women's movements are associations in a considerably looser sense than their counterparts of the late nineteenth and early twentieth centuries.

More generally, voluntary activity of all kinds is changing. In Britain, traditional women's organisations such as the Women's Institutes are experiencing a long-term and apparently inexorable decline, as are some types of youth groups and sports clubs; this decline also affected the trade unions and some service organisations (e.g. the Red Cross) during the 1980s. As in the USA, these tendencies have sometimes been taken to herald a decline in voluntary engagement (Putnam, 2000). Overall, though, there has been a slow but steady expansion in association membership in Britain since the 1970s, apparently affecting all social groups and all generations, but particularly among women (Hall, 1999, 421-4). Given that a close association exists between sociability in voluntary associations and the effectiveness of informal learning (Field and Spence, 2000), these trends are highly significant. Moreover, the growth in associational membership appears to be itself closely associated with rising educational standards, again particularly among women (Hall, 1999, 436-7; Li *et al*, 2003). However, these trends have helped reshape the overall picture of associational membership, as newer social movements and local forms of engagement have overtaken some of the more traditional and national organisations. And this has in turn altered the prospects for informal learning.

Rather than lamenting the decline of collective values, it makes more sense to explore the potential for reconciling the search for individual autonomy with new forms of social integration (Beck and Sopp, 1997). Yet again it is important to distinguish individualism on the one hand, and isolated egotism or monism on the other. The new adult learners, for instance, are clearly looking, among other things, for ways in which to situate themselves in a social world where nothing is certain any longer. In so far as they undertake learning through civic engagement, it may be through the membership of 'imaginary communities' that provide ready access to (selected) information which members may sift and judge for themselves, rather than by face-to-face involvement in routine meetings and structured collective action.

The new adult learning is a part of a much broader process. As individuals come to rely less on traditional institutions and the authority figures associated with them – church leaders, parents, aristocracy – to guide their behaviour, so they become more self-directed. At least in principle, they can select from a variety of possible role models; traditional role models certainly do not disappear – indeed, they are an important if little-understood resource for fundamentalist movements – but to select any role model requires that individuals face up to an increasing range of biographical options (Jansen and Klaassen, 1994, 77). And those who are most reliant upon self-direction, and are most likely to espouse post-materialist values, are placed in a position where refusing to learn is simply not an option. On the contrary, those who actively embrace self-direction and post-materialism are most likely to favour learning as a positive lifestyle feature, a sign that they can cope with chaos. And if it is hardly surprising that many adults enjoy learning on their own, interestingly, it is among young people that the support of a group is most highly valued, at least in Britain (Campaign for Learning, 1998, 20-21). It should be emphasised that we are discussing individualisation as a process and not egotism as a chiefly negative attribute – it is not necessarily either a selfish or a self-centred process. Empirically, the relationship appears to be rather complex: while there is substantial survey evidence of greater individualisation across the Western nations, it appears that individualism (or egotism) is limited to specific domains where individuals believe that they should single-mindedly pursue their own interests (Halman, 1996, 200-209).

This is not to glorify individualism or to see it as invariably untainted by egotism and self-aggrandisement. It is perfectly possible for the new adult learning to be extremely materialistic. The increasing popularity of investment clubs – whose members come together to learn about and invest in the stock market – is a good example of the potential combination of self-directed learning, sociability, and a concern for the financial bottom line. Spreading rapidly from their origins in the USA, there were by 1999 some 70 such clubs in the Republic of Ireland alone. Clubs are typically formed from those who have insufficient capital or expertise to make solo investment a worthwhile option, and they invariably consist of people who have some common basis for trusting one another; thus the mba.ie investment club, with 20 members and a £IR 50 monthly subscription, is drawn from people who met through their association with an MBA programme in Dublin City University. Individual club members carry out an agreed process of research into potential investment areas, reporting back to the monthly meetings which then vote on how the pooled funds are to be invested (Ward, 1999, 3).

Furthermore, the situation of learners in the new adult education can be highly contradictory. It may be difficult to reconcile the values of self-direction and autonomy with dependency on a teacher, particularly when this is combined with the risks of exposure or even humiliation in front of one's peers. One solution may be to opt out of institutionalised instruction altogether, studying alone rather than in a group, from materials rather than from direct instruction. Another is for learners to deal with the conflict between their adult roles and identities on the one hand and the childish status of returning to school by seizing control of interpersonal relations within the classroom, even if only temporarily. Mike Baynham has convincingly argued that classroom humour and 'off-task exchanges' frequently provide a way for 'participants, teachers and students, to manage being in the classroom together, with all the potential for conflict of unequal power/knowledge situations' (Baynham, 1996, 197-8). Banter and entertainment do help to keep up recruitment levels (Salisbury and Murcott, 1992, 563-8). Naturally, this is not new: in 1921, Basil Yeaxlee noted that 'study is the adult's recreation ... In adult education the pupil must enjoy himself' (Yeaxlee, 1921, 33). But pointing out that adult education has always involved a bit of fun as a way of keeping up the numbers is only part of the story. Baynham is surely right to see humour and 'off-task exchanges' – particularly when student-driven – as ways of handling the complex status of being both learner and adult. They are a way of working actively and creating an identity.

Reflexive modernisation

How are we to understand this expanding world of highly individualistic and consumer-oriented learning? Individuals' lives are
changing, and the world of adult learning is being transformed as a
result. I have tried to stress that this process does not arise solely
from economic factors but is also deeply bound up with cultural and
social change. This is an important point. Because the policy case for
lifelong learning is so closely bound up with skills and com-
petitivess, it is easy to lose sight of the profound transformation of
individual biographies, in respect not just of work but also of home,
leisure, consumption, or even intimate relationships. All have become more unpredictable, all now require us actively to make decisions about what we plan to do with our lives, and to weigh up a
range of often contradictory information and knowledge as we do
so. One group of social theorists – already liberally referred to in this
essay – has described these changes as part of a wider process of
'reflexive modernisation'. As their work has considerable importance
for our understanding of lifelong learning, it may be helpful briefly
to summarise here some of their main ideas.

Perhaps the best known among this group are Ulrich Beck, Professor
of Sociology at the University of Munich, and Anthony Giddens,
until recently the Director of the London School of Economics.
While differing in some key respects, they have reached similar conclusions concerning the central role of knowledge in contemporary
societies. In some respects, both writers stand in the mainstream of
sociological analysis, with clear debts to the founding fathers,
Durkheim and Weber. In emphasising that humans are agents of
their fate and not simply the passive bearers of positions within the
social structure, both Beck and Giddens are faced with the problem
of explaining how the modern world differs from the past. Rejecting
post-modernist theories as offering no explanation at all, both focus
in on what Beck calls the individualising tendencies of late modernity. Giddens puts it like this: each individual is faced with the fact
that their social relationships are becoming disembedded from the
specific contexts associated with habit and tradition, and are therefore increasingly contingent upon choice and reflection. In turn, this
disembedding process is being achieved as a result of three forces.
First, globalising tendencies not only foster a degree of standardisation on the one hand but also encourage individuals to compare
their own situation with information about what appears to work
perfectly well in other contexts. Second, 'symbolic tokens', such as
money but also the specialised languages of science and business,

are increasingly spanning all kinds of localised boundaries, and thanks to information technologies they do so not only in space but also in time. Third, expert systems, or rationally structured orders of knowledge, are growing in importance and are increasingly accessible to wide ranges of citizens. For both Beck and Giddens, the importance of this account is that it draws attention to the ways in which a whole host of social practices – from the broadest to the most intimate – are always being re-examined in the light of new information.

For Beck, the key characteristic of late modernity is 'risk' (Beck, 1992). While Beck accepts that knowledge now plays a central role in contemporary capitalist economies, he also draws attention to the unintended consequences that frequently seem to follow on from the application of new knowledge. The most obvious example of this process is environmental degradation and pollution. But at individual level also, people are more reluctant to place their fate in the hands of organisations – whether state or corporation, neither of whom has proved to be all-wise in recent years – yet are aware that there may be unintended consequences of taking responsibility for their own, individual futures. Underpinned by his notion of the 'risk society', Beck places a strong emphasis upon the individualisation of both life situations and biographical patterns. This is not the same as egotism or atomisation; on the contrary, individualisation is for Beck a profoundly social process, in which the ability reflexively to plan, choose and maintain one's relationships and practices becomes central for individuals to be able to negotiate the unpredictable risks of modernity. For Beck, this raises the prospect of new forms of inequality, thanks to an inherently unequal distribution not only of the 'goods' of modernisation but also of the 'bads' (Beck, 1996).

Although developed separately, Giddens' work shows many similarities to Beck's. Although similarly attracted by the idea of risk and uncertainty as fundamental features of contemporary existence, Giddens emphasises that humans have always faced these phenomena, often on a scale now virtually unknown, at least in the comfort zones of the Western world. What is new is the pervasive awareness of 'manufactured risk' – that is, risk that arises precisely out of human activity, and particularly out of the application of knowledge, rather than from natural phenomena: food scares and radioactive contamination, say, rather than plague and famine. Giddens also differs from Beck in emphasising the importance of the social sciences in fostering a thorough-going, radical reflexivity:

70

> The reflexivity of modern life consists in the fact that social practices are constantly examined and reformed in the light of incoming information about those very practices, thus constitutively altering their character... In all cultures, social practices are routinely altered in the light of ongoing discoveries which feed into them. But only in the era of modernity is the revision of convention radicalised to apply (in principle) to all aspects of human life. (Giddens, 1990, 38-9)

Examples of this process offered by Giddens himself include decisions over gender identity or genetic inheritance, as well as more day-to-day decisions about relationships or diet. In one extended study, Giddens has examined the way in which social psychology is popularised through self-help manuals, designed to appeal to people who are re-examining their relationships (Giddens, 1992). For Giddens, these are evidence that no social practice is too small-scale and too intimate to escape the disembedding processes that are typical of late modern society. All behaviour and all relationships can be, and frequently are, subjected to the process of institutionalised reflexivity.

How do these social theories contribute to our understanding of lifelong learning? First, their very existence commands attention. Not to put too fine a point on it, some of our most prominent social thinkers regard knowledge and reflexivity as the central levers of change in modern society. This alone should encourage us to take stock of the implications; even if Beck and Giddens have got it badly wrong, they are nonetheless highly influential figures, and not only in their own fields. Giddens and Beck are also leading theorists of the 'Third Way' school of political thought (Giddens, 1998). Since both place permanent learning ('reflexivity') at the heart of their theoretical contribution, this should ensure that they are of some interest at least to those who are concerned with lifelong learning.

Second, Giddens' and Beck's theories may have a more direct bearing upon the nature of lifelong learning (Hake, 1998; Schemmann, 2002). Their direct relevance will depend largely on whether their accounts hold water. In my view, they certainly contribute something to our understanding of the scope of lifelong learning, as well as of its ultimate significance. They are not the only theoretical fish in our practical sea, and other contributions are drawn upon often enough in this account, but their work seems to me central in grasping the underlying function and place of lifelong learning in contemporary societies.

From Giddens' and Beck's accounts of institutionalised reflexivity, at least two conclusions stand out. The first is that lifelong learning can be as much about the 'small things' of everyday life as about the grand objects of conventional discourse. Second, institutionalised reflexivity will not simply go away. Increasingly, it is the medium of human action and interaction, and its associated problems – uncertainty, insecurity, change for the sake of change, inequalities of distribution and access – will need to be tackled. Third, they offer a complex and nuanced account of the interaction between the large impersonal forces that shape human destiny – globalisation, technological change, changing values and so on – and the social practices of individual actors. Giddens and Beck can be faulted for understating the role of faddism and situational constraints, both of which strike me as fundamental to the processes of institutionalised reflexivity as they are operationalised in given social practices. I also worry about the all-embracing nature of their analysis, suggesting as it does that these tendencies affect more or less everyone, to a more or less equal extent (on this, see the discussion below of the more discriminating analysis to be found in Vester, 1997). But the emphasis upon human agency, reflexivity and trust is central to the understanding of lifelong learning presented here.

Trust is particularly significant since open situations are also, potentially, full of uncertainty and risk. In principle, they may lead to more subjective decision-taking and choice in life planning; but they also confront the individual with the possibility of taking decisions that may inadvertently lead to a dead end or even a reversal, affecting not only oneself but possibly also intimate others (Jansen and Klaassen, 1994, 77-8). Little wonder, then, that the discourse of self-development and self-actualisation is such an important part of self-help therapy. One irony is that 'Although this expertise forms an essential and very substantial theme in public discourse, it is a rhetoric that is oriented to private lives' (Chaney, 1998, 541).

Some have argued that, far from becoming increasingly reflexive and innovative, late modern societies are virtually trapped in a cycle of mistrust and fear. In particular, the growth of new forms of personal development and growth such as counselling or alternative therapy are marks of 'a society that lacks confidence about its future direction' and is unclear about how to handle relationships (Furedi, 1997, 132-3). However, for Anthony Giddens 'the ethos of self-growth signals major social transformation in late modernity as a whole ... burgeoning institutional reflexivity, the disembedding of social relations by abstract systems, and the consequent interpenetration of the local and global' (Giddens, 1991, 209). For Giddens and Beck, it is precisely the continuous and active engagement between individuals and knowledge that characterises late modernity. Yet while these theories offer significant insights into the importance of lifelong learning, they also have limitations.

One drawback with reflexive modernisation theories is their tendency to project the key shifts onto the entire adult population. Yet none of these trends – globalising tendencies, abstract know-ledge, institutional reflexivity – impacts equally upon the entire population. Even in relatively affluent and cohesive societies such as those of Western Europe and North America, reflexive modernisa-tion has an extremely uneven impact. Examining contemporary social and cultural change in Germany, Michael Vester has used Bourdieu's concept of the social space to distinguish four broad groupings, each differently affected by – and grappling with – the tendencies towards change:

- the highly individualised, critically engaged with modernising tendencies, concentrated in the upper and most modernised social groupings, and thriving on their ability to ride out un-certainty

- the insecure middle-of-the-road, largely drawn from the middle generations of those workers who in Germany enjoy a middle-income and middle-education, some of whom are becoming disillusioned with aspects of modernity as a result of growing insecurity

- the comfortable conservatives, relatively well-situated finan-cially but experiencing a tendency for their children to move away from the traditionalism espoused by their parents

- those 'declassé' groups most damaged by the collapse of esta-blished social ties and increasingly confined to the darker shadows of modernity, showing a tendency either to withdraw into apathy from public life or to sympathise with aggressive radicalism, often of the neo-right variety (Vester, 1997, 115-17)

Extending this analysis somewhat speculatively, Vester's distinctions might usefully be applied between different parts of the population in respect of lifelong learning (figure 1, page 74).

Does this mean lightweight learning?

In an overview of sports and leisure trends in the 1990s, Ian Henry discerns 'a picture of increased individualism, privatisation and

Figure One: Lifelong learning in the social space

The permanent learners

■ Learning and self-development a core part of identity

■ Highly motivated to learn

■ Adept at self-directed learning

■ 'Learning pioneers' who espouse new methods

■ Critical of 'outmoded' established providers

The instrumental learners

■ Willing to learn when asked by employer

■ Learning is a means to an end

■ Accept the provider chosen by superiors

■ Strong preference for well-tried and tested methods

The traditional learners

■ Learning a core part of identity

■ Subject-driven values within an academic hierarchy

■ Highly motivated to learn

■ Strong preference for well-tried and tested methods

■ Great respect for academic providers

The non-learners

■ Non-(or anti-)academic self-identity

■ Organised learning either avoided or undertaken under pressure

■ No belief in the effectiveness of learning

■ Resentment of all providers

social polarisation' (Henry, 1999, 287). The same might be said of a great deal of the new adult learning, which has attracted much derision from its critics. One eminent English adult educator, for instance, has attacked the heritage industry as a 'virulent form' of 'lower case history' (Fieldhouse, 1997, 5). Others suggest that the new adult learning represents a 'worship of technique', at the expense of anything more substantial or purposive (Biesta, 2004). This pervades even our most intimate moments: 'We turn to books to learn how to make love and in consequence sex comes to be thought of as mainly a technique' (Barrett, 1979, 25). And this critique is certainly not lacking in power. But this knee-jerk rejection misses the point. The sheer extent to which economic activities and social values have changed since the 1940s means that old boundaries between 'real learning' and 'trivial learning' are becoming blurred; much that seemed trivial in the past assumes a new significance as we learn to handle fluid social relationships and an increasingly insecure economy. There is a growing fluidity to adult identities, accompanied by an increasing tendency for certainties to be replaced by provisional knowledge. Lightly-worn learning, a capacity to live with uncertainty and a preoccupation with the personal and individual are the counterpart of the fluid identities that Bauman sees as characteristic of post-modernity: 'the life itinerary of most individuals', he writes, 'is likely to be strewn with discarded and lost identities' (Bauman, 1998, 28). For some, the capacity to handle the new and surf the uncertain is itself an important defining characteristic of the self. Laue Traberg Smidt has noted the way in which education programmes delivered through a new technology will tend to recruit 'pioneer types who are attracted by a new medium' (Smidt, 1999, 44).

And all this has consequences for the established formal sector. Rather than turning away from the new adult learning, established providers appear to be going half way towards meeting learner expectations. This has become a key strategy for survival. The ability to spot a trend – Tai Chi, line dancing – is crucial to the management of an adult education programme. Personal qualities such as warmth, humour and tact are vital tools for the adult education tutor. Using participant observation, a study of two adult evening classes in the early 1990s noted that the tutor's ability to entertain her students was central in holding up student numbers. In one language class, 'there were times when fun and the mechanisms for creating it were far more prevalent than the learning. However, the fact remains that student recruitment to French 2 held up for three terms' (Salisbury and Murcott, 1992, 564). Such tendencies are even clearer in IT-based learning, where the technologies are usually familiar to learners from their experiences of home-based entertainment.

When a major national museum analysed use of its web site in the winter of 1997/98, it found that the number of visitors was rising sharply, reaching over 23,000 by February 1998. But in each month the average visitor only looked at one or two other pages after the home page, and less than one tenth visited the education section (Thomas and Paterson, 1998). In order to attract visitors and retain them, educational packages have no alternative but to be entertaining. Understanding this, the Director of the Institute for the Learning Sciences at Northwestern University in Illinois encourages staff to contrive their learning materials accordingly: 'We designed Road Trip (a geography programme) for the student who would rather be home watching television than in school' (Schrank, 1994, 5). As education and entertainment borrow one another's clothes, it is inevitable that some of the new adult learning will be lightweight, superficial, and transient in its impact. This is not to say that the new adult learning does not pose serious challenges to the providers of adult education and training. If established providers ignore these trends, they may be overtaken by events; if they adopt them, they may be colluding in a trivialisation of knowledge.

Yet it is not at all clear whether established providers have much of a future. In a world of unbounded adult learning, the role of the specialised adult education institution and its workforce of specialised adult education teachers is far from clear. If learning takes place everywhere, much of it informally or without an instructor, then adult education workers and institutions have at best a somewhat secondary role. Tendencies towards the recognition and valuing of informal learning, at least by employers if not by many formal educational institutions (Felstead *et al,* 2004), are further eroding the notion of the adult education worker as a source of expertise. At the same time, all sorts of people can suddenly find themselves defined as adult educators – people with such diverse job titles as human resource developers, facilitators, trainers, counsellors, personal advisers, community developers, or learning brokers. Yet in a world of knowing, reflexive citizens, the expertise of the adult education worker resides less in their mastery of a subject or skill than in their ability to recognise the perspectives and experiences of learners, and engage them in further learning (Vehviläinen, 2001). Once more, this is not necessarily a comfortable location: Karin Filander accords human resource developers the evocative title of 'homeless experts' (Filander, 2003, 103), whose narratives of work express a culture of ambiguity, marginality, unmanageability and conflicting expectations. The once small, cosy, relatively coherent, institutionalised and somewhat marginal world of the adult education profession has been replaced by a much more diverse, fragmented, uncertain and larger universe of people who in one way or another help to facilitate the learning of others (Edwards, 1997).

Here we are, already in a learning society. I have tried to avoid, in this chapter, more than a glancing mention of vocational lifelong learning, simply because some prominent critics have complained that the notions of lifelong learning and a learning society are obsessed with work and competitiveness to the exclusion of a more general and generous definition (Coffield, 1999; Tight, 1998b). Still ignoring the world of work for a moment, it is possible to say that more people are taking part in a wider range of organised learning; more post-school institutions are reaching adult learners; our informal learning now tries to deal, however unsatisfactorily, with fundamental questions of our individual identity and intimate relations. Moreover, these have now become defining characteristics of our way of life. When Giddens or Ulrich Beck speak of the reflexivity of late modernity, when Manuel Castells writes about the informational society, they define our world as one where learning has become a key resource for individuals and groups. By navigating our lives as 'permanently learning subjects' (Dumazadier, 1995), we are living different lives and attaching different meanings to them from those who in earlier times took their body shape, their linguistic skills, their sexual techniques and their handling of family relationships as given.

Beneath the feathery layer of policy debate lies a much more substantial process of social and economic transformation. I have tried to emphasise the extent to which the learning society is driven by changes in the wider context of individual values, social relationships and living patterns, rather than by economic factors alone. Far from being a simplistic process of dumbing down, the new adult learning mirrors a profound social shift. It both exemplifies and is a key part of the wider processes of reflexive modernisation, and of tendencies towards individualisation. It is in this wider context of socio-economic change that the opportunities and excitement of lifelong learning – as well as the risks and dangers – must be understood.

3
The Learning Economy

Work is changing, though it is doing so in ways that are complex and uneven. Manual work, once the backbone of every industrial or agrarian economy, is in deep decline, particularly in its unskilled forms; service occupations are expanding in size and importance. In the remaining core areas of manufacturing, the new production methods require greater individual responsibility and autonomy from the workforce, while traditional skills are disintegrating. And right across the economy, higher flexibility and adaptability appear to be common features of the vast majority of occupations. For managers, maintaining quality and productivity requires increased attention to the training and development of the entire workforce. For workers, continuing employment depends ever more upon 'readiness to learn over lengthy periods of the working biography', and increasingly 'it is the subjects that, independently and with growing levels of individual risk, must regulate their own vocational capabilities' (Alheit, 1994, 85).

Many have seen this process as heralding a new social order, founded on knowledge. Since the 1970s, there has been debate over the idea of a post-industrial economic order, dominated by highly educated information service workers (Bell, 1973). Robert Reich, Secretary for Labor in President Clinton's first cabinet, has argued that even if highly educated knowledge workers are not numerically dominant in every given economy, the central role is now invariably played by what he calls the 'symbolic analysts' – that is, those whose role is to manipulate and process information (Reich, 1993). This account has become a central element in the 'Third Way' thinking of contemporary social democrats (Giddens, 1998), with potentially far-reaching implications. Tom Bentley, director of a British think-tank that has strongly influenced Third Way policies, claimed in the late '90s that 'We are entering an era in which the most important productive resource is knowledge', and that as a result a new division of labour is emerging which is networked rather than hierarchical, co-ordinated 'not through command and control, but through collaboration' (Bentley, 1998, 101-2). For Bentley as for many others, the new economy promotes equity and openness, with learning opportunities for all.

But this view has not gone unchallenged. In the early 1970s, Harry Braverman argued forcefully that the new technologies and production methods, far from increasing the knowledge component of labour, were in fact deskilling work, and his scepticism has been embraced by a number of critics ever since (Braverman, 1974; see also Gorz, 1994, 56-7). Others have used the evidence of change to reach depressingly negative conclusions. For Richard Sennett, work in the new capitalism can no longer provide a secure social and ethical anchorage for workers to fix a stable identity; the new capitalism is, accordingly, leading to the 'corrosion of character' (Sennett, 1998; see also Crowther, 2004). Claude Dubar has similarly argued that the collapse of stable employment based relationships is producing a 'crisis of identities' for many people (Dubar, 2000). The idea that the 'new economy' is inherently more equitable than the old one has also been vigorously challenged, particularly by feminists (Fenwick, 2004).

Given the prominence of economic concerns in the discourse of lifelong learning, it is important to investigate the context in which these concerns have evolved. Are we really on the verge of a skills revolution? How far is it true that labour is becoming more mobile, or indeed that more mobile labour is required? Surveying the evidence of contemporary labour market developments, this chapter concludes that although policy makers have tended to exaggerate the extent of change, the language of the learning economy has now assumed a momentum of its own. It has done so, though, partly because this discourse chimes with other more dominant forces, including the tendencies to individualism, reflexivity and consumer affluence that have already been sketched out in the previous chapter. Much of the discourse of lifelong learning avoids these social and cultural concerns, centring instead upon a narrow range of largely economic reference points.

Occupational change and the changing skills mix

Work is not what it used to be. The decline of manufacturing occupations, already apparent in the 1970s, has continued inexorably ever since. De-industrialisation has been accompanied by a parallel rise in service sector occupations. In the second half of the twentieth century, the British economy lost some 5 million jobs in manufacturing and agriculture, and gained some 8 million in services. Approximately three quarters of all employees in Britain were working in the service sector by the late 1990s, and only one quarter in manufacturing; agriculture employed a mere 2.3 per cent. Moreover, this trend was set to continue: it was expected that nine out of every ten jobs created in the future would be in services (Armistead, 1994). To varying degrees, the same trends are visible in Australasia, North America, the rest of Europe and Japan.

As well as a general growth in service sector employment and the decline of manufacturing, the period since the Second World War has seen steady growth in occupations that can be classed as professional or highly skilled. The number of Britons working in managerial occupations rose by around a half between 1981 and 1996, as did the number in personal and protective services; the number classed as associate professionals and technicians rose by over a third, as did those working in the professions themselves (Lindley and Wilson, 1998). The greatest decline has been in manual trades and unskilled work. Between 1981 and 1996, the number of skilled manual workers fell by around a fifth, and the number of plant or machine operatives by around a sixth. There was even a small decline (just under 6%) in the number working in secretarial and clerical occupations.

The factors at work in this story of change are relatively familiar. First, the removal of trade barriers and other globalising tendencies in production and distribution have helped to shift the centre of gravity of manufacturing away from the older industrial lands. In an increasingly global market place, the new industrial heartlands of the Pacific Rim have benefited from relatively low labour costs and rapidly rising skills levels. Even within Europe, the once-communist nations are attracting inward investment, thanks to high educational standards combined with lower labour costs than those found in the West. Second, new technologies are being adopted with dramatic consequences for workers. In Britain, three-quarters of the workforce – and almost all non-manual workers – use computerised equipment on an everyday basis (Felstead *et al*, 2005, 48). Third, and often in combination with the most flexible of the new technologies, many managers are starting to reorganise the way work is carried out. Attitudes to such developments as home-based working have undergone a sea-change among both employers and workers since they were first explored – perhaps revived would be a better word – in the 1980s. At the same time, though, growing numbers of office workers are based in communal spaces, or enjoy the mixed benefits of a 'mobile office', which might be their own car (Felstead, *et al*, 2005, 42-44). Many workers are employed on a contingent basis – as contract workers, self-employed, or part-timers – in an attempt to adapt to turbulence in the market place.

The first three sets of shifts can be located largely inside the workplace, though they are also visible in wider civil society. But civil society also influences the workplace, directly and indirectly. Fourth, then, consumer expectations have had a growing impact on workers' everyday experience. This is most obvious in face-to-face encounters where workers meet directly with consumers, but it is also apparent inside many large organisations, including public sector enterprises, and it often affects relations within the workplace as much as those with outside stakeholders. Claude Dubar has claimed that the redefinition of 'labour as a service relationship', so that each worker is a client and provides for clients (internal and external, in public and private sectors), is the most significant recent transformations in work (Dubar, 2000, 113). Fifth, and partly as a consequence of consumer market forces, government regulation has helped to reshape work. This is a particularly well developed phenomenon in Western Europe, where much regulation is direct, stemming as it does from decisions of the European Commission. Even in the much more deregulated labour markets of the USA, though, the long arm of the law can make itself felt, through resort to litigation.

Lastly, changing social values are affecting work. The most obvious is the feminisation of work, something which both reflects and fosters the changing status of women more generally. The proportion of women has grown particularly rapidly in expanding areas of the economy and in the public sector. And while many women are employed in low status, low wage and low security jobs, the last three decades have seen a marked change in the status of work undertaken by women, particularly younger women. While young men tend to be in lower status jobs than their older counterparts, younger women tend to be in higher status and better paid jobs than do middle aged and older women workers. While part of this is caused by a tendency for women to re-enter the labour market at a lower level after child-rearing, it also reflects the entry of young women into managerial and professional occupations since the 1970s (Lindley and Wilson, 1998, 15; Savage, 2000, 137). But value change can also be witnessed in other ways, such as the development of 'divergent perceptions of practice' (Beckett and Hager, 2002, 13) that can be found in many occupations; examples include the ways that alternative medicines, home schooling and organic farming are all challenging existing practices.

A few words of caution help us to avoid the dangers of exaggerating either the degree or the direction of occupational change. First, the bald statistics need careful treatment, as ever. Part of the reported growth in service sector occupations is caused by reclassification of what were previously treated as manufacturing-sector jobs, largely arising from such restructuring processes as outsourcing and subcontracting of what were previously in-house activities (OECD, 1994, 157-60). There has also been some inflation in the definition of managerial positions, particularly in private service sector employment. So some apparent changes may be a product of terminological shifts, though it should be said that this is also sometimes itself a product of changing circumstances in the workplace.

Second, employment in the service sector does not automatically equate to engagement in knowledge work. Much service sector employment is far from being highly skilled. The word 'McJobs' has been invented precisely to describe the routine service jobs that have grown up in retail, security, cleaning and private health-care industries as well as in catering (Ritzer, 1998). A high proportion of newly-created jobs in the UK during the 1990s, for example, came in areas such as the hotel and catering industry or in domestic and other cleaning services (Keep and Mayhew, 1999), many of them typically involving routinised, even Taylorist forms of work. Conversely, though, a 'service orientation' has spread across many occupations, including manufacturing. Some commentators suggest that the redefinition of manual labour (however skilled) as a form of service relationship has helped to identify it 'as a form of subordinate and dependent labour' (Savage, 2000, 134), while middle class work has assumed a new visibility as the archetype of individualism and autonomy. In a parallel development, service work has often required affective skills that were largely dispensable in manufacturing and extractive jobs, and often these are skills that have been customarily associated with femininity – and frequently, therefore, undervalued as compared with the 'hard' skills of male craft workers (Fenwick, 2004, 174-6). Much service work also requires attention to appearance and image: a study of retail and catering organisations in Glasgow showed that over half of employers regarded employees' appearance as critical, and a further 40 per cent judged it important, with particular attention to factors such as age, physical looks, dress sense and voice or accent (Nickson *et al*, 2004, 18).

Third, the expansion has disproportionately been in flexible and even contingent forms of employment. In Britain the proportion of employees in temporary work grew significantly from the mid-1980s, with a particular upturn in the 1990s. While male temporary employment rates grew more rapidly than those for women, a higher proportion of women workers is engaged in temporary work (Purcell, 1998, 71-2). A similar pattern of growth in part-time employment in Britain, by contrast, has been largely concentrated among women working in the service sector. Self-employment has also risen in Britain and elsewhere, among both men and women, often as a rather precarious form of sub-contracting to larger and more stable organisations. These developments are particularly marked in the new economy: the percentage of part-time, temporary, contract and self-employed workers in Silicon Valley, for example, leapt from 19 per cent in the 1980s to 42 per cent in 2000 (Rosenfeld, 2002, 24).

Flexible and contingent working is a broad category, and the effects on workers' views of training and learning are somewhat complex. Certainly it seems sensible to conclude that such working typically brings about an 'individualisation of labour relations' (Commission of the European Communities 2003, 36), though part of this appears to arise from some people's preference for autonomy and independence. This being so, flexibilisation is broadly associated with other factors that are tending to place responsibility for upskilling on the worker themselves. Dubar suggests, on the basis of a number of French studies, that inevitably such contingent workers identify less closely with their job or employer of today, and much more with their own evolving and unpredictable career, with direct consequences for the way they view the value of investing in new knowledge and skills (Dubar, 2000). This is probably true for certain types of routine work, but in other cases contingent workers can over-identify with their job, so that they suffer stress and overlook outside relationships and interests. In particular, home-based 'knowledge workers' seem to be prone to work long hours and neglect both their own health and the health of their relationships (Commission of the European Communities, 2003, 35). So these are important qualifications to any simplistic model of upskilling as a result of a switch from manufacturing to services, but if anything they serve to accentuate the extent to which occupational patterns have changed and are continuing to change.

Occupational change is one issue. Just as important is the extent to which boundaries are becoming blurred between jobs, employment status, sectors, industries and perhaps even labour markets. A UK government advisory committee went so far as to argue that 'Many jobs have in fact lost any clear occupational descriptor, and acquired general titles backed by specific complex skill sets' (National Skills Task Force, 1999, 81). Training employees for such flexible and complex work poses a number of challenges. Repeatedly, researchers have found that managements persistently pursue a preference for narrow and plant-specific skills rather than the broad and general competences that might support the adaptability and scope required for the new types of work (Elger, 1991, 55). Moreover, many of these new jobs emerge and evolve incrementally, by adding one or two extra tasks, rather than by the sudden appearance of a new occupation (Thompson, 1989, 226). One example is the evolving role of the secretary in many organisations (DfEE, 1999c, 16-17). While increased computerisation has reduced the number of mundane tasks (and also allowed other workers to perform for themselves what were once defined as specialised secretarial tasks), secretaries have developed new skills such as spreadsheet management and desk-top management. More importantly for the purposes of this study, secretaries are also assuming an increasingly important role as internal ICT trainers and help-desk operators. These are often informal roles, and frequently go unrecognised and largely unrewarded.

Multi-tasking is one consequence of boundary-blurring. Increasingly, specialists need to work in teams, pooling their knowledge and skills in what is intended to be a holistic manner. As is explained in a recent guide for mental health professionals: 'Multi-disciplinary teams offer a way of reconciling the rapid growth in knowledge and specialisation among professionals with the increasing appreciation of the inter-connectedness of many problems and the effect of fragmented services on the consumer' (McGrath, 1991, 1). Yet this process – increasingly common in a range of industries – itself poses a new demand for teamwork, communications and leadership skills. Nor are these skills always easy to learn and retain from one problem to another. What may be involved are teams which are not necessarily permanent and stable, with an unchanging membership, but also those which perform as loose-knit coalitions who come to-gether to achieve particular tasks. What works for one team may not work for the next.

Regulation is another factor. Environmental regulations, health and safety legislation and food hygiene regulations all require training to set standards and often generate further training needs as managers and others try to keep abreast of the implications of the latest legis-lation. Some may also learn informally, usually from one another, how to bend the rules and keep costs down. Quality standards fall into this broad category: a range of training is required as a condi-tion of registration in the ISO (International Standards Organisa-tion) 9000 series of quality standards, as well as in the ISO 14000 series of environmental standards, and this tends to be reflected in firms down the supply chain being asked to train employees to the set standards (Rothery, 1995). Purchasers may well insist that a sup-plier switches to online trading or implements new quality stan-dards within a given time limit of perhaps a few months, forcing the supplier to engage in an intensive programme of change (including large-scale training) or to risk losing the contract. Many profes-sionals must undertake continuing professional development (CPD) as a condition of maintaining their registration with their pro-fessional association. For instance, nurses in the UK must provide evidence over any three-year period that they have undertaken at least 35 hours of organised learning (UKCC, 1992). Accountants in the UK are expected to undertake 'structured' and 'unstructured' development, with each individual keeping a record of their training and self-directed learning as a condition of membership of their professional association; evidence of CPD forms a mandatory element of the firm's audit registration and professional indemnity insurance (Fuller *et al*, 2003, 78). There is abundant evidence of a wider and growing pattern of pressure and even compulsion to train, not in order to improve skills or job-related knowledge as de-fined by employer or employee, but in order to meet the demands of third parties (see the next chapter for further discussion of this trend).

Market conditions have also affected skills needs. Whether we are speaking of organisations or individuals, it seems that consumers in general have become both more confident and more demanding. At the individual level, it is reported that more sophisticated and price-aware consumers are likely to be sensitive to the availability of higher perceived service levels. Such consumers are also said to be more promiscuous: during the course of 1996, one consumer in five switched their main grocery store (Reynolds, 1998, 38). Fashion also affects the learning climate more directly. Apparently National Grid stopped using the term 'apprentice' in 1989 because its senior staff believed that young people were being deterred from applying for positions because they thought the status of apprentice to be old-fashioned. At the same time, ironically the language of apprenticeship was being introduced in non-manufacturing areas, precisely because it was unfamiliar (Unwin, 1996, 60). Novelty and fashion play a part, then, in workplace learning just as they do in learning that is not related to work. But their significance is related to a much wider pattern of increased consumer expectations, often backed by a willingness to resort to legal action, which has also placed a premium upon adaptability, flexibility and a broad range of occupational skills.

Finally, the decline of trades unionism has been both a consequence of other changes and itself a significant feature of the landscape. The headline figures are clear: right across the industrial (and increasingly post-industrial) world, union membership rates have plummeted since the 1970s. Since the onset of industrialisation, craft workers' unions in particular had played an important role in determining the conditions of apprenticeship systems (which they often used as a means of controlling entry into skilled jobs). However, with important exceptions such as the German-speaking countries, unions largely lost this role during the collapse of major manufacturing industries in the 1970s. Yet they found it difficult to adjust to the new workplace politics of training in the 1980s and 1990s (Field, 1996), despite growing evidence that they can serve as important intermediaries in gaining commitment among both workers and managers when new training programmes are being considered (Rosenfeld, 2002, 40-1; Forrester, 2004; Trades Union Congress, 2004). In the absence of trade union structures, many workplaces lack legitimate and established channels of communication and representation that are trusted by workers. And while the major reasons for declining union membership have to do with deindustrialisation and a largely unfavourable policy climate, I would speculate that there may also be some connection with a more general process of dis-identification between many workers and their jobs.

It is widely acknowledged that the changing nature of work has, on balance, produced steady growth in demand for skilled and qualified workers, and a steady decline in the demand for less skilled and poorly qualified workers. A detailed analysis of a series of national representative surveys conducted in Britain between the mid-1980s and 2001 has produced a convincing portrait of the way these broad trends have developed in one country (Felstead *et al*, 2002).

This analysis confirmed the findings of other studies with respect to the general tendency for formal qualifications required for jobs to rise over time, with particularly steep growth in the numbers of jobs requiring a degree. It also showed a rise in the time that workers themselves believe is needed in order to learn how to do the job properly, with a marked fall in the number of jobs that can be learned in less than one month (Felstead, *et al*, 2002, 113). Women workers were particularly likely to report pressures to upskill, leading to a significant narrowing of the gap between the skills requirements of men's and women's jobs (Felstead *et al*, 2002, 44), though this is not to say that women workers automatically found it equally easy to access appropriate learning opportunities. Moreover, these broad trends affected virtually all occupational groups; the only exceptions were transport, financial services and health and social work (Felstead *et al*, 2002, 45). Almost all categories of generic skill were affected, other than physical skills (largely affecting male workers), which remained static. By far the largest growth was in the use of computing, with smaller rises being recorded for social skills, communications skills and numeracy skills (Felstead *et al*, 2002, 52-3). Furthermore, in all occupations, Gallie has shown that those employees who reported increased skills requirements also reported a greater degree of 'task discretion'. He concluded that as tasks were becoming more complex, so employers were increasingly obliged to rely on the judgement of individual employees (Gallie, 1996, 138-9). Finally, workers also reported modest but significant growth in the perceived requirement to learn new things on the job itself (Felstead *et al*, 2002, 54).

This body of work is particularly convincing because it is based on not only the opinions of managers as to the skills requirements of particular jobs but also on the perceptions of workers themselves. On this count, the work of Felstead, Gallie and Green is compelling: most workers believe that the skills needed to do their job properly have risen steadily over the last two decades. Overall, then, there is a wide variety of pressures towards upskilling and flexibilisation, driven by a range of changes in the nature of work and its organisation. Quite evidently, those pressures are not experienced evenly across the economy. For many firms, deskilling may appear a more attractive prospect, since it clearly fits into a strategy of cost control or reduction, which in turn helps the firm to compete on grounds of price. This strategy may appear particularly promising in those sectors and countries where price is a particularly important consideration for consumers (Keep and Mayhew, 1999). Elsewhere, the argument may not be so appealing. Rather than accept the low-cost, low-skills equation, many policy makers and firms express a preference for a 'knowledge economy', built around the 'high performance workplace', requiring a constant reinvestment in skills and knowledge for all workers, right across the board (OECD, 1996). Is this goal as desirable as it seems – and if so, how might it be achieved?

The learning organisation

Permanent innovation, unstable and highly competitive markets, new technologies and flexible specialisation – how are firms, and workers, to respond? In particular, how does this constellation of change affect learning in and for work? Are there ways in which the weightless economy can engage its human resources in learning that is not empty-headed?

Changes in work are not just driven by technology but also by new ways of organising and regulating the workplace. In broad terms, this is sometimes presented as a somewhat uneven move away from the dominant 'Fordist' model of management towards a more open and consultative approach. As a strategy for organising workers in complex organisations, Fordism is often associated with the name of Frederick W. Taylor, the theorist of assembly-line production. Writing from a Marxist perspective, Bill Schwartz suggests that Taylor's vision of management was centrally concerned with

> the expansion of regulation into new areas of social life including the increasingly sophisticated control of the labour process, the massive accumulation of new data and new knowledge by the dominant classes, and the consequent extension of capital's power throughout the social formation. (Schwartz, 1985, 202)

Essentially, this approach sees managers as highly skilled specialists in organisational control, whose job it is to act as the guardians of a rational division of labour, with strict separation of conception (thinking, innovation, design) from execution (assembly, distribution, sales).

Following Paul Thompson, we might label the more recent approach as the neo-human-relations school of work organisation (Thompson, 1989, 18). Drawing on the humanistic social psychology of Maslow and Herzberg, those who hold this approach take the view that Taylorism has more or less lost any rationale it once had. Rather than treating the worker as a largely passive factor of production, it emphasises the inherent human need for self-fulfilment, status and belonging in work as in other activities. To capitalise on these drives, and to harness them to greater productivity and commitment, management must change. Typical products of this approach are such ideas as the theory of the learning organisation (Argyris and Schön, 1978).

In an influential contribution to the debate, two Danish economists have argued that recent changes in technology, organisation and markets mean that training and development strategies must be revolutionised. In the 'learning economy',

> First, there is a growing need for a broader participation in learning processes. Swift and efficient innovation processes must involve all layers in the firm. Second, multi-skilling and networking skills become of crucial importance. Third, the capability to learn in and to apply learning to the processes of production and sales becomes the most important dimension to the viability of the modern firm. Management skills become related to the establishment of routines and rules which stimulate interactive learning. (Lundvall and Johnson, 1994, 25-6)

This implies a more holistic approach to work-related learning than that which has dominated until the recent present, as well as a more rounded and inclusive definition of what counts as potentially useful skills or knowledge. More radically still, it suggests that firms thrive best when they provide a working environment that not only stimulates productivity and application but also fosters continual learning – in other words, which restructures the workplace itself so that it actively favours the sharing and acquisition of new knowledge and skills.

Hence the importance of such concepts as the learning organisation. This concept originally found favour among human resource management specialists, both scholarly and professional, in the early 1990s (Jones and Hendry, 1994). But its roots go back much further, arguably to the human relations school of industrial management in the 1920s and 1930s, and certainly to such humanistic management theorists as Reg Revans, whose work on action learning was seminal (Revans, 1982), and to Chris Argyris and Donald Schön (Argyris and Schön, 1978). In the 1980s and early 1990s, with the growing focus on the link between training and company performance and competitiveness, human resource managers became increasingly attracted to the idea of maximising the organisation's capacity for constant improvement and change by encouraging all employees to acquire new skills and abilities throughout their working lives. For Jones and Hendry, this implies that a starting point comes when an enterprise

> ... recognises the need for change, focussing on issues to do with leadership, power, the devolution of initiative and personal development, linked to the needs of the organisation and the wider community. The ensuing transformation is most likely to entail a 'mindshift'. (Jones and Hendry, 1994, 160)

The implications are nothing short of revolutionary. As it is no easy option, relatively few organisations have pursued this route for any great distance.

Where in practice are organisations taking this concept? One approach pioneered in the 1980s and 1990s was the creation of corporate universities, initially as a rebadging of the training department, subsequently as a broader-based and more strategic approach towards corporate learning, and then as a way of managing and distributing the range of knowledge within the organisation. Corporate universities have generally attracted press coverage because of their perceived threat to traditional university systems (Hague, 1991, Jarvis, 2000). Yet at least for the foreseeable future, it seems likely that corporate universities will work in partnership with existing universities rather than displacing them. Thus among the first courses offered when the Daimler-Benz University opened in 1998 was a five-day summer school at Hong Kong University. Its other partners included the Harvard Business School (whose Dean joined the Daimler-Benz University Council) and the Institute for Management Development in Lausanne (Füller, 1998, 13).

By 1999, there were an estimated 1,200 corporate universities worldwide. For most, higher education as conventionally defined was a minor part of their activity. Rather, they generally represented an attempt to change attitudes towards learning. Unipart University provides an illuminating example. Created by a management buyout of the British Leyland components arm in 1987, a decade later Unipart had expanded into a range of activities within and beyond the automotive industry. Unipart University, opened in 1993, was designated as the core learning function for the entire organisation, involving all employees at all levels and increasingly extending its reach to other stakeholders, such as smaller firms in the supply chain (Millar and Stewart, 1999). Arguably, though, the high point of the corporate university movement has passed. The failure of

Britain's National Health Service University, created in date to improve learning in the country's largest single employer, is indicative. Despite the enthusiasm of the Minister of Health, steps were taken in 2005 to close the NHSU down when he was replaced in a government reshuffle. After some twenty years of experiment, the corporate university movement looks increasingly like a rebadging exercise, an attempt to make training sexier by giving it a new image. The more recently established Arriva Development Academy, for example, focuses primarily on leadership training, usually for graduate employees alone (Arriva plc, 2004, 22).

The case of Rover Learning Business, created by Britain's largest car manufacturer in the 1980s as part of a process of raising quality by systematic upskilling, illustrates some of the problems as well as potential (Rover Group, 1998). Rover's approach attracted widespread acclaim for its breadth and vision from academics and management specialists alike. It won awards for its commitment to the learning organisation and was described by two highly respected scholars as 'an organisation which, perhaps more than any other, had taken seriously the imperative to manage learning and to create a 'learning laboratory' environment', an achievement which they summarise as 'extraordinary by any standard' (Matthews and Candy, 1999, 55-6). Yet the learning company concept was not sufficiently persuasive to outlive a transfer to German ownership, with the accompanying shift in management expectations that followed. Two years after buying Rover in 1994, BMW closed down Rover Learning Business, recreating the old department of Group Training and Development – a title chosen partly because it seemed more focused upon skills and the bottom line. Moreover, despite a decade as the model learning company, Rover's performance remained poor. In the last half of 1999, the workforce at Rover's Longbridge plant shrank from 14,000 to just 9,000 (Griffiths, 1999, 6). BMW then sold the company on to a group of British financiers. By mid-2005, the future of Rover's car production was uncertain.

At one level then, the Rover story tells us that learning certainly is not enough. Even after a decade, the model learning company could neither compete nor share its vision with its new owners, and so it could not deliver the new psychological contract whereby workers devoted themselves to flexibility and adaptability in exchange for employability. Of course, there are other versions of this story. The most convincing account would stress that, in a rapidly moving global market place, it is very rare indeed for training and development alone to help a company survive. Competitive strategies can be built on a range of other factors.

Much of the skills debate has tended to assume that the best competitive strategy, at least for the high wage economies, is through constant improvements in quality. Yet this is to ignore the continuing benefits of competing on the basis of price, which is why – to take one example – 'no frills' airlines like Ryanair and EasyJet were able to bite into the market share of flagship airlines like Lufthansa or British Airways. Like Rover, BA has won awards for the quality and range of its training. Ryanair, by contrast, treats training as a cost, and has strategically aimed to reduce its financial impact. It has a reputation for tough dealing with airport authorities: in its contract with Charleroi Airport (financed by the Belgian Walloon authority), Ryanair secured a grant of €768,000 for training crew (Clarke, 2005, 5). At the same time, Ryanair has shifted part of the cost burden onto its employees. Increasingly recruiting in central and eastern Europe rather than Ireland in an attempt to drive down wage costs, the company normally seeks new staff from agencies who charge their applicants fees for initial training courses. Ryanair told existing pilots, who were required to retrain when the company upgraded its fleet, that they would have to contribute substantially towards the costs of their course and would have to repay the full costs of €15,000 if they left the company within five years of retraining. Pilots who challenged these terms in the Irish industrial courts were then issued with redundancy notices (Creaton, 2005, 1). While some customers may be unhappy with service levels, most appear to be more than willing to take advantage of Ryanair's prices, which suggests that the company's controversial managers have found a highly successful strategy that depends primarily on price advantage. Competitive strategies based on price rather than quality are usually successful where there is a lively market for cheap products or services.

In other cases, training is undertaken largely to reduce headcount – often subsidised by external public agencies – rather than improve internal human capital. In the British coal industry, for example, far more mineworkers were receiving training designed to help find work outside the industry than were being trained for new roles within it (UK Coal plc, 2004, 9). Much of this activity was funded by the European Commission, and the remainder came from the British government, channelled through its Selby Coalfield Task Force. In the context of a much reduced industry, UK Coal's largest asset was not really its workforce, whatever the company said, but its land.

Nor is it clear that many senior managers themselves, whatever they may say in public, really do place a high value on training and development. According to one survey in 1999, the attributes which earned most respect from top company executives were a strong and well-thought-out strategy, maximising customer satisfaction and loyalty and strong business leadership. There was little regard for any concept resembling continuous development or lifelong learning (Bounds, 1999). Even in the most competitive companies, training and development remain marginal in the average board-room. They will help create high performance firms only where they are locked firmly into a wider corporate strategy that is consistent with, and constantly upholds, the organisation's mission for learning (Keep and Mayhew, 1999).

More practically, can workers actually relate their learning gains from undergoing training, to their work? For all the rhetoric of the learning economy and the breakdown of hierarchy, in reality most employees face an experience of continued subordination. Take the example of Volkswagen, the German car manufacturer, which started to experiment with teamwork, flatter hierarchies, job-sharing and shared responsibilities in the late 1980s. While in many ways the company apparently regarded the experiment as satisfactory, it found that workers objected, not unsurprisingly, to taking on tasks and responsibilities they saw as traditionally belonging to management, unless they received additional payments (Goudevert, 1993, 12). British researchers have shown that workers who have acquired new skills and knowledge but are then unable to apply them to their job tend to experience higher levels of anxiety and dissatisfaction as a result (Green and Gallie, 2002, 10). While workers who enjoyed high skills combined with high levels of task discretion were the most enthusiastic about their work, many people continue to work in jobs that are relatively routine and undemanding (Green and Gallie, 2002, 8).

Similarly, empirical studies of the 'flat organisation' suggest grounds for caution (Fairbrother, 1991). Unfortunately, most of these studies concentrate on the impact on managers – few researchers have thought it worth their while to study the experiences of shop floor workers. Nevertheless, the evidence is still of interest. One study of the impact of delayering on middle managers in 50 organisations found some evidence of increasing empowerment over individual work roles, leading to higher levels of self-reported job satisfaction. The downside was that not only did this also bring increased levels of stress, managers also found themselves increasingly frustrated, since the reward they expected for taking on greater responsibility and showing higher levels of commitment – namely, progression through the career ladder – was also disappearing as a result of downsizing and delayering (Thomas and Dunkerley, 1999). Another team which examined the impact of downsizing and delayering among 'blue chip' companies, found that there was considerably more rhetoric than practical measures, concluding that the outcome appeared to be 'a revised version of the traditional career model for managers' (McGovern *et al*, 1998, 472).

Nor is this necessarily limited to those working in large companies. A study of women working as carers noted that the move from training into employment came as a 'stark revelation' for most of the women facing for the first time the experience – as they saw it – of penny-pinching, petty bureaucracy and profiteering. Little wonder that, although their subjective identities as carers remained as firm as ever, these women developed 'an almost total cynicism about the courses' which had sought to prepare them for employment (Skeggs, 1997, 71). Similarly, there seems little empirical support for the view that modern employment practices are being re-engineered in order to empower workers and allow them to apply their learning to develop and enhance their jobs (Harley, 1999, 47-59).

One difficulty is that within any workplace, there will be a range of departments and units whose interests lie in seizing control over the distribution of knowledge, rather than in democratising it. The fate of the 'knowledge management' idea may help to illustrate this. Although training and human resource development professionals have shown interest in relating the concept of 'knowledge management' to their own related ideas of 'the learning company', in practice this has proved hard to achieve. One survey by the Institute of Personnel and Development in the UK showed that in many organisations, knowledge management is strongly associated with the information technology department, where it has been narrowed down to cover such relatively limited and specialist issues as the application of new IT tools like groupware and intranets. According to the IPD's consultant, the technologies seemed 'to be blinding managers to the realities of the way people actually use and share information' (Scarbrough, 1999, 68).

This raises the obvious question: has post-Fordism really created a dynamic market for flexible and mobile workers? Evidence of a general rise in skills in countries such as Britain is overwhelming, but it also seems that the overall picture of upskilling hides considerable unevenness, with many workers experiencing little change in the skill requirements of their everyday working lives (Felstead *et al*, 2002; Felstead *et al*, 2004). In the light of recent studies of the labour market, it seems that expectations of a more mobile and flexible workforce have been exaggerated. While some workers are undoubtedly experiencing these tendencies, others – probably the vast majority – are not. Even in such globalised industries as management consultancy, mobility is constrained. The more a job involves communication and interaction with other workers and customers – especially where much of the mutual understanding is tacit and context-specific – the more likely it is that the worker will be tied to a particular culture and place, regardless of her formal skills or qualifications.

Furthermore, the steady growth in the skills requirements of jobs is rarely in step with the skills levels of the labour force. Again, the British experience nicely illustrates this tendency for skills demand and skills supply to march to the beat of different drums. Despite an overall trend towards growth in both the skills levels and formal qualifications required by jobs, the average skills and qualifications levels of workers appear to have grown even more quickly. Felstead, Gallie and Green estimate that the aggregate supply of highly qualified workers in Britain has more or less kept pace with the numbers of jobs requiring high level qualifications, though even an overall balance may well hide a degree of mismatch in some particular disciplines or occupational areas. They also found some evidence of 'credentialism' – that is, new entrants being asked for qualifications at a level higher than that which they believed necessary to do their jobs – and of 'over-qualification'. The level at which workers' qualifications most significantly outstripped demand – whether perceived or 'real' – was at the craft and trade level. And with rapid growth numbers of workers holding qualifications, there was a large apparent excess of jobs with no qualifications requirements over the numbers of people without qualifications – an excess that they estimated at some 3.6 millions of jobs (Felstead *et al*, 2002, 54). As with over-skilling, workers whose qualifications are higher than those expected tended to be more dissatisfied in their work (Green and Gallie, 2002, 10).

Gallie and Green show that workers in highly skilled jobs are often relatively contented in their work but exhibit higher levels of anxiety and self-reported stress than those in less skilled work (Green and Gallie, 2002, 8). One likely reason for this is that the most highly skilled are also expected to work hardest (Green and Gallie, 2002, 17). Moreover, typically post-Fordist flexible forms of employment are associated with low levels of mutual support among workers, whereas flexible employment 'nourishes competition within its own skilled workforce as each employee is at pains to keep his job' (Petrella, 1997, 23). Similar side-effects have been found in the public sector. One case study of a health service trust in Britain, for instance, concluded that structural change had 'destroyed the conditions necessary for experienced staff to pass on their tacit skills and knowledge to their less experienced peers' – a process that occurred despite formal hierarchies, as when senior ward sisters passed on experience to junior doctors (Fuller *et al*, 2003, 48). We could go further, and suggest that the flexible employee is likely to place limits on his or her trust in their employer, creating a turnover problem as key workers seek more secure or highly paid employment elsewhere.

Finally, many of the demands of the new economy can be met without much in the way of training. One obvious example is the importance of 'looking good': this attribute is absolutely central in many industries, particularly those that face out directly to clients, such as downtown bar-cafés and restaurants or personalised consultancy firms, where a degree of aesthetic appeal helps to sell a service or product (Nickson *et al*, 1998). In many service middle class occupations, including training and teaching, a well-groomed and professional image appears to help build trust between client and worker, as well as apparently helping workers feel good about themselves. The growth of 'aesthetic labour' as an aspect of work in service industries is a major factor in the rapid growth of the beauty industry since the early 1990s, a pattern that increasingly impacts on men as well as women (Black, 2004). And in so far as visiting the beauty salon helps workers invest in their human capital and enhance their employability and performance, it may provide a far better return than training.

Thus much of the learning explosion of recent times has been more apparent that real. Much political and employer pressure has been applied to encourage employees to train. Yet inevitably this is to some extent a zero sum game. If company A is competing head-on with company B, training will only provide temporary help, as sooner or later company B will copy any new skills that are being used in company A as a result of its training. Company B may even have the advantage of knowing which ways of using the new skills worked and which were a dead end. In the end, both companies will train simply in order to keep up with one another, and much the same applies on a wider scale to nations. The idea that training and development is the only source of sustainable advantage is well-intended and optimistic, but it simply cannot work in the longer term. But in this case, what can?

One possible solution lies in the developing debate about socially-embedded learning. As a group of Nordic economists put it, in an argument that deserves to be widely heard,

> It is a logical and interesting – though usually overlooked – consequence of the present development towards a knowledge-based economy that the more easily codified (tradeable) knowledge is accessed by everyone, *the more crucial does tacit knowledge become* in sustaining or enhancing the competitive position of the firm. (Maskell *et al*, 1998, 42; emphasis in original)

One approach has of course been that associated with ideas of the learning organisation. But the Nordic group's analysis lends itself readily to the idea of the learning industrial cluster, in that it involves recognition of the networks that pass information and ideas between individual firms in an area or sector.

In policy terms, this approach has become associated with the goal of the learning region. Economic drivers have often been quite strong in developing local learning cultures. In South Wales, for example, inward investment has markedly affected regional capacities for lifelong learning. By facing local actors with the expectation that employees will actively acquire new – if plant-specific – skills, and providers will help them, inward investors have helped build capacity that is open for others to adopt (Rees and Thomas, 1994, 54).

Mobility, flexibility and the learning imperative

Regardless of the ambiguities of research evidence, policy makers continue to place a high priority on skills, flexibility and mobility. Moreover, they are inextricably linked, as the following communiqué from the Cologne summit of the G8 nations demonstrates:

> The next century will be defined by flexibility and change; more than ever there will be a demand for mobility. Today, a passport and a ticket allow people to travel anywhere in the world. In the future, the passport to mobility will be education and lifelong learning. This passport to mobility must be offered to everyone. (Group of Eight, 1999, 1)

But what is this passport to be in practice? The question is worth asking, since much of the policy emphasis has focused in recent years on qualifications. From a post-Fordist perspective, formalised qualifications have been criticised as leading to rigidity and undermining lifelong learning. Two senior civil servants in the European Commission once complained that much education and training still engenders 'standardised' and congealed skills, sanctioned by diplomas that are acquired once-for-all' (Riché-Magnier and Metthay, 1995, 420). But qualifications also neatly fit the preoccupations of the new public management, with its concern for performance measurement, audit and payment by results. In Britain, public funding has often been allocated towards providing agencies on the basis of qualifications awarded, rather than on more traditional criteria.

This tension is also mirrored in the academic debate between those who see qualifications as diminishing in importance and those who argue that they represent a means of enabling labour mobility. From the former group, Kjell Rubenson argues that

> ... the internal labour market will play an increased role as training costs increase ... Employers can be expected to give even more consideration to education as a screening device since the role of training will be – or at least will be perceived to be – more crucial in the economy. (Rubenson, 1992, 27)

However, others have argued that shifts towards post-Fordism imply

> ... a shift from prevailing internal labour market structures with their inherent limitations in an era of increasing economic volatility towards a model of 'professional' labour markets, involving a stronger emphasis on general, transferable skills and thereby allowing a higher degree of functional flexibility and worker mobility (Buechtemann and Soloff, 1994, 237).

Outside Britain, where the creation of a new national system of vocational qualifications stimulated much empirical research, we still have less evidence on this subject than dogmatic assertion and polemic, much of it highly normative and exhortatory.

To take one example, unitisation – that is, breaking learning programmes down into discrete units – and the assessment of prior learning (APL) are often presented in a positive light. Thus the French national approach to the assessment of vocational experiential learning 'la validation des acquis professionels', has been praised for facilitating, despite its time-consuming procedures, 'the individualisation of training, that is to say balancing between the individual characteristics of the employees and a collective process' (Feutrie and Verdier, 1993, 474). The aim of such processes is to identify, in a more or less formal way, the tacit skills and knowledge of workers. APL may well be used to regulate employee performance, as in Jenoptik, which seeks to:

bring the employees' hidden talents out into the open, including their foreign language and computer skills, and even their personal communicational and presentational abilities. As a result, the employees' individual target agreements can be expanded to reflect their personal potential and their future development needs. (Jenoptik, 2004, 52)

Together, APL and unitisation may potentially offer a means of sorting and making clear the various skills and knowledge that adults possess as a result of their educational, vocational, cultural and social experience. Against this, flexibility may be gained at the loss of coherence and grasp of the basics, opportunities for cooperative learning are reduced, the importance of theoretical underpinnings of practice is downplayed, and the supply of training is regulated through individuals' choices (Banks, 1993, 40; Colardy and Durand, 1998, 246). Furthermore, as with any form of in-house accreditation, the external value of APL rests heavily upon the reputation of the establishment that has conducted the assessment (Feutrie and Verdier, 1993, 483-4).

Underlying these reforms is a belief that a more transparent qualifications system will promote flexibility and mobility. To what extent is this well founded? An instructive example comes from the European Commission's attempts to establish a transparent framework for vocational qualifications across the EU, in the hope of building a single market for labour, accompanying the single market for goods, capital and services (Field, 1998, 116-27; Gordon, 1999). Following a series of relatively small-scale initiatives, the commission embarked in 1985 upon a large scale process of mapping the content of vocational qualifications across the (then twelve) member states, with a view to ensuring their comparability. This task was devolved to the Berlin-based Centre européenne pour la développement de la formation professionelle (CEDEFOP), which in turn created a series of sectoral working parties consisting of employers' representatives, trade unionists and occupational experts. The outcome of a time-consuming series of task-analytic studies was a large number of lengthy, detailed and occupationally-specific lists of the skills and knowledge represented by particular qualifications in each industry in such of the member states as were able to supply accurate information.

Complementing these studies, the Commission also legislated, introducing a series of specific directives covering particular occupations such as nursing, followed in 1988 by two general directives requiring employers and governments in member states to recog-

nise the equivalence of all university degrees and vocational qualifications gained after at least two years' post-secondary training,
provided that they had been issued by a 'competent authority' in an
EU member state (Field, 1998, 124). This cut through the problem of
comparability and transparency by deeming that a degree was a
degree and a trade qualification was a trade qualification. And
despite a degree of resistance and a small number of exemptions
(for example, those designed to protect minority languages like
Irish), the courts have been rigorous in upholding these directives.

By the time the single market was created in 1992, much had been
done to remove what the commission saw as artificial barriers to
mobility. But what were the results? In the event, Europeans were
happy to exploit the possibilities of a borderless union for leisure
purposes, but proved remarkably reluctant to leave home in search
of employment. Ironically, the numbers of EU migrants within most
member states actually fell between the mid-1970s and late 1980s,
simply because rising unemployment had removed opportunities
for unskilled labour (Werner, 1994, 42). Of those who did move in the
late 1980s and early 1990s, the vast majority moved along well-established pathways, where the recognition of qualifications posed few
problems (Marsden, 1994). By far the largest group, for instance, was
the Irish, most of whom moved to Britain where their qualifications
were widely understood by employers and education providers;
similarly, most Danish migrants went to other Nordic nations such
as Sweden or Finland, both of which were still outside the EU (Field,
1998, 128-9).

Within the EU, then, demand for flexible and mobile labour has not
risen as a result of policies designed to reduce barriers to movement.
In particular, it appears to have little impact on demand for employees who possess the highest levels of skills and qualifications,
despite the fact that this was the group at which the 1980s policies
were aimed. While there are several reasons for this, such as unemployment rates, language difficulties, and the hidden costs of
mobility such as housing and education, one important factor is the
relatively low significance for employers of explicit and codified
skills, as against tacit knowledge and social capital. Thus one study
of personnel managers in British-owned multinationals suggested
that those companies which were developing a European approach
tended to rely less on British expatriates and more on locally-re-
cruited managers (Walsh, 1996), and a rather smaller survey of the
largest German firms came to a similar conclusion (Hoffritz, 1997).
Those well-qualified employees who do move across borders tend

frequently to be transients who are appointed for a fixed term and are used because of their knowledge of the firm and its key people (Boyle *et al*, 1996). While there has been an explosion since the mid-1980s in short burst journeys by managers and professionals, this had arisen from the general globalisation of ownership and activity and is as strongly associated with firms under American or Asian ownership as with the EU (Forster and Whipp, 1995). So despite tendencies towards convergence, then, the labour market in Europe remains heavily segmented along national lines (Marsden, 1994), and the exceptions to this rule tend to be well-established. As for the CEDEFOP tables, even the staff in the EU's own employment service made little or no use of this information – half of them did not even know of its existence (Field, 1998, 122). Even within member states, most geographical mobility is relatively short distance. In Britain, overall mobility rates – whether local or inter-regional – remained more or less constant during the 1990s, despite rapid economic change (Dixon, 2003).

Labour is, it seems, a remarkably 'sticky' factor of production. Many skills do not transfer easily from one setting to another, presumably because they are often embedded in dense networks of workplace relationships. There are two puzzles requiring resolution. One is the historically stubborn pattern of migration among most Europeans: those who move around do so along well-established tracks, outside or inside the EU. There are several reasons: labour markets are not only economic but also cultural and social, there are hidden barriers to movement, and demand for inwardly mobile labour is depressed by the risks inherent in taking on someone on the sole basis of their qualification. The second puzzle is why the European Commission persisted in its efforts long after it became clear that they were largely fruitless. But this ceases to be a puzzle if we see the Commission's activities as driven more by internal political forces – at a time of tension over the extension of the EU's 'competences' (or 'sovereignty') – than by sober economic calculation. This is by no means a pattern that is solely confined to European political institutions, nor indeed to European labour markets. One study of the financial returns to migrants' skills in Canada concluded that 'it may be harder to translate human capital to a new country the less manual are the skills involved' (Ferrer *et al*, 2004, 22). Thus even in a labour market accustomed to high levels of inward migration the complexities of ensuring that all the relevant actors are adept at recognising, applying and rewarding knowledge and skills acquired abroad are substantial.

Employable workers as economic nomads?

Nevertheless, recent studies of the labour market have shown rising levels of mobility. And strikingly this involves employees in not only switching employers but also making more career moves than was reported in the past. While most employees perform a particular job for some time, a high proportion change their career when they switch to a different employer, and for a surprisingly large number, this appears to involve a lateral career change rather than conventional, linear career advancement (Arthur *et al*, 1999, 37; Collin and Watts, 1996, 387-88). Talk of 'boundaryless careers' (Arthur *et al*, 1999, 11) is still, it seems, hyperbole. Most people, for most of their lives, are working in the same occupation as when they first entered full-time employment and, whether or not they have been promoted, we have seen that for most people this remains their expectation. But for a growing minority, flexible or multiple career paths are the norm, and inevitably it has been suggested that this is both a growing trend and one for which existing education and training systems have left workers ill-prepared.

A flood of negative consequences is said to have flowed from this. Tom Bentley asserts that 'Poor employability in the UK was recently estimated to cost an annual £8 billion, without taking into account the social costs of crime and unemployment' (Bentley, 1998, 99). As a consequence, Bentley joins those who argue that, in place of the traditional focus of training for *employment* what is now needed is training for *employability*, and that particularly for individuals this may make a great deal of sense. This was, in fact, a common policy theme in the late 1990s. Employability was enthusiastically adopted as a policy goal in Western Europe, which had experienced considerable difficulty in the 1970s and 1980s as a consequence of structural unemployment. The European employment ministers in 1997 identified employability, along with adaptability, entrepreneurship and equal opportunities, as one of the four 'pillars' of a common employment policy, and defined lifelong learning as one of the chief means of building employability (CEC, 1997).

Enhancing employability is, accordingly, as in so many other aspects of lifelong learning, closely associated with individualising tendencies. Summarising a study of trends in careers management in the 1990s, one UK government agency asserted in the mid-nineties that because of diminishing security of employment,

> Individuals must therefore be prepared to cope with changes in employer, location, home and type or style of work. This means

> developing skills of managing transitions and settling in quickly to new environments. It may mean learning how to establish good relationships in an environment without becoming so immersed that moving out becomes traumatic. (Skills and Enterprise Network, 1996, 3)

Similar trends are found elsewhere. One Dutch survey of trends in human resource development concluded that

> Employees must have an insight into the opportunities and limitations of their own competencies and learn to anticipate possible new roles that they could fill within their own organisation or elsewhere in the (near) future... What can be observed is that organisations are becoming more transitory and that both bonds between employers and employees are based more on interdependence and less on loyalty. (Streumer *et al*, 1999, 272)

Previously the concern of employers, the shape and content of career development (and protection) are shifting inexorably towards the employee.

In an unpredictable and turbulent environment, employability is easier to aspire to than to promote (van den Toren, 1999). First, there is a clear tension between the firm's interests in reducing turnover (particularly of key skilled workers) and the broader societal interest in ensuring that employees are able to move. Given that the risks of 'poaching' are already widely cited as a deterrent to employer investment in skills training, there is no reason to suppose that firms will be any more enthusiastic about interventions consciously designed to enable workers to become more footloose. In countries where trade union membership is high, as in the Netherlands, employability is increasingly covered during collective bargaining, but this option has limited relevance in the majority of Western nations, where trade union membership is relatively low (and often concentrated in public sector employment). Second, motivating employees to undertake general education and training not directly related to their current job poses an obvious challenge, and carries the risk that those who take part most willingly will be those who wish either to leave or alternatively to embed themselves even more firmly in their current company. Third, identification with an occupation has often been associated with a willingness to invest one's energies and emotions in improving performance, and there is a risk that this may be eroded. Richard Sennett has lamented the tendency for workers in modern capitalism to feel a relatively weak attachment to their job (Sennett, 1999). If groups of workers con-

tinue to feel part of a strong occupational culture, it may well be because their job demands a high level of loyalty and group identity rather than simply because of the skills involved. Some uniformed services, such as the armed forces or fire service, provide an obvious example.

Highly employable and ambitious individuals who are alert to the risks of remaining with a single employer, may also represent a risk to employers. High labour turnover is costly enough in the short term, but the fast-fix solutions that go with short term horizons can wreak lasting damage (Ramsay, 1996). On the one hand, managers are exploring the possibility of loyalty programmes, seeking to promote and reward commitment to the firm, and examining the tacit dimensions of the 'psychological contract' between worker and firm, in order to find out why it is that some people stay while others leave. However, these interventions are also costly. Their effectiveness is largely unproven and may be due to their novelty. They may even encourage the kind of footloose behaviour they are intended to discourage, by setting up a process of counterbidding as employees compare their firm's loyalty programme with those of competititors. And they contribute nothing to the wider goals of the firm.

Self-direction and employment

We have seen that a multitude of pressures is forcing individual employees to pay more attention to their own development. In an official report on key skills in Britain, for instance, it was recently asserted that:

> One of the most important is the ability to plan and manage one's own career. This involves understanding the opportunities available in the labour market; how to apply for jobs and present oneself at interviews; and being able to plan and arrange one's own career development. (National Skills Task Force, 1999, 57)

Similarly, the European Commission claims that 'learners must become proactive and more autonomous, prepared to renew their knowledge continuously and to respond constructively to changing constellations of problems and contexts' (CEC, 1999b, 9).

Generally, responsibility for achieving this ideal state appears to lie with individuals, who are urged to acquire the skills and habits of self-regulation and self-monitoring. The health education professional, it is suggested, is a ''reflective practitioner', whose work is marked by an aptitude for self-appraisal, critical analysis of practice and pursuit of effectiveness' (HEBS, 1997). Similarly, according to the UK's national professional code of conduct for nurses, it is for the individual to take responsibility for identifying their own short-comings and planning their own learning, and ensuring that they meet the requirements for continuing professional development (UKCC, 1992). There are also increasing demands for workers to share and transmit their skills, with employers asserting their ownership of workers' intellectual capital. Formally and informally, the use of coaching and mentoring rose steeply from the mid- to late-1990s, especially among workers who had line management or supervisory responsibilities of some kind (Felstead *et al*, 2002, 53-4).

Individualisation of responsibility also flows from corporate vul-nerability to competitive pressures. This can be seen in the strategy of a large British-based confectionery firm, which in the late 1980s became increasingly aggressively involved in the US soft drinks market, as well as in less ruthless but still risky fields in Central and Eastern Europe. By redirecting human resources strategy to focus on high added value, the firm's directors claimed that

> The Group's ability to sustain a competitive advantage over the long term will depend in large part on the continuous development of the Group's employees. For this reason the Group is committed to pro-viding an environment which values continuous learning and which provides learning and development opportunities both within busi-ness units and across the Group. Development is a shared respon-sibility, and employees for their part must possess the drive and initiative to take advantage of the available learning and develop-ment opportunities. (Cadbury Schweppes, 1999, 27)

In some cases, there is also no doubt a desire to minimise the costs of financing training and development programmes and not just share responsibility for making sure that the learning happens. The consequence, though, is a trend towards greater involvement of the employee as individual in taking ownership of the decision to acquire new skills and knowledge, engaging in greater self-monitor-ing and regulation, and demonstrating to employers and potential employers that they possess the 'drive and initiative' to make a com-petent employee.

This is not simply a matter of preparing young people for job-seek-ing at some stage in their future, adult lives. It extends throughout the working life. Claude Dubar contends that the principal features of the new employability are 'maintaining oneself in a state of com-petence, of competitiveness in the market (as one keeps oneself in 'good shape' physically)' in order that one is prepared for a variety of specific tasks (Dubar, 2000, 112). Fundamentally, the principle of employability represents a radical individualisation of the 'psychological contract' between workers and the state of employment. Some business writers have described

> ... a new covenant under which the employer and the employee share responsibility for maintaining – even enhancing – the individual's employability inside and outside the company. . . . Under the new covenant, employers give individuals the opportunity to develop greatly enhanced employability in exchange for better productivity and some degree of commitment to company purpose and community for as long as the employee works there. (Waterman *et al*, 1996, 207-8)

Nor is this necessarily an unwelcome development although, as we will see, the amount of pressure can at times be close to coercion.

So is all this imposed upon workers? Is it a new, more subtle form of top-down management, as Marxists believe (Crowther, 2004)? And is individualisation experienced by workers as an oppressive burden, imposed upon them from above and breaking down the resources of solidarity and fraternity that previously afforded them protection against exploitation? Partly so, perhaps, but it is worth emphasising the extent to which people embrace the same values at work as they do in other areas of their lives. People who share the values of autonomy and self-realisation are just as likely to try to express them in the workplace and in their professional development as in other spheres of life. Rather than dependency upon an employer – what might be called the parent/child model – they may be highly attracted to the idea of self-reliance and 'career-resilience'. Rather than experiencing individualisation as an alien imposition, perhaps workers experience these tendencies both as the exercise of power relations from above and as the exercise of autonomy – in short, as part of a wider and 'complex interweaving of class and individual identity' (Savage, 2000, 101).

At any rate, a sense that workers have some responsibility for maintaining their own employability is now widespread (Dubar, 2000,113). It is perhaps predictable that this approach has been taken furthest by high-technology companies with a relatively young and mobile workforce, such as Apple Computers, Sun Microsystems and Raychem Corporation (Waterman *et al*, 1996, 208-16). As yet, though, there are relatively few empirical studies of this phenomenon. In their review of North American research into self-directed learning, Ralph Brockett and Roger Hiemstra list several studies of teachers, but no other occupation group appears to have received much attention. They also note the comparatively small number of serious studies of self-directed learning among manual and clerical workers (Brockett and Hiemstra, 1991, 96-7).

Some evidence is provided for Britain by the 2003 Pathways in Adult Learning Survey (PALS) and the related 2002 National Adult Learning Survey (NALS). Both surveys distinguished between 'taught' and 'non-taught' types of learning. First, PALS provides an important gauge of the extent of self-directed learning. Excluding those still in full-time education, over half of the respondents (52%) had undertaken some taught learning in the three years before the survey, and a similar proportion (53%) had undertaken some non-taught learning. Significantly, two-thirds of these had undertaken both taught and non-taught learning (Snape *et al*, 2004, 179). Taken together with the findings from earlier surveys in the same series (Beinart and Smith, 1998; Fitzgerald *et al*, 2003), these figures confirm that non-taught learning is an extensive activity, and that it frequently seems to be undertaken by people who are also engaged in taught learning.

NALS and PALS also provide important clues as to the nature of non-taught learning. It is almost never used to work towards a qualification: only 8 per cent of non-directed learners were studying for a qualification, as compared with 48 per cent of learners on taught courses (Snape *et al*, 2004, 97). Broadly, their motives appear to have been a balance between a general interest in the subject and largely work-related reasons. Six out of ten involved in non-taught learning said they were learning new skills for their job at the time; some 48 per cent said they were learning in order to improve their career prospects, while 44 per cent were aiming at job satisfaction (Snape *et al*, 2004, 49). Generally speaking, non-vocational reasons such as general interest were less common, but were still important; thus 32 per cent of non-taught learners claimed a general curiosity about the subject, while 29 per cent wanted to 'do something interesting' (Snape *et al*, 2004, 51). An earlier study in the NALS series found that those who were working towards a qualification were usually doing so by following a package of materials, almost always written, provided by a college or employer; the new technologies appear to have made very little impact on this form of training (Beinart and Smith, 1998, 204).

Among self-directed learners in NALS, the vast majority gave work-related reasons for their study. Almost half of all workers (47%) said it would help with their current job, and a third of those not in work (32%) that it would help with a future job; 10 per cent mentioned some sort of voluntary activity (Fitzgerald *et al*, 2003, 85). Self-directed learners were by no means homogeneous, however: managers and professionals were the most likely to be learning in order to improve their career prospects or their job satisfaction; people in routine and semi-routine jobs were most likely to be learning in order to change their job; and workers in lower supervisory and technical occupations were most likely to be learning to keep their job. In terms of subject studied, most non-taught learners were pursuing computing (30%), leisure activities (23%) and roughly equal numbers were interested in specific occupational subjects (26%), leisure activities (26%) and professional training (19%), while other subjects attracted rather smaller numbers (Fitzgerald *et al*, 2003, 83). An earlier survey found that, of the 15 per cent who said they were using a learning package of some sort, virtually all were using written materials and around a third were using a computer software package, usually together with written materials (Beinart and Smith, 1998, 214).

On the surface, this pattern looks highly consistent with the policy shifts that see self-direction in learning as an integral component of employability in the future. Yet this undoubted flowering of self-directed learning may prove a shaky prop for policy-making, whether at national or company level. In particular, a dramatic shift towards the use of new technologies to promote self-directed learning appears unlikely. Thus a 1999 survey of British Institute of Personnel and Development members found that while over two-thirds expected to see a marked expansion in the use of ICTs in their organisation, many were extremely sceptical about their value in practice, giving it a relatively low rating in comparison with more traditional approaches. A significant proportion simply did not know how effective the new technologies were: over 40 per cent of those who had used the internet for training purposes said they were 'unsure' about its effectiveness when compared with 'traditional' so-called stand-up classroom teaching (Cannell, 1999). If professional trainers lack confidence and knowledge over these new approaches, their spread among the wider public may be seen more as a part of the individual toolkit than as an integral element to organisational strategy.

Much training is developed on the assumption that the employee is a self-directed learner (Brockett and Hiemstra, 1991; Streumer *et al*, 1999, 273). Thus the Arriva Learning and Development Gateway gives all employees access to online resources and courses, complementing trade union-led open learning centres where workers can access Learndirect programmes (Arriva plc, 2004, 23). In general, though, we have seen that the actual introduction of electronic resources at the workplace is limited, at least in so far as their use for training and development is concerned (Beinart and Smith, 1998, 204). While there are strong expectations that the new technologies will transform the possibilities for a shift towards self-directed learning, there is little evidence that adult workers possess the skills required to utilise these methods. On the contrary, many continue to express a strong preference for traditional taught methods. The authors of one major survey report were surprised to find that, although many people stated that their preference was to learn by 'doing practical things', their preferred method of learning by a large margin was through books or other written materials. Attending lectures came second (Campaign for Learning, 1998, 21). One study of managers in small firms found that although they strongly favoured the use of work-based learning for their employees, their own preference was for attending a taught course (Martin, 1999). Most people seem to rate information technology relatively low in terms of how useful it is as a learning tool (Campaign for Learning, 1998, 22). Hence the importance of higher level metacognitive abilities and strategies, as well as motivation for self-directed learning.

These qualifications matter because many policy-makers view a combination of self-direction with the new technologies as providing a robust basis for expanding, and widening, participation in adult learning. This is how the UK government views its University for Industry, for example. However, self-directed learning and IT-based learning are, at present, largely separate and different phenomena. Despite the patchy take-up, survey and other data suggest that individual interest in and practice of self-directed learning is already extremely widespread. IT-based learning on the other hand was initially chased largely by 'pioneers', whether individuals or organisations – its status remains somewhat experimental. For most trainers, its potential lies in the future and is as yet unproven. What is clear at this stage is that the most reluctant learners, and the most excluded and peripheral groups within the workforce more generally, are unlikely to embrace learning through ICTs any more than they are attracted by more conventional approaches.

Learning to labour, learning from labour

Is the world of work being overturned? I think not, or at least not entirely. Many people still work in jobs that require little or no skill, some of them created by the very forces of globalisation and high technology that are conventionally said to be driving the economic revolution of our times. Many people work in one trade and even for one employer for most of their working lives. Levels of geographical mobility, far from being at an all-time high, have not even risen within the borderless world of the European Union. Certainly there are important, even dramatic changes. But these should not be exaggerated, and neither should their consequences be overstated. The constant talk of a new learning economy is expressed most crudely in the straightforward demand that employees start to acquire new skills and mentalities, so as to become more adaptable and mobile. At a more sophisticated level, it is reflected in the popularity of such notions as knowledge management and the learning company. But some of this rhetoric is misplaced, or even in bad faith. Management gurus are selling their books, managers are trying to show themselves to be ahead of the trend, business leaders are trying to screw down wages, companies are trying to fool the consumers. These factors matter for a number of reasons, not least because they shape the context in which people do acquire new abilities which they may apply to their jobs. At some stage, people will see through the rhetoric and identify the bad faith. If people think that trainers, or the companies and policy-makers that set the training agenda, are selling snake oil, that too will become part of the context, in the shape of increased cynicism among those being offered the training. Reflexive citizens tend to make reflexive workers – and reflexive trainees.

Yet, as was shown at the start of this chapter, the nature of work is changing. And as it does so, learning appears to play a central role for both workers and employers. This is hardly surprising – dynamism lies at the very heart of capitalism, and change – as Marx often remarked – is one of its constant features. But changes in work are related to, and sometimes produced by, broader social and cultural transformations, and together they appear to be leading to a restructuring of social and economic relationships across the board. Some of the forces driving changes at work accordingly have little to do with upskilling or employability, but arise from changes in the wider culture. As individual citizens become more cynical about authority outside the workplace – in the political sphere, or in broadcasting – so they come to doubt the all-knowing wisdom of their managers within it, and prefer to learn in ways that respect their wish for autonomy and control. As consumers seek pleasurable experiences from their learning activities at home, so they prefer forms of training and development that are fun. And so on. The permanently learning worker with her reflexive autobiography experiences her job as one part of a wider set of relationships, responsibilities and – yes – pleasures. And as we have seen, individualisation processes now play a powerful part in shaping these experiences, as a new form of subjection but equally as a new form of emancipation.

4
Who is being left behind?

For much of the twentieth century, public education policy has served as a vehicle for securing greater social equality. With public attention focusing mainly on the school system and higher education, adult learning stood somewhat to the margins of this broad policy consensus. Pioneering adult education organisations espoused the goal of social equality, such as the Workers' Educational Association or the labour college movement, dedicating themselves to training active citizens and labour leaders who might then be in a position to pursue changes in the wider society, for example by championing greater equality in school and university systems.

Until the 1960s, adult education and training were only rarely provided in order to promote social equality directly. When they were, it often smacked of the remedial or compensatory. Even the types of adult education that really were designed to compensate for earlier failings tended to attract a protective sheeting of radical language. Paolo Freire, the radical Brazilian adult educator, was widely cited by both practitioners and those who trained adult educators. For many, it seems to have been enough simply to quote Freire's name (Field, Lovell and Weller, 1991). Concrete references to his thinking – and to its roots in liberation theology – were relatively rare, and this remains the case despite current interest in spirituality and adult learning. But if Freire's name was sometimes used to help adult educators come to terms with the distinctly unradical nature of their daily work, it also helped inspire an entirely admirable willingness to engage with excluded groups.

Meanwhile, adult education organisations also came into contact with the radical ideas of the new social movements of the 1960s and 1970s. While feminism was the most influential in the longer term, the general themes of the new social movements – autonomy, emancipation, democracy, individual human rights – were largely accepted by many professional adult educators, along with a general scepticism about what many saw as the exaggerated claims made on behalf of a schools system that appeared to fail large parts of the population. From this perspective, a major task for adult education was to tackle the massive inequalities perpetuated, and even partly created, by schools designed to prepare youngsters for adult life in industrial society and an elitist higher education system that functioned as a finishing school for the children of the middle classes.

How has the dawn of our learning society affected the situation? Lifelong learning is actively reproducing inequality. It may even be creating new sources of inequality, as well as providing a new legitimacy for power and privilege. Proposing a study of adult learning and social inclusion, the OECD's Centre for Educational Research and Innovation stated this starkly:

> In today's 'knowledge economies' and 'learning societies', knowledge, skills and learning have come to be recognised as fundamental for participation by individuals in modern life, as well as the hallmarks of dynamic economic units and thriving social communities. ... For those who have successful experience of education, and who see themselves as capable learners, continuing learning is an enriching experience, which increases their sense of control over their own lives and their society. For those who are excluded from this process, however, or who choose not to participate, the generalisation of lifelong learning may only have the effect of increasing their isolation from the world of the 'knowledge-rich'. The consequences are economic, in under-used human capacity and increased welfare expenditure, and social, in terms of alienation and decaying social infrastructure. (OECD, 1997b, 1)

A parliamentary committee in Britain similarly expressed concern that 'A side-effect of the substantial improvement in overall participation during the last two decades has been to widen the gap between the educational 'haves' and the 'have-nots'' (Select Committee on Education and Employment, 1999). Another official report noted 'a worrying trend for the skills-rich to extend their learning and competence while the skills-poor fall further behind' (DfEE, 2000, 9).

Moreover, this process is said to affect not only individuals or sub-groups within a particular society, but also whole regions and even nations. For Manuel Castells, for example, the networked society has made large parts of the globe virtually irrelevant; possessing no skills or knowledge of any value, they fall into the 'black holes of informational capitalism' (Castells, 1998, 162). Typically, towns and regions who lack a significant higher education infrastructure are likely to fall behind in the race for knowledge-based advantage (Sotarauta, 2005). The presence of a large labour force, with or without specialised craft skills, is no longer able to attract the investment in productive capacity that created nineteenth century industrial giants like Manchester, Pittsburgh, Tampere or the Ruhr. In Bauman's deliberately provocative analysis, the question in our own time is whether the new poor no longer form a reserve army of labour, but are largely unwanted and redundant (Bauman, 1998).

Social exclusion and the redundancy of the poor

'Failure', Richard Sennett has written, 'is the great modern taboo' (Sennett, 1999, 118). Our new learning society is awash with books, tapes, CDs, videos and radio and TV programmes that tell you how to succeed, and reality TV cheerfully puts failure – and humiliation – into the public gaze, but few authorities tell you how to cope with failure. Yet in a more fluid, fast-moving and individualised society, in which the path is cleared for new opportunities open to people from groups previously excluded – most obviously women – the risk of failure is faced by the middle class as well as the poor and disadvantaged. Old forms of protection – the school tie, the club, the stock trading company, even the family – no longer offer a convincing remedy. But if established middle class groups are exposed to the risk of sudden failure, old and familiar forms of poverty and exclusion are often remarkably persistent. The new forms of exclusion are not destroying the old; rather, they are overlaying them, creating new and more complex patterns of inequality which may, by virtue of their complexity, be harder to resolve.

Social exclusion tends to be a cumulative process, but the new emphasis upon knowledge is a further complicating factor. In Britain, the incoming Labour government accepted that in 1997 it had 'inherited a situation of growing welfare dependency and increasing deprivation in some sections of society' (DfEE, 1997, 6). Taking income inequality as a key indicator, this judgement seems quite an understatement. While the majority of families has continued to enjoy a more or less continuous increase in real earnings since the late 1960s, the bottom tenth have seen a decline, not just relative to the majority but in real terms (Hills, 1998). Nor is this a simple matter of growing income inequality. As well as income polarisation, it seems that the same period has seen growing inequality in access to those less tangible resources – networks, trust and social contacts – that constitute social capital (Putnam, 2000). While Britons generally have become more active in voluntary associations since the 1970s, membership levels have fallen substantially among manual workers and their families, with a lingering if diminishing gender gap. In consequence,

> It is those in working-class positions, poorly-educated and without service-class friends who are most likely to be disengaged from, hence deprived of access to, any formal channels of social capital. This is particularly true of women in these positions. (Li *et al*, 2003).

This is particularly important, as it is through contacts and information networks that many people are able to convert their education and training into tangible assets in the labour market, or indeed in other areas of daily life (Emler and McNamara, 1996; Field, 2005).

The general move towards lifelong learning, which usually looks as though it is increasing opportunities, has also helped increase tendencies towards greater inequality, and may have helped entrench existing ones. This apparently paradoxical development is happening for a number of reasons, four of which are particularly significant. These are: (1) the closure of options for those deemed unskilled; (2) rising general expectations; (3) the new politics of poverty and welfare; and (4) the way in which absence from the new learning culture can also become a mechanism for legitimating inequalities – inequalities which may themselves be arising partly from a general acceptance of the idea and practice of lifelong learning.

First, there are fewer jobs for people without recognised skills. One of the most marked features of recent changes in the labour market is a steady fall since the early 1980s in the number of jobs open to people without qualifications or experience: between 1986 and 1992, for example, the proportion of jobs where no qualifications were required in Britain fell by 6 per cent (Gallie and White, 1993, 21). Nor is this simply a British phenomenon, for the International Adult Literacy Study found that in the mid-1990s the unemployment rate among those with limited literacy was almost 18 per cent, while it was under 8 per cent for the remainder of the workforce (OECD, 1997a, 164). While this process is partly a by-product of 'credential inflation', as Chapter Three has shown it is also associated with a general longer term process of upskilling (Dore, 1997; Felstead *et al*, 2002).

There are still many jobs that require no skills or qualifications, or fewer than were needed than in the past. Bar codes mean that check-out operators do not need to be able to read and count, while assistants in burger joints are able to operate the cash register simply by pressing a button with the appropriate icon (a steaming cup for coffee, and so on). But there are fewer of these jobs than there used to be, particularly in sectors where global competitors can offer un-skilled labour at considerably lower costs than can the West. More-over, the rise of the knowledge economy may make it harder rather than easier to obtain positions solely on the basis of informal con-tacts and family, which is how many unskilled workers found jobs in the past. Rapid changes in technique and organisation not only affect skills and know-how, but may also render insider networks obsolete. The value of an individual's social capital can fall as well as rise, and in those circumstances qualifications play an increasingly important role as a screening device (Rubenson, 1992, 27). In a knowledge economy, there is simply less space for those who lack recognised skills.

Moreover, the gap between the highly qualified and the unqualified seems to be growing. In Australia, for example, the relative value of post-school credentials is falling over the long term as the number of degree-holders in the population rises, but the penalties for the wholly non-qualified are also rising, and they are rising more steeply than the rewards for credentials are falling. This means that the value of qualifications relative to non-qualification has been en-hanced (Marginson, 1995, 69-71). Similar patterns can be seen in the United States, where increases in income between the mid-1980s and the mid-1990s were 34 per cent more for workers with a degree than for those without a high school diploma (Sennett, 1999, 88).

Are similar tendencies affecting adult learning? It certainly seems that the new adult education has been embraced most enthusias-tically by those who are already relatively well qualified. In a com-parison of British survey data between 1996 and 1999, at a time when overall participation rates were stable, the proportion from the professional and managerial social groups who were current or recent learners rose from 53 per cent to 58 per cent. Interestingly, when it came to age group, the largest rise was among the 45-54 age group, from 36 per cent to 41 per cent (Tuckett and Sargant, 1999, 12). In Finland, participation in adult learning rose by 31 per cent for those with higher education qualifications and by fewer than 16 per cent for those with secondary schooling only (Tuomisto, 1998, 158). At the top end of the social order it seems that learning inequalities are being piled upon material inequalities.

Some have gone further, suggesting that there may no longer be a persuasive case for tackling poverty at all. Both Manuel Castells and Zygmunt Bauman, for instance, claim that in a post-industrial world, the reserve army of labour is now virtually useless (Castells, 1998; Bauman, 1998). Bauman states his case starkly: 'The poor are not needed and so they are unwanted. And because they are un-wanted, they can be, without much regret or compunction, forsaken' (Bauman, 1998, 91). For Castells, the poor are a new 'Fourth World', excluded by virtue of their irrelevance to informa-tional capitalism (Castells, 1998, 162-4). The poor may be always with us, but we no longer require their services.

This is almost certainly an exaggeration. Demand for unskilled labour continues to be high, as argued above, even if it is declining, but even in relatively prosperous nations there have certainly been important changes in the nature of poverty, as well as its treatment. To take only one example, the steady demise of Fordist type indus-tries in western countries has tended to disadvantage unskilled older workers (often male) and inexperienced younger workers (particularly migrants and ethnic minorities), creating a growing population of long term unemployed. In Germany, for instance, the rise in long-term unemployed was more than twice the level in 2004 as the general rise in unemployment; the growth was particularly high among the over-55s and the under-25s (*Frankfurter Allgemeine Zeitung*, 2005). Consequently there are marked tendencies towards ghettoization – some groups in the labour market find themselves in a far more precarious and exposed situation than others. But are they really redundant, completely worthless in the eyes of twenty-first century turbocapitalism?

In an important critique of Bauman's thesis, David Byrne argues that far from being an irrelevance, the poor are indispensable precisely because they alone are available for 'poor work' – that is, badly paid and insecure jobs, not least in the shadowy activities that stand at the margins of, but nevertheless flow into and support, the economic mainstream. They 'are necessary ... to the continued accumulation process in the new form of capitalism which is being created' (Byrne, 1999, 56). It is because they lack qualifications and skills, as conventionally defined, that the socially excluded have been marginalised, but these very defects are an asset in the new capitalism, whose extremes of flexibility create spaces not just for short term jobs, but for sporadic jobs, semi-legal jobs and a variety of informal arrangements, from house cleaning and nannying to the milder forms of crime, such as selling recreational drugs or driving vanloads of beer and cigarettes across tax borders. For these sporadic or informal jobs, being 'streetwise' is all the education that is needed. At the margins of the new capitalism, knowing too much might be risky. But there is rarely much of a future at the margins.

Rising expectations

While the least advantaged are subject to marginalisation and pre-cariousness, elsewhere social expectations are rising. People routinely assume that in a modern society, those whom they en-counter on a daily basis will be broadly able to handle reading, writing and numbers, and maintain a coherent conversation. And this is true for most of the population, who have benefited from far higher quality schooling than did earlier generations. It is certainly true that many older adults now enjoy relatively affluent lives, to an extent that their 'consumer-led retirement lifestyle' puts them in 'part of a social vanguard' (Gilleard, 1996, 490). Companies who target middle-aged consumers talk in terms of 'the young-old' market. Retirement patterns have emerged that embrace later learning. Initially flourishing in university extramural classes and similar forms of public provision, this later lifestyle learning now appears to have migrated into the non-formal sector. This group – affluent, mobile, confident in its cultural capital – is not by any means an isolated minority (Gilleard, 1996, 491); yet its experiences are not shared by all older people.

The myth of declining standards is itself an illustration of the way public expectations are changing. A series of surveys of literacy and numeracy standards has shown that in Western countries like Britain, those who left school recently are generally more literate and numerate than older people who left school in a different era. Particularly solid evidence was offered in the International Adult Literacy Survey, which used an internationally-standardised instru-ment to measure the literacy and numeracy levels of the adult popu-lation in twelve nations (OECD, 1997a). Older adults were more likely to be found in the groups of low literacy, while younger people were in the highest performing groups. The only exception, at least in the case of the UK, appears to be among those whose school ex-perience spanned the 1970s and early 1980s, who performed less well than both their older and younger compatriots (Sweeney *et al*, 1998). It is reasonable from this to conclude that, with minor variations in different countries, school standards in most Western nations have improved somewhat over the last 50 or 60 years. But that is not how most people see it. Newspaper editorials and politicians alike constantly bemoan the falling standards of literacy and numeracy among young people.

As IALS and other surveys show, it is not that standards of literacy and numeracy are falling among today's school-leavers; on the contrary, they are getting better. What has changed are our expectations. We now regard it as normal for everyone to be able to read fairly simple texts such as safety instructions, video recorder manuals, health and safety regulations, maps and memos. And as our expectations have risen, so the gap has become wider for those who are unable to carry out these tasks, which are so routine for the rest of us. In an information society, poor literacy means that even identifying relevant learning opportunities is a major challenge.

The politics of poverty and the discourse of exclusion

The third major change concerns the politics of poverty. With the construction of the welfare state in the late 1940s, most European societies acknowledged that public policy should seek to integrate all citizens into the world of full employment, while providing a degree of financial and other support for those unable to work. Extremes of inequality were both economically damaging and a risk to social cohesion. The post-1945 settlement rested on the management of social inequality in ways that avoided extremes of poverty and wealth of the kind that was so visible in Europe and America in the 1920s and 1930s. It also rested broadly on the principle that social inequality should be legitimate, and based on factors that people largely accepted as fair – such as educational achievement (Marshall, 1992; Strathdee, 2005).

Several authoritative figures have suggested that this period has now come to an end. Globalisation and rapid technological change, leading to increasingly intense competition, are generating new pressures on the most vulnerable, leading in turn to increased social exclusion. By the 1990s, instead of using the language of poverty or inequality to describe those who had fewer resources than the rest of us, policy makers throughout Europe had started to speak of social exclusion and social inclusion. Did the shift in language also denote a change in political attitudes? I think so. The very fact that policymakers throughout Western Europe latched on to the language of exclusion, as did senior figures in such intergovernmental agencies as the OECD and the European Commission, was a signal of a shift under way (Field, 1998, 141-2). It also formed part of a wider linguistic shift in Europe during the 1980s and 1990s, with policy makers increasingly using terms such as 'insertion sociale' and employability to foreground their intentions (Dubar, 2000, 111-12).

At its simplest, the changing language reflected a move away from any concern with social change, and an acceptance that capitalism is now the only game in town. Rather than struggling against the structural causes of inequality, the new language of exclusion implies that government's task is to promote 'inclusion' into the existing social order. But we can go further. In the past, the poor were poor; some saw them as authors of their own fate, while others viewed them as victims of forces beyond their control. Today, failure can affect increasing numbers of people – typesetters, miners and steelworkers, but also stockholders, software engineers, designers and college lecturers.

At the same time, the vast majority of citizens have become more comfortable, and electorates across the Western world have been voting for tax reductions. Logically enough, the politics of poverty and inequality has also changed, not least because of the move towards a knowledge society. In industrial society, organised labour could demand universal welfare services as a vital guarantee of security for working class families. But as Ulrich Beck points out, the replacement of labour by knowledge and equipment – which itself usually embodies knowledge – has meant that organised labour has lost much of its power and influence across the Western world (Beck, 1997, 166). Contemporary social and economic changes have particularly destabilised the social and political environment of the manual working class. Peter Alheit has described this process in detail for the urban working class in Germany, suggesting that as the 'life world' of worker milieus is de-traditionalised and loses much of its meaning, there are winners (Alheit mentions working-class daughters who no longer face the narrowing pressures of family and community to hang around feeding the menfolk) and losers (such as young men who lose their orientation and may become profoundly alienated), as well as many who stand somewhere in between these extremes (Alheit, 1994, 186-7).

Along with social change has come a waning sense of the social obligation of the 'haves' towards the 'have-nots'. Beck attributes this erosion of a sense of duty towards the less fortunate to secularisation and the increasingly global identities of the affluent (Beck, 1997, 166-7). But it is at least equally plausible to suggest that the more people are investing in private health care, housing, pensions and education, the harder it becomes to persuade them to vote for political parties promising high taxation and a strong welfare state. This is particularly important given that some of the most affluent individuals in contemporary Western societies have come from groups judged, in welfarist terms, as among the most vulnerable. Chris Gilleard has argued, for instance, that the prevalence of affluent, consumer-oriented lifestyles among sizeable numbers of older adults now 'threatens to undermine the established certainties surrounding the welfarist construction of later life' (Gilleard, 1996, 490).

Rather than appealing to social solidarity, the language of inclusion offers a humanistic response to middle class fears of the poor. The fear of exclusion damaging the whole society is remarkably widespread. Thus the UK government's National Advisory Council on Education and Training Targets warned in 1998 that

> Social exclusion is expensive, not merely because of the burden that it imposes on the social security system, but also because of the indirect costs that arise from, for example, juvenile delinquency and the greater levels of ill-health that poorer members of society suffer. (NACETT, 1998, 13)

Further, the excluded pass on their exclusion to their children (Bentley, 1998, 106). In more extreme versions, this shades over into a fear of the excluded themselves, who have been described by some commentators as becoming effectively an underclass. In arguing that there is a risk of creating a sub-group that has effectively dropped out from wider social networks, living from a mixture of crime and welfare benefits, proponents of this hypothesis focus particularly on the perceived problems in a number of advanced societies with 'lower-class young males' who have become detached from the labour market and therefore from society as a whole (Murray, 1990, 18-19). In the United States, Murray has claimed that experience shows training and education programmes to be relatively powerless as they 'don't reach the people who need them most' (Murray, 1990, 33). While such views are less widespread in Europe than in the USA, perceived associations between exclusion and anti-social behaviour can be used to justify the coercion with respect to vocational training, which was noted in the preceding chapter. At the very least, they provide a language and framework for defining and debating problems.

Relations between lifelong learning and social inequality increasingly affect other policy areas. In most Western countries, welfare state provision is being reformed in order to transfer responsibility away from government and towards the individual. Increasingly, the role of the State is allegedly to facilitate employability and well-being, by providing personalised support and information services. Thus in Germany, where the so-called Hartz reforms of welfare provoked considerable opposition from trade unions and others, unemployment policy rests less and less on the provision of high levels of financial support and increasingly on the use of support services such as 'Ich-AG' (or Myself plc) and the labour offices' Personal-Service-Agenturen and Programme Jump (see for example *Frankfurt Allgemeine Zeitung*, 2005). Similar features can be found in Britain's various New Deal programmes, which rely heavily on focused and individualised support through personal advisers and individual guidance. The importance of personal support in boosting confidence and self-legitimation has been shown in some detail in studies of the New Deal for Musicians and the New Deal for disabled people (Cloonan, 2004; Heenan, 2002).

Yet the use of such support without access to other resources is bound to create new problems. In the field of health promotion, for example, it has reasonably been argued that 'there is a contradiction between offering people information on which to make lifestyle choices if they do not have the personal resources to make choice possible' (West Belfast Economic Forum, 1994, 6). The same might be said of personal financial planning, of caring for those with disability, or of housing policy. This argument can be taken further: in a learning society, the fact that individuals are treated as though they can acquire and understand the implications of new information about their well-being becomes in turn a justification for reducing the resources that are made available through public services. Although this can amount to a form of 'structural discrimination', it is one that largely passes unnoticed and unchallenged. By individualising the characteristics which justify employers and others in treating people differently, the trend towards lifelong learning also helps fragment the excluded, and encourages a search for individual solutions. And this pattern is reproduced through other areas of public life, as the welfare state switches its focus from 'passive support' to 'active strategies of insertion' – the most significant of which include training, so that individuals can acquire the skills and knowledge required for them to take active responsibility for their own well-being (Rosanvallon, 1995).

Legitimate inequalities

Finally, lifelong learning may also serve to legitimate inequality. In a more individualised society, which positively embraces a culture of continuous lifelong learning, successful participation in organised education and training functions as a mechanism for disguising and naturalising hierarchies (Stauber and Walther, 1998, 38-40). Where equal opportunities legislation exists to outlaw discrimination, for example, it is standard practice to state in job advertisements precisely which qualifications are required from successful candidates, but the uneven distribution of qualifications among different categories of the population means that access to jobs is not really equal in practice. The ready availability of self-help texts on the market means that all are equally able to buy and use such texts to help build identities and performances that signal our willingness to learn, but the bulk of self-help publishing is directed explicitly and consciously at young, managerial or professional adults who are already focused on the project of the self (Hancock and Tyler, 2004, 623).

From this perspective, lifelong learning plays a central part in the processes of inclusion and exclusion. It is not simply affected, more or less passively, by processes taking take place elsewhere. It is actively used by particular groups and individuals to advance their interests and underpin their claims, and it is becoming more significant as an external marker of whether or not an individual or community is likely to prove a worthwhile investment for the future. And part of its success lies in the overwhelmingly positive image that lifelong learning enjoys (Stauber and Walther, 1998, 40). Frequently, this means that the disenfranchised are likely to accept their exclusion as the (just) penalty for their own failure.

Anthony Giddens has suggested that such exclusionary processes are not simply imposed on others, in a passive and one-sided manner. Unfortunately, their impact is all the greater in that they can also be internalised by individual actors in ways that are profoundly damaging to their sense of worth and value:

> To the effects of material deprivation are added a disqualification from reflexive incorporation in the wider social order. Exclusionary mechanisms here ... concern not only subjection to modes of power coming from the technical control of knowledge-based systems, but also attack the integrity of the self. (Giddens, 1994, 90)

Given the importance of self-confidence and intrinsic motivation to much adult learning, this internalisation of self-doubt and anxiety is bound to undermine and attack the very possibility of building up a firm identity as a capable lifelong learner.

Not that this is entirely new. Early industrialisation was associated with a similar stratification within the working class, associated with the acquisition of skill and know-how among particular groups. Charles Dickens and Frederick Engels, among many Victorian commentators, both wrote of the skilled artisans as an 'aristocracy of labour', and how their earnest dedication to self-improvement often served as a badge of respectability, marking them as a distinctive group who had little in common with the unrespectable poor (Field, 1979). So is the difference today between knowledge-rich and knowledge-poor simply a difference of degree? Or, in the information society, is something more substantial at stake? For if it is, the policy solutions of the past – securing more equal access to initial education and training, and to compensatory or remedial education for the adults who missed out the first time round – will not do.

Who are the 'knowledge poor'?

Lifelong learning has raised the stakes and helped embed inequality. At the same time, it is both an expression and a cause of social openness and fluidity. Issues of equality and inequality are therefore of substantial importance in understanding the social consequences of the trend towards lifelong learning in Western societies. So who are the new knowledge poor, and what are the prospects facing them?

Social class, according to one authoritative UK survey, 'continues to be the key discriminator in understanding participation in learning' (Sargant et al, 1997, 12). In an authoritative 1999 study, well over half of those from the upper and middle classes (that is, social groups A and B) described themselves as current or recent learners, as against a third of skilled workers (group C2) and a quarter of the unskilled (groups D and E). These differences were just as marked when it came to future intentions, with 50 per cent of ABs indicating that they were likely to take up learning, compared with 34 per cent of C2s and 27 per cent of DEs (Tuckett and Sargant 1999, 13).

While the NIACE surveys use a relatively clear definition of learning, the categories used to analyse the participation patterns of different groups are – perhaps inevitably – crude. A more differentiated approach was used in the 1997 national adult learning survey, though its value is affected by the breadth of definition of learning that was used. In terms of this broad definition, participation was highest amongst professional and managerial groups, reaching 95 per cent amongst professionals and associate professionals (see Table 1). This survey also suggested that professionals and associate professionals had the highest levels of participation in non-vocational learning, as well as vocationally-oriented learning (Beinart and Smith, 1998, 55). Being in work is also a key divider; over a four and a half year period, over 90 per cent of those in work told researchers in 1999 that they had done some organised learning, against 47 per cent for those not in work (La Valle and Finch, 1999, 10).

Furthermore, some industries spend more on training than others, with particularly high levels being recorded in non-tradable services and high-tech areas, as well as in sectors with generally high levels of research and development spending (Greenhalgh and Mavrotas, 1996, 139; Felstead *et al*, 2002). According to one analysis of the Labour Force Survey (DfEE, 200, 9), there is growing polarisation in Britain between those firms that provide training and the substantial minority that provide little or none. Participation in training is lowest among the self-employed and people working in family enterprises, a pattern that is found in the wealthier Pacific Rim nations as well as in the older industrial lands (Wu, 2000, 160).

Table 1: Percentage within each occupational grouping who had done some recent learning (excluding those still in full-time continuous education)

Occupational group	% of learners	% of vocational learners	% of non-vocational learners
Managers and administrators	79	74	30
Professional occupations	95	92	39
Associate prof/technical	95	92	41
Clerical and secretarial	83	76	36
Craft and related	71	66	26
Personal and protective service	78	73	25
Sales	73	67	26
Plant and machine operatives	64	59	17
Other occupations	60	53	22

Source: Beinart and Smith 1998, 55.

From one point of view, the social class bias of lifelong learning is to be expected. It is certainly not new. Adult education has always tended to attract earnest middle class improvers: in the early nineteenth century, bourgeois supporters of the Mechanics' Institutes were fond of complaining that their audience consisted too much of the lower middle classes and that the manual workers at whom they were aimed were staying away (Wright, 1996).

Why should contemporary societies be any different? Part of the answer is that social class is now increasingly correlated with the ability to handle new knowledge and develop new skills. To take one example, it is widely suggested that 'graduates, far from being insulated from rapid and pervasive change, are in fact especially vulnerable to the effects of this turbulence, especially when they work in professional areas that are themselves undergoing rapid transformation' (Candy *et al*, 1994, 33). A positive orientation towards learning – which can include favourable attitudes, for example the view that new ideas and approaches are exciting or fun, as well as more conventional learning attributes – is increasingly a prerequisite of success in graduate and professional careers. As lifelong learning becomes an important dimension of social class, so the significance of the 'learning divide' has grown.

If social class is one determining factor, gender is a second. Unlike social class, gender appears to have only a limited effect on crude participation. The NIACE surveys suggested that although slightly more men than women participate in learning (41% as against 40% defined themselves as current or recent learners in the 1999 survey, for example), the gap was not only small but appeared to be narrowing; future plans to learn were more or less indistinguishable for men and women (Tuckett and Sargant, 1999, 7). Using a wider definition of what counts as learning, the national adult learning survey reported a slightly larger gender differential – 78% of men and 70% of women described themselves as current or recent learners – suggesting that men may be more likely than women to take part in very short episodes of learning (Beinart and Smith, 1998, 38). Over a four and a half-year period, 85 per cent of men reported doing some learning, compared with 77 per cent of women (La Valle and Finch, 1999, 11). However, the gender pattern looks different for different types of learning. The 1997, 1999 and 2002 surveys all showed that men were more likely to engage in self-directed learning than women, mainly because non-taught learning was mostly connected with work (Beinart and Smith, 1998, 210; La Valle and Finch, 1999, 11; Fitzgerald *et al*, 2003, 21).

At aggregate level, there was little gender difference in either survey in respect of taught learning. Superficially, women seem to be catching up with the men, and arguably even overtaking them. However, this picture of apparent equality is misleading. When taught learning was subdivided into vocational and non-vocational learning, a marked gender effect was apparent; in vocational learning, the gap between women and men rose to 11 per cent, while in non-vocational learning women were more likely to take part than men (Beinart and Smith, 1998, 51; this finding was also reported in Fitzgerald *et al*, 2003, 20). Admittedly, such raw data tell us nothing about the qualitative difference between women's and men's experiences of learning (see Fenwick, 2004), but they do confirm that, below the superficial similarities in aggregate data, gender inequalities continue to play a significant part in the distribution of learning opportunities. By the same token, gender probably plays a role in the distribution of compulsory learning, since much vocational learning is mandatory rather than voluntary.

Along with class and gender, age constitutes the third great determinant of participation. However, the case of age also shows how hard it is to equate simple participation with advantage. If participation is understood simplistically as a Good Thing, then the facts are clear: the young get most and the elderly get least. This is as true for informal and self-directed learning as it is for taught learning: the 1997 British survey found that 34 per cent of people in their twenties had done some self-taught learning in the previous three years, against only, 20 per cent of people in their sixties (Beinart and Smith 1998, 210). But there is another way of looking at this: one benefit of becoming older may be the weakening or even disappearance of pressures to take courses and examinations.

There is considerable evidence that participation among older adults is falling. British survey data for 1999 and 1996 show a marked rise in current and recent participation in all age groups of adults under 65, yet participation rates fell from 19 per cent to 16 per cent, for the 65 to 74-year old group and from 15 per cent to 9 per cent for those aged 75 and over (Tuckett and Sargant, 1999, 11; Aldridge and Tuckett, 2005; but note the contrary evidence in Fitzgerald *et al*, 2003, 20). It is not yet clear whether this is a distinctively British pattern, created by policies adopted during the 1980s and early 1990s, or whether it represents a more substantial underlying trend. This group has lost out from the rise of the new adult learning and the collapse of more established patterns of adult education provision. Thus local authority adult education and university extramural provision, which were particularly popular with older adults in Britain, were particularly hard hit as a result of policy changes introduced in the early 1990s and largely maintained after 1997. At the same time, those who have left the labour force through retirement or ill health have been unable to benefit from the expansion of work-based learning.

Yet we should be as cautious about overgeneralisation on grounds of age as in any other case. Much debate over age inequality concerns the supposed disadvantages of the elderly. This is understandable: contemporary Western values tend to praise youth and deride the old. Yet to accept this discourse at face value, and to see the young as privileged simply because images of youth, in idealised form, dominate the public space, would be extremely misleading. In particular it would ignore the systematic and structural forces that have functioned since the late 1970s to push young people into 'poor work' and to exclude them from the more protected and less vulnerable areas of employment. In the mid-1990s, for instance, two-fifths of all those aged 25 to 34 in Britain had experienced at least one episode of unemployment – far the highest of any age group in the labour market. Byrne notes what he calls an 'age-related effect' (but which might more accurately be called a generational effect), in that those 'who entered the labour market as it has become post-Fordist experience the disadvantage of that directly. Those with a history of work under Fordism retain some of the advantages of that system' (Byrne, 1999, 92-3). An EU-wide survey of labour market conditions noted similarly that both the collapse of the youth labour market and the decline of opportunities for the unskilled since the mid-1970s has been combined with an upturn in the supply of female labour to fill many of the new jobs that are appearing (Rubery and Smith, 1999, 18). At the same time, much of the learning undertaken by young people consists of mandatory training courses, often followed as an alternative to unemployment.

If survey data are any guide, ethnicity appears to play a relatively minor part in determining participation in countries such as Britain. According to the 1997 national adult learning survey in Britain, there were no significant differences between the participation levels of those who described themselves as 'white' and those from other ethnic groups (Beinart and Smith, 1998, 45). This is an important finding, though it must again be stressed that this cannot be interpreted as meaning that participation is necessarily a signal of equality between different groups. Beyond this, large scale survey evidence is of limited help, as the numbers of ethnic minority respondents involved will generally be too small to allow for further analysis – out of 5131 respondents in the 1997 British adult learning survey, for example, only 179 did not describe themselves as 'white'.

Much of the evidence about participation rests on such broad survey data. This type of evidence tells us little about either the consequences or the meanings of participation (Usher and Bryant, 1989, 109). Indeed, Richard Edwards has challenged the very notion of participation as a meaningful category of analysis, since it encompasses such a wide and diverse set of activities and variables (Edwards, 1997, 117). Drawing on his study of adult returners to higher education, Linden West argues that 'the answers people give to researchers are shaped by the questions asked as well as the methods employed and the assumptions which underlie them'. In the case of adult learning surveys, respondents are likely to assume that vocational motives will be more easily understood and accepted as legitimate than enjoyment and self-fulfilment. Thus 'Kathy', one of West's interviewees, initially couched her account of an access course in terms of her desire to qualify for a professional occupation; but her reasons turned out to be at least as much concerned with self-fulfilment and development as with work. West concludes that 'vocational aspiration might be but one element in a longer story of individual struggles for identity and self' (West, 1996, 34, 206).

But even this does not complete the story. West still assumes that the characteristic learning narrative is a positive, emancipatory quest for meaning. It is an assumption that I often find myself making, and presumably it is shared by many other people who work in educational institutions. Yet there are many for whom participation is a story of coercion, boredom and repeated failure. For many, participation is not a matter of personal choice and identity; it is a matter of following instructions.

Conscription and resistance

If so much rides on lifelong learning – individual employability, company survival, national competitiveness – what is to be done about those who, once all the barriers are removed, are reluctant members of the learning society? As the discourse of permanent lifelong learning has spread, and worked itself through into the language and practices of continuing professional development and constant updating, so a degree of coercion has also emerged, often gaining widespread acceptance as people come to see lifelong learning as a basic survival mechanism. Internalised expectations mean that a significant number of adults – perhaps a majority – regard learning as something they have to do if they are to survive and thrive in the risk society. Thus over half of all Europeans sampled in a survey agreed that 'continual education and training is a necessity' for themselves (CEC, 1996b).

For most people, the learning imperative is implicit and largely un-spoken. Increasingly, though, it has become explicit. A recent policy paper in the Netherlands which outlined the contribution of its National Action Programme for Lifelong Learning towards removing obstacles and offering relevant opportunities, went on to insist that:

> This is achieved by involving everyone. However, a chain is only as strong as its weakest link ... All people, young and old, are firstly and naturally responsible for themselves. You have to learn how to take care of yourself, and therefore you must want to acquire the know-ledge and skills to do that. Those who do not take part will be re-minded of their responsibilities. (Ministry of Culture, Education and Science, 1998, 9)

The use of similar rhetoric in Britain led Frank Coffield, who had directed a major research programme on the Learning Society, to suggest that lifelong learning had become 'the latest form of social control', stamped by 'moral authoritarianism' and backed up by 'threats of compulsion' (Coffield, 1999, 9-10). After all, a large pro-portion of the wider adult population has no particular interest in taking up the so-called 'opportunities' that are on offer. To take one small example, a recent international survey showed that consider-able numbers of people are neither taking part in education or train-ing at present, nor have any wish to do so. The proportion ranged from 34 per cent of those sampled in Denmark to 75 per cent in Hungary (Boudard and Morlaix, 2003, 510). Moreover, those who have benefited least from educational opportunities in the past are also far the most likely to express little or no wish to return to educa-tion in the future, as are people from manual working class back-grounds and older people (Aldridge and Tuckett, 2005, 15-17). Social democratic governments, such as the New Labour government in Britain, are therefore particularly likely to adopt a mixture of induce-ment and compulsion in order to engage low participation groups in continuing education and training.

Yet these trends were already well established in the 1980s. Indeed, they can frequently be traced back to the depression of the 1930s, when many governments – including Britain's – required unemployed workers to undergo retraining (Field, 1992). In recent years, though, the use of compulsion has been extended to a large part of the adult population, and above all the working population. It is easy to forget just how commonplace the conscription of adults into training has become. A long list exists of activities that are not open to people who refuse to take part in training. Some of these are long established: driving a car, for example, is a common public activity that is only open to those who pass a formally verifiable test. No one complains much about the social control exercised over those who refuse to conform to this expectation, nor is it likely that anyone would lament the fact that airline pilots or nurses are expected to update their skills on a regular basis, or that professional athletes are called in for specialised coaching on an almost daily basis.

These are the tips of a much larger iceberg. For a growing number of people, for lengthening periods of their lives, lifelong learning is compulsory. While this is particularly true for those who are in paid employment or who are receiving welfare benefits, it increasingly affects other people as well.

Most of the factors that produce coercion are external ones, and have relatively little to do with the skills – as conventionally defined – that help employees carry out their job. Among the most important of these external factors are:

- statutory requirements, such as the EU's occupational safety and health regime which demands that member states transcribe into their national legislation a requirement that workplace representatives be trained to the specified standards

- regulatory frameworks, which may encompass training to set standards as a condition of continued practice in a particular industry or occupation

- contract compliance, such as when a purchaser requires a major change in procedures, for example a shift to online trading, so that staff must be trained in new methods and processes

- customer or client expectations, as with, for example, the decision after the Stephen Lawrence murder enquiry that the Metropolitan Police should undergo a wide range of antiracism training activities

- professional association requirements, which may go well beyond specifying the entry qualifications to encompass mandatory continuing professional development

In addition to these external forces, some organisations have established their own internal demands. Some employers have gone so far as to apply a form of training conscription to the entire workforce. AlliedSignal Inc., the New-Jersey based industrial conglomerate, with a workforce of some 70,000 in more than 40 countries, insists that each employee completes at least 40 hours of training every year (Wilson, 1999, 51). At a more intimate level, some employers require compulsory counselling for workers whose performance is judged below par, as an alternative to taking disciplinary action (MacEarlean, 1999, 9).

The scale of these developments is remarkable. When asked in the National Adult Learning Survey in 2002, six out of ten workers who had taken courses related to their current job said that the course was not compulsory. The remainder said that the course was made compulsory by their employer (33%), their professional body (4%) or by legislation (4%) (Fitzgerald *et al*, 2003, 69). In a more detailed survey of 20,667 households across the West Midlands region, an estimated 36 per cent of the labour force had undertaken some job-related education and training, and of these, the largest subject of training was in areas subjected to statutory regulation; 26 per cent said their training was in health and safety or environmental health alone (West Midlands Regional TECs 1998, 73). With most respondents reporting that they had done the training because their employer required it, the report's authors concluded that 'employer compulsion is clearly the main reason for training in the region' (West Midlands Regional TECs 1998, 74).

Much of this training may be of very short duration, and have only a remote connection with skill as conventionally defined – First Aid at Work courses, for instance, usually last one day. While the workforce are the main target of these regulatory pressures, they can also extend to all kinds of other organisations, including voluntary bodies. Within my own recent experience, for example, training is now compulsory for the mums who make hot dogs for youngsters at our local rugby club (food hygiene training) as well as for volunteer stewards at a yearly folk music week.

In addition to the employed workforce, conscription is virtually routine for the unemployed. In nations which have a public benefits system, it is normal for the unemployed to be required to undertake training as a condition of receiving their benefit. Because much training for unemployed people is part-financed through the European Commission's Structural Funds (for details see Field, 1998), it is common within the EU for training to become compulsory at well-defined stages: after six months of unemployment for the under-25s and after two years for the over-25s. As the following comments from a private sector trainer demonstrate, the participants are certainly not attending out of their own motivation:

> A: The big group for us, the adults, they're really just drop-outs. That's right, isn't it. They're drop-outs and they don't see why they have to go back to class after ten years away from class. That's what they call it, class, that's how they would see it, and they don't want it, to go back to school. It's very, very difficult to bring them round. (Training Focus Group, Newtownabbey, 21 October 1997)

In most Western societies the unemployed constitute a sizeable group of learning conscripts: in its first six months, the New Deal programme for unemployed young people recruited some 60,000 in England alone (DfEE, 1998b). In general, at least in the UK, relatively few individuals ever experience withdrawal of benefit, and one qualitative study found that even those who had been sanctioned saw coercion as legitimate in principle; the civil servants who worked as New Deal Personal Advisers were even more likely to accept sanctions as a useful tool (Wilkinson, 2003, 22). A requirement to train seems to have high legitimacy in the eyes of the wider population.

It is not simply the scale of compulsion that is important. The development of widespread compulsion also forces us to reconsider our views of participation. Conventionally, non-participants have always been seen by adult education writers as victims of social structures or psychological deficits, denied equal access to a positive opportunity. Participants, on the other hand, are regarded as willing volunteers. This view of the willing learner has become embedded in the pedagogy of adult teaching, which is said to be characterised by its ability to 'develop and maintain symmetrical relations between teachers and learners', using 'democratic and participatory pedagogies' to help learners access and even create knowledge (CEC, 1998b, 9). Yet as lifelong learning becomes generalised, and adult participation ceases to be largely voluntary in nature, these accepted wisdoms must be challenged.

One obvious set of difficulties is centred on motivation and what, with younger learners, might be called active 'disaffection'. In the focus group discussion already cited, one trainer had faced physical intimidation:

> A: That's the reality at the coalface. We are the ones who have to face them and try to get them to do something useful for once. It isn't all

doom and gloom, you do have the ones that you feel are the success stories. But some of them, they will, they will come in because
they have been sent there and they will start to wreck the place.

For another, motivating this group represented an extraordinarily
difficult, if sometimes rewarding, challenge:

B: No, some have no interest, not all of them but some, they're just
parked there. They're pushed into it. Some will get more interested.
It's very, very hard, so it is, getting them interested. (Training Focus
Group, Newtownabbey, 21 October 1997)

Once more, this is best interpreted as a rational response to exclusion. The truth is that long term unemployment disproportionately hits those who are already disadvantaged in terms of their
skills, knowledge and qualifications (and also, often, in terms of
other characteristics such as physical appearance and even post-
code). It erodes not only the skills, motivation and social networks of
the unemployed themselves; it can trigger discriminatory responses
by employers, and help ensure that any return to work is usually to
those jobs that are the most precarious. From this perspective, participation in a scheme designed specifically to help the unemployed
can itself be highly dysfunctional, serving to label the participants
while inculcating skills they cannot apply.

As well as seeing non-participants as excluded victims, though, it is
also possible to see non-participation as a form of active self-ex-
clusion. The German writer Dirk Axmacher goes too far in describing this as a form of 'resistance' (Axmacher, 1989, 36-7). The truth is
that we know almost nothing about the positive meaning of non-
participation as a self-definition, other than that it appears to be
quite widely – and deeply felt. In Britain, for example, respondents
in a national survey who claimed to have undertaken no post-school
learning in the previous three years (this came to around one
quarter of the total survey sample) were asked what might encourage them to do some learning. In reply, half of these 'non-
learners' said that there was nothing that might encourage them to
learn (Beinart and Smith, 1998, 239). In this group, older adults were
far more likely than younger people to say that nothing would encourage them: 70 per cent of 'non-learners' in their sixties gave this
reply, as against 20 per cent of those aged between 16 and 19. Non-
learners were also more likely to believe that knowing people is more
important than qualifications in getting jobs, and that employers
will usually choose a younger applicant than an older one despite
their qualifications. Slightly surprisingly, perhaps, having enjoyed

school made virtually no difference (Beinart and Smith, 1998, 236-45).

Of course, the identity of 'non-learner' is not always quite as fixed as at first appears. Over a quarter of those who described themselves as 'non-learners' in the 1997 survey reported 18 months later that they had undertaken some learning – usually related to their job (La Valle and Finch, 1999, 5). In a qualitative study in Scotland, some people who defined themselves as 'non-learners' appeared to be doing so as a way of expressing their independence and in some cases their masculinity. This group was made up predominantly of older working class men (Field, 2001). And where there is resistance, it comes from unlikely sources. Tilda Gaskell, in a study of older adults, reported that 'aging members of the 'new middle class" very much disliked being told how they should learn new skills in order to maintain their health and autonomy (Gaskell, 2005, 375). It seems that members of the service middle class, who are accustomed to exercising a degree of control over others through education and training, may be particularly hostile to the same message when it is directed at themselves. It may be strictly inaccurate to describe either group as 'non-learners' since they must have learned a fair amount over the ten year period covered in the survey, but what matters more is the cultural depth with which this view is held. For many people, particularly older men and women, not being a 'school type' forms a positive part of their self-identity. And it is the older adults – those who have left or are leaving active employment – who are free to enjoy the identity of 'non-learner'. For many others, learning remains a matter of compulsion rather than choice, and this changes the rules of the game for providers as well as for learners.

Compulsion is not simply a matter of social control, nor of the dominance of work-related preoccupations. Rising expectations among consumers for autonomy, increasing individualisation and choice, and concern for public health and environmental sustainability have all contributed to help change public expectations. We noted the widespread if largely tacit acceptance of the importance of self-development and upskilling as a way of seeking to balance the risks of insecurity and uncertainty. However, those who have internalised 'the rules of the (lifelong learning) game' are not the most likely to face the more naked forms of external coercion. Rather, the most coercive forms of conscription are likely to be applied to those who stand outside the learning society, for whatever reason.

Human capital and social capital

Much of the public investment in lifelong learning is targeted on training programmes for various excluded groups. In particular, public investment is channelled into skills programmes for the unemployed, as well as into literacy programmes for those with the lowest levels of formal literacy. The justification for these investments is simple: it is said that people are unemployed because they lack the skills employers are looking for, and training programmes which help the unemployed acquire valued skills represent good value for money. In particular, marginalised groups such as the long term unemployed or ex-prisoners suffer from much lower levels of literacy than those with whom they are competing in the labour market. If successful, programmes of this nature will cut public spending by taking people off benefits and putting them into work. And because so much lifelong learning is work-related, the state can then leave it to employers and individuals to take care of their own skills development once they are in a job. Potentially, then, the pay-off in terms of social inclusion is considerable. How well does this approach work in practice?

Obviously, the results of any targeted training programme will depend on a variety of factors, some of them external to the programme. In the UK, for instance, the New Deal programme was introduced in 1997, at a time when the economy was undergoing a period of steady growth, accompanied by a net expansion in employment. A macro-evaluation of the first full year of the programme suggested that it had reduced youth unemployment by roughly 30,000 relative to what it would otherwise have been – equivalent to a reduction of almost 40 per cent (Anderton *et al*, 1999, 13). But New Deal is a relatively high cost programme. It provides for an intensive period of individualised counselling, followed by one of a number of options, including subsidised employment, each of which involves at least some training leading to a recognised qualification, all aimed at helping participants to find work. Such mixtures of job advice, training and job placement have been widely adopted across the European Union, exemplifying policy-makers' efforts to identify more active and pre-emptive policies towards both welfare and the labour market (Rosanvallon, 1995).

Targeted training of this kind therefore looks attractive as a solution to relative disadvantage. However, publicly funded training programmes also face well-known difficulties. One is the tendency for employers to hire programme participants (either actual or prospective) rather than other workers, in order to benefit from subsidies. As well as this tendency towards what economists call substitution, there is also the possibility that job subsidies will give participating firms an artificial advantage over their competitors, or that other job seekers will be denied help because they do not happen to meet the programme's criteria. While the New Deal appears to have experienced relatively low levels of substitution in its first years, things might have been very different had labour market conditions been less favourable (Atkinson, 1999, 17). Further, some of the public spending will be wasted, because it will be spent on people who would have found work anyway, or on training that employers and individuals would otherwise have paid for – a phenomenon known to economists as 'deadweight'. Typically, active labour market programmes involve a deadweight loss of around a half – as did the New Deal in Britain, in its first full year (Atkinson, 1999, 14).

The risk with any training programme is that the better its reputation, the more likely it is that it will cream off those most likely to succeed. In a self-reinforcing cycle, the most disadvantaged are concentrated disproportionately in the least effective types of active labour market programme, powerfully reinforcing their disadvantage (Campbell *et al*, 1998, 21). During its first full year, only a fifth of those leaving the New Deal had taken up subsidised employment, with most of the rest either entering full-time education and training, or finding ordinary, unsubsidised jobs (Anderton *et al*, 1999, 9-10). The implication is that many young unemployed people found work through the routine operation of the labour market, at a time of relatively high demand for labour, rather than as a direct result of the New Deal. Moreover, the least advantaged trainees were likely to experience the least favourable outcomes. A national survey of New Deal entrants showed that young unemployed adults from minority ethnic communities were considerably more likely to fetch up in full-time education and training, and less likely to end up in jobs, than were their white counterparts (Bryson, Knight and White, 2000, 72-3). The reason was that while members of ethnic minorities were just as likely as white to be submitted for the employment option, employers were then screening them out (Hasluck, 2000, 34-5). That said, it has been claimed that the New Deal proved a comparatively positive experience for disabled people, a group that has continually suffered from discrimination and prejudice in earlier training schemes (Heenan, 2002).

Finally, state-managed programmes are often ill-suited to the flexibility and adaptability of a post-Fordist labour market. Hence the need for partnerships, involving employers and other inter-mediaries such as voluntary organisations. Yet bureaucratic regulation and tight monitoring requirements still tend to override the needs of individuals or employers. Frequently, target groups are defined in terms of their status as receivers of welfare benefits. The New Deal in Britain provides a telling example: because the pro-gramme's reputation among the long term unemployed is relatively high, some unemployed people were trying to enter although they had not been on welfare benefits long enough to meet the entry criteria (Atkinson, 1999). These criteria in turn derive not solely from the demands of the UK government's Employment Service but also from the framework regulations of the European Structural Funds, which partly finance such schemes. There is, then, always a tension within state-funded programmes between the tendency towards bureaucratic regulation that is required to manage and monitor a large scale programme, and the flexibility and adaptability that are such widely-noted features of post-Fordist labour markets.

Evidence suggests that conventional supply-side strategies on their own have a limited impact upon inclusion. Inward investors into Wales, for instance, have preferred to recruit overwhelmingly from those who already have jobs rather than from the unemployed (Rees and Thomas, 1996, 53). Simply giving people new skills does not help unless they are able (a) to constantly apply them in practice and (b) to supplement this codified knowledge with tacit knowledge, for example by acquiring new social capital – that is, by building up their networks of contacts and communications so that they can find work by word-of-mouth and on the basis of personal knowledge rather than through formal qualifications and the public media alone. One interesting finding from studies of the New Deals is that well-connected personal advisers are particularly important in help-ing to build confidence and connections among those who are most disengaged, whether through serious disadvantage (Heenan, 2002) or lifestyle and disposition (Cloonan, 2004).

Social connections are important in creating disadvantage, and it is logical that they might play a critical role in overcoming it. Parti-cipation in organised adult learning is closely correlated with involvement in wider networks and in civic activity (Field, 2005). This is not a new discovery: in a much-cited report on a develop-mental adult education programme undertaken in a coalfield com-munity during the 1970s, with the explicit goal of recruiting from manual working-class groups, Jacques Hedoux suggested that 'parti-cipants in ACF (Action Collective de Formation) constitute a socially-active minority who, in order to access adult education, must benefit from an important number of favourable circumstances' (Hedoux, 1982, 254-5). (This finding was taken up in an influential survey by Veronica McGivney (1991), and has been widely discussed since, albeit with little apparent subsequent reference to Hedoux's original findings and methods).

Can social capital be built up, through positive strategies of human resource investment? While it has not often been formulated in this precise way, the question is not new, as Hedoux's work demonstrates. Four points are worth emphasising.

First, Hedoux discovered that the tendency to participate is associated with a wide range of factors. Among other characteristics, participants were more likely to be skilled workers, to have a spouse who was in work, to subscribe to a magazine, to believe themselves likely to face unemployment, and have undergone 'downward intergenerational mobility' – that is, to have fetched up in a lower status job than their parents. Civic engagement was therefore only one factor among many. Second, Hedoux's findings indicated that some types of civic engagement were more likely to be associated with organised learning than others. Involvement in 'traditional societies' such as patriotic groups, sports clubs and musical ensembles had a relatively limited association. Rather stronger influences appeared to derive from membership of 'socio-cultural associations' like youth clubs, campaigning groups such as consumer movements, and political parties, which in the area in question at that time included the communist party. There was also a strong association between participation and involvement in such communal festivals as local fêtes and May Day assemblies (Hedoux, 1982, 265-7). This picture of vibrant civic engagement, so typical of a working class community in the 1970s, is now badly dated; the hollowing out of popular – albeit largely male – socialist movements and the collapse of other working class associations has accordingly helped to reinforce social exclusion in many such communities (Li *et al*, 2003). Third, it should be stressed that Hedoux's fieldwork took place in a well-established coalmining area with relatively high levels of unionisation and steady male income levels – large-scale male unemployment, although widely anticipated, then still lay in the future. It is highly unlikely that his findings hold true for post-industrial communities. Fourth, Hedoux himself concluded that while participation might importantly reduce social disparities between the social classes, this should not be allowed to 'mask the considerable perpetuation of inegalitarian social processes within the working class' (Hedoux, 1982, 273).

Civic activity is concentrated among those who are already well-educated. This appears to be a general characteristic of virtually all forms of voluntary associational activity, whether well-established or relatively new. However, in recent years there has been a marked decline in the membership of the major voluntary organisations; trade unions, political parties and the Women's Institutes are prominent among the organisations affected in this way. On the other hand, local action groups and new movements such as environmentalism are reporting increasing membership levels (Hall, 1999). But these are not quite the same type of organisation. While local action groups draw from a quite diverse membership, among the so-called new social movements such as feminism and environmentalism, it is common for active members and supporters to have completed third-level education. In one intensive study of feminists and environmentalists in a northern English city, Mary Searle-Chatterjee found that her subjects shared at least three decisive characteristics: they had studied at university, were largely employed as cultural workers, and came from family backgrounds where activism and independence were highly valued (Searle-Chatterjee, 1999, 270-2). Even among the wider arena of sympathisers and occasional activists, education appears to play a role: in the mid-1980s, German Green Party voters were reportedly three times as likely to have completed their *Abitur* as the electorate at large (Hülsberg, 1988, 115). The new social movements may well be important for the promotion of adult learning (see Chapter Five) but their relatively narrow constituency of membership means that they have limited relevance for the challenges of social inclusion.

Finally, much social capital is very local in its nature. Close relations based on kinship and neighbourhood are often a highly effective source of reciprocal help and support, but these localised sources of social capital tend to provide access to a limited range of benefits and resources (Campbell *et al*, 1999; Field and Spence, 2000). Dense and close ties can constrain as much as they empower. As Pahl and Spencer observe in their study of friendships, 'if people are to cope with a risk society and gain full opportunities from a flexible labour market', inward looking ties such as those of kinship and ethnicity are unlikely to help (Pahl and Spencer, 1997, 102). Rather, individuals and groups need to develop 'bridging ties' that will help them to access resources from outside their own immediate circles.

Social capital – that is, the existence of shared networks, norms and trust – provides a key setting for informal learning (Field and Spence, 2000). When people are able to expect reciprocal support, and enjoy a high degree of mutual trust, their social capital usually allows them to share ideas, information and skills. This in turn appears to allow them to adopt innovation more rapidly, and take common action to achieve their ends (see also Maskell *et al*, 1998). But social capital can also be used to exclude as well as to include; communications may not be shared with outsider groups, and new ideas and skills may be ignored because they come from outside the network of those who are known to be trustworthy. To take one example, immigrants are often poorly rewarded for experience and qualifications gained outside their host society. A Canadian study showed that even where they appear to have the same skills as native born workers, immigrant workers enjoy comparatively low returns for skills acquired through foreign experience – though the same study also showed that migrants were rewarded for learning acquired within Canada, where local supervisors were presumably able to form their own direct judgements about the worker's cognitive abilities (Ferrer *et al*, 2004). So even when it comes to experiential learning the returns to learning seem to be deeply dependent on the social relations within which it occurs.

Without careful policy intervention, then, social capital will usually serve to reinforce inequalities, not least by providing the excluded with ways of adapting to their inequality. Partly because well-informed and trustworthy networks are the best way of keeping afloat in a turbulent environment, and partly because the new forms of governance place so much weight on working with voluntary and community bodies, the importance of this exclusionary mechanism is likely to grow rather than diminish.

The learning society brings many enriching opportunities for growth, development and fulfilment. It stands in the Enlightenment tradition, as part of humanity's struggle to free itself from the ties of superstition and traditional hierarchy. It is part of a more open society, enabling knowledgeable individuals and groups to achieve their goals by virtue of their own efforts. It is a testimony to the openness of the learning society that this chapter has not dwelt at length on the position of women, for example; nor, in most countries, would it even be possible to consider women as a homogeneous group.

But the learning society also poses the risk of an increasing polarisation between the information-rich and the information-poor. At the end of the 1960s, Torsten Husén predicted that as knowledge displaced industry as the main source of wealth,

> Society towards the year 2000 will confer status decreasingly on the basis of social background or, assuming there is any left, inherited wealth. To a growing extent, *educated ability*, will be democracy's replacement for passed-on social prerogatives. (Husén, 1974, 238)

More than two decades later, the same point was made by Riccardo Petrella:

> A new process of social stratification is now setting apart the segment of the skilled and highly skilled workforce who find well-paid, stable and guaranteed employment (the new 'nobility' of excellent ability, education and competence) from all the remainder, mostly individuals with no or only limited skills, who at best might have the chance of getting a precarious, poorly paid and socially stigmatised job. (Petrella, 1997, 24)

The individual's ability to benefit from initial education or training is therefore an important element in the wider, multifaceted process of exclusion. Its importance as a source of inequality appears, indeed, to be growing.

Precisely because the individual's capacity for learning across the lifespan is such a vital resource, the ideal of the learning society has explanations for failure at the ready: people, organisations, and nations fail to thrive because they are not making the most of their talents. In turn, an inability to handle new ideas and skills is seen as an acceptable basis for inequality. But this is overlaid upon much older inequalities. If gender roles have become more fluid in and through the learning society, so much the worse for those women who have been left behind, and the same holds true for other excluded groups too. Moreover, the very idea of 'information-rich' and 'information-poor' is itself a gross over-simplification. Part of the difficulty is that the inequalities generated by the learning society are complex in the extreme; like the changes in the external environment and in our own identities to which the learning society corresponds, they are also fluid and frequently lack transparency or predictability. As a result, inequalities in the learning society are a multiple, moving target with open boundaries.

5
New Educational Order

Lifelong learning is an uncertain business. It can be joyous, fruitful and deeply satisfying. And it can be painful, exhausting and deeply disturbing. Yet, whatever we think of it, ours is a world where lifelong learning is pervasive. What are we to do about it? Thus far, I have mainly offered a critical perspective on what lifelong learning is, and what it is creating. My starting point is that we already live in a learning society, with all the difficulties, opportunities and risks this involves. I have argued here that the drive towards the learning society has been accelerated at least as much by the force of social and cultural change as by economic and technological developments. One consequence of these shifts has been that lifelong learning itself becomes a key dimension in the process of social exclusion and inequality – not only in the sphere of employment and earnings, but also in such fields as consumption, individual well-being, health and citizenship.

What is to be done? In our cynical age, we have to consider the obvious question: is it worth doing anything at all? Surely, the idea of progress of any kind, but above all progress through education and learning, has been comprehensively debunked? Is this not one of those grand totalising narratives, dreamed up by the Enlightenment philosophers, which have been abandoned by postmodernism? This is an intriguing argument, not least because it presents precisely the same story of ignorance – Enlightenment positivism – overturned by knowledge – postmodernism – as the one that it claims to critique. Postmodernism is a dead end, though it can be quite an interesting dead end. Its existence is itself evidence of the way our fast-moving knowledge economy is partly driven by fads; just as structuralism and then post-structuralism were advanced and then abandoned by scholarly trendsetters, so postmodernism is already becoming the emblem of the intellectual fashion victim. Taken more seriously, it offers possible insights into complex and fast-moving areas of life, albeit insights whose scope is rapidly exhausted. In the end, though, postmodernism is just not interesting enough, above all for those who believe that some of the big ideas are still worth struggling for. Indeed, I see it as part of the problem. It is our *trahison des clercs* – a safe consumer revolt, by the knowing, against a surfeit of indigestible knowledge. It is quite remarkable to me that post-modern and post-structural thought have arisen at a time when structures are so visibly powerful and important in shaping our destinies – a time when, as two Finnish educationists say, '*the whole world* has been colonised by multinational corporate power' (Suoranta and Tomperi, 2002, 33). In the end, postmodernism reaches the same policy conclusion as those who believe that adults are responsible for managing their own learning, celebrating the many-faceted diversity of individual consumer preferences.

Out there in the world, evidence that learning matters is indisputable. The economic benefits of learning are widely understood, though they are usually measured by rather crude yardsticks. It is well known that in most countries, having a university degree is likely to bring substantial financial rewards, and the vast majority of degree holders find that these advantages greatly outweigh the initial financial costs of study. Those rewards are gained independent of other advantages held by those who possess a degree, such as having comparatively affluent parents and being relatively well connected; in most cases, university students come from relatively advantaged backgrounds, so that the advantages of higher education are helping to reproduce existing income inequalities.

At the other end of the educational scale, there is growing evidence of the financial benefits that derive from basic cognitive skills such as literacy. Indeed, it seems that the returns from investment in basic literacy are more significant proportionately than those from investment in university study (Ferrer *et al*, 2004). For those who are unpersuaded by the evidence of economic benefits from learning – though most of the sceptics I have encountered are well endowed themselves with formal qualifications – there is also a growing and persuasive body of evidence of the non-economic benefits from learning. Much recent work has confirmed the direct wider benefits that derive from cognitive gains such as growing confidence and self-efficacy, which appear to be associated with improved mental and emotional well-being (Morrell *et al*, 2004). There is also evidence linking learning to benefits that are probably best seen as indirect consequences, such as civic engagement, personal safety or health (Schuller *et al*, 2004). In short, learning is a way of exerting agency by (re)gaining control over at least some aspects of your life.

In a complex society that is increasingly based on its ability to develop and manipulate knowledge, the capacity to recognise useful and reliable knowledge becomes ever more significant – and ever more burdensome. Further, new knowledge is created all the time, and its application in different contexts creates new possibilities – as well as new problems – that then enable further change, including hybridised applications of different types of knowledge. Ulrich Beck's concept of the 'risk society' is precisely intended to draw attention to the ways in which these spiralling processes of innovation and continual (re)discovery then have unintended consequences, some of them appallingly negative, which can span the entire gamut of our lives. So any single set of solutions to the problems and opportunities of the learning society will be profoundly inappropriate.

In developing future strategies for lifelong learning, significant lessons can be learned from the experiences of a number of governments who have sought to promote a learning society. The British case has been particularly well documented, in part because the UK government has actively promoted research into lifelong learning, and in part because of a lively body of critical analysis, much of it by professional adult education specialists. A prominent adult eductor has concluded that the years between 1997 and 2004 witnessed 'predictable but modest advance' under the Labour governments of Tony Blair, as well as some aspects of continuity with the policy assumptions of the Conservatives who held power from 1979 to 1997 (Taylor, 2005).

Certainly, the available evidence indicates that Labour policies have indeed achieved some practical successes in engaging with traditionally excluded groups, particularly through programmes aimed at community based and workplace learning, developed in partnership with national adult education agencies and trades unions (Morrell *et al*, 2004; Forrester, 2004). There is some evidence that Britain's investment in information, advice and guidance has also helped engage new learners (Tyers and Sinclair, 2004). By contrast, Britain's recent record on e-learning has been mixed. There is some evidence that the government's *learndirect* programme has attracted learners who are less well qualified and more likely to lack a recent history of learning than the national population of adult learners (Tyers and Sinclair, 2004), but the *learndirect* courses are usually offered in partnership with established providers, and mostly consist of a mixture of remote and face-to-face activities; its online activities are usually supported by local learning centres. By contrast, the UK's e-university, launched in 2003 with an initial public investment of £62 millions, failed to recruit students and was closed after one year of operation, leading to an enquiry by the House of Commons (House of Commons Education and Skills Committee, 2005). The government's experiment with learning credits, in the form of Individual Learning Accounts, also enjoyed mixed success: while ILAs were taken up much more rapidly than anticipated, some of the funding was used by people who would have paid for their own courses, and some was diverted by unscrupulous enterprises towards non-educational ends. Overall, then, the UK experience suggests that certain lines of action are certainly worth pursuing, while others remain at best unproven.

Yet Taylor is surely right to see the UK government as unambitious, and unwilling to challenge fundamentally conservative assumptions about our education and training system (Taylor, 2005). Given the scale of the challenges facing us, a rather more radical re-orientation is required. The experiences of European and other governments in the last ten or fifteen years are at best halting early attempts to grapple with some of the more pressing problems.

This chapter explores five, and only five elements of a future strategy, singled out either because they are inherently important or because they are being neglected. These are:

- rethinking the role of schooling in a learning society
- widening participation in adult learning
- developing the workplace as a site of learning
- building active citizenship by investing in social capital
- pursuing the search for meaning

Overshadowing each of these five elements is a sixth: the need to balance our own aspirations and goals with the growing requirement for environmental responsibility.

Schooling in a learning society

Many discussions of lifelong learning pay most attention to the post-school phases. This is not surprising: OECD studies suggest that the traditional front-loading of education systems has intensified since Edgar Faure's pioneering report appeared in 1972; new patterns of upper secondary and third level education have resulted in only limited blurring of the boundaries between schooling and working life (Istance, 2003, 94-5). Since resources, policy and public attention are already abundant for schools and higher education, surely we should concentrate on learning in adult life?

I think this is short-sighted. The effects of schooling upon the ability to learn later in life have been well-known for many years (Cross, 1981; La Valle and Finch, 1999). Any adult educator will have met plenty of people who left school as 'accredited failures', with profound damage to their learning identities in later life. It is also clear that early family background can play at least as important a role as schooling in influencing participation in later life (Gorard *et al*, 1999a, 43). Many of the key factors that explain adult learning behaviours are already in place while the child is completing its schooling. If the consequences of the learning society are as momentous as they appear, it makes no sense whatever to plan and manage schooling as though nothing has changed. Yet that is what seems to be happening. And there are some who would like school to become a bastion of traditional values and established certainties.

Schooling processes will be expected to give pride of place to teaching young people how to learn. This is not a new message: Torsten Husén was saying much the same thing in the late 1960s (Husén, 1974). Nor is it as simple as it sounds. It means rejecting much of the intellectual baggage that has dominated policy thinking for decades (Strain, 2000). In particular, we must break out of the prison of human capital theory, which measures inputs in terms of years of schooling completed. Conventionally, policy makers have taken a highly conservative view of schooling's contribution to lifelong learning. By extending the number of years spent in full-time initial education and improving the performance of the initial education system, several Western governments argue that they are in fact promoting lifelong learning. This was, for example, a key component of the British government's approach to lifelong learning, which was based on a sizeable increase in the number of young people remaining in full-time education and training (DfEE, 1998a). Internationally, rates of participation among 16-17 year olds and 18-21 year olds are conventionally used to represent the quality of inputs into national education systems.

Ironically, the front-loaded approach to lifelong learning may in fact have quite the opposite consequences from those intended. For many young people, full-time study in further or higher education functions as a kind of warehouse, where they are shelved between leaving school and starting work, rather than as a positive choice. This has obvious and predictable consequences for their motivation, and so for their ability to succeed. Thus New Deal providers in Britain in 1999 found that 'motivation/attitude difficulties' among the young unemployed were the most difficult problems to overcome, and over two-thirds saw this as the main factor in client dropout (Tavistock Institute, 1999, 17).

Nor are things that different among young university students. Mature students frequently express surprise, even shock, at the low levels of interest shown by their younger colleagues in their studies (Merrill, 1999). In Scotland and Northern Ireland, where the APR had already reached 50 per cent by the mid-1990s, the extension of initial education for young people is not associated with greater interest in adult learning; on the contrary, participation in adult learning – whether in universities or elsewhere – is rather lower than elsewhere in the UK (Schuller and Field, 1999). Extending the initial system, then, may simply replicate and deepen a culture of low achievement, strengthening an instrumental view of education and training as things that other people do to you, rather than as continual and active learning processes for which you shoulder much of the responsibility.

So what type of schooling is needed in a learning society? Five broad propositions are considered here. The first and most obvious is that learning how to learn becomes a priority. Unambiguously, the focus must be on learning rather than on teaching, and this is not nearly as simple as it sounds. As the European Commission argued in the late 1990s,

> Placing learners and learning at the centre of education and training methods and processes is by no means a new idea, but in practice, the established framing of pedagogic practices in most formal contexts has privileged teaching rather than learning... In a high-technology knowledge society, this kind of teaching-learning relation loses efficacy: learners must become proactive and more autonomous, prepared to renew their knowledge continuously and to respond constructively to changing constellations of problems and contexts. The teacher's role becomes one of accompaniment, facilitation, mentoring, support and guidance in the service of learners' own efforts to access, use and ultimately create knowledge. (CEC, 1998b, 9)

This means moving away from teaching on the basis of simple precepts – 'what works' – towards a more context-dependent, responsive and above all active approach to learner support (Bentley, 1998). Unfortunately, this sounds suspiciously akin to the educational progressivism that has been caricatured in Britain as the negative inheritance of the 1960s. Yet in the present context, there is a growing number of areas – information technology being the most obvious example – where teachers, like other adults, may know little more than their pupils. The challenge is how to design a curriculum that enables young people to develop the confidence and skills to become effective learners throughout their lives.

Second, a paradigm shift is taking place, away from the ideas of teaching and training towards the concept of learning. By implication, this involves also a switch from a 'supply-driven' view to a 'learner-centred' approach. Rather than focusing chiefly upon didactic skills and the formal curriculum, a new importance must be attached to the creation of *learning environments*, of which the classroom or workshop is but one (Ziehe, 1998). For some years, the UK government has promoted the strengthening of ties between schools and other environments for learning. This may include both 'vertical' connections between schools and other educational institutions – kindergarten, higher education, vocational training institutions – and 'horizontal' connections with other important sites of what we might call lifewide as well as lifelong learning – families, communities, voluntary associations and employers.

The benefits are many, not least because schooling can only effectively foster certain types of knowledge. This feature was identified during the debate over lifelong education in the 1970s (Cropley, 1979, 17-8), and in most countries there have been substantial changes in relationships between schools and other sources of knowledge. However, the advances have taken place along a relatively narrow front; while many young people undergo periods of work placement or visit museums and universities, similar connections with adult education centres or voluntary organisations are relatively rare. Further, as noted in Chapter Four, the bias of informal learning tends to be towards those who are already well placed in terms of their networks and formal educational attainment.

Third, the curriculum of schooling can no longer limit itself to the retention and repetition of propositional knowledge, much of it already out of date and confused by the time it is first learned. The sociologist Anthony Giddens, whose thinking has helped shape the left-of-centre politics known as 'the Third Way', has argued in a brief passage on lifelong learning that 'Although training in specific skills may be necessary for many job transitions, more important is the development of cognitive and emotional competence' (Giddens, 1998 125). As well as the capacity to manage one's own learning and apply knowledge in a variety of contexts, the idea of cognitive competence also embraces such aims as creativity and curiosity. However, if the idea of cognitive competence is reasonably familiar, that of emotional competence is relatively new. Embraced during the later 1990s as something of a management fad, the idea of emotional intelligence was defined as a series of qualities that might be linked to improved organisational performance – while some were probably inherent, others could to an extent be developed by planned interventions (Dulewicz and Higgs, 1998).

One widely canvassed solution to these problems has been the idea of 'key skills' as part of the curriculum. This is a widespread notion, whose ubiquity is suggested by the fact that the same term springs up in a variety of languages – *Schlüsselqualifikationen* in German, *compétences cléfs* in French, and so on. But despite this consensus on the general desirability of key skills, there is little agreement on what they might be, beyond a rather instrumental minimum of literacy and numeracy skills combined with some familiarity with the new technologies. Some even challenge the very idea of key skills, at least as it is conventionally expressed. Two British critics, for example, dismiss the idea as 'educationally untenable' (Hyland and Johnson, 1998, 164), since there is no shared understanding of what these skills might be, and anyway all the skills involved can be shown to be context-specific. Drawing upon a conceptual framework first developed by Pierre Bourdieu, Beverley Skeggs defines the new interpersonal competences as a series of dispositions and predispositions, many of which are fundamental to the learner's concept of self. As a result, Skeggs argues, the curriculum regains much of the legitimacy that has otherwise been eroded by tendencies to scepticism and relativism (Skeggs, 1997, 69). There are therefore real problems in developing the curriculum in this direction, not only for policy-makers but for learners themselves.

Moreover, moving towards a competence-led curriculum requires a different approach to qualifications. Two senior EU policy advisers whose thinking influenced the European Commission's policies for both education and technology development during the mid-90s, wrote that much teaching 'still rests on schemas inherited from the industrial period: it engenders 'standardised and congealed skills, sanctioned by diplomas that are acquired once for all' (Riché-

152

Magnier and Metthey, 1995, 420). In a British context, it is more usual to fix on the way in which qualifications systems are mostly geared to a single, academic outcome. As Tom Bentley comments, these systems are a poor guide to performance in less academic contexts (Bentley, 1998, 121). Critics of French legislation on continuing education have alleged that it has fostered short-duration training, geared narrowly towards task-specific skills that are poorly suited to technological or organisational transformation, let alone to mobility in the external labour market (Feutrie and Verdier, 1993, 469). On this view, a fixed framework of credentials contributes to rigidity and standardisation at a time when what is needed is flexibility, creativity, performance *and* a focus on understanding.

Fourth, and paradoxically, none of this means abandoning what we now believe to be the core function of the school. In a learning society, every child needs access to the 'basics'. Literacy and numeracy are truly 'key skills' unlocking doors to further learning. Whether as citizens or as workers, it seems that those who have the poorest skills to start with begin to lose them sooner. This appears to be particularly true for numeracy skills (Bynner and Parsons, 1998, 8-9). Again, this sounds suspiciously like educational traditionalism, but it is not. My argument is not that everyone should know the date of the Battle of Hastings, or have a grasp of Jane Austen's prose style or even Maya Angelou's, attractive though these may be, but that a school system which fails to deliver on basic skills of literacy and numeracy is not geared to the demands of a learning society. Agreeing what 'the basics' are is now something of a challenge, as the goal posts are moving. Agreeing how to deliver the basics is also harder than it might appear, requiring a concerted effort between home and school, so that skills are constantly being improved and rehearsed in living environments, rather than in the classroom alone. And this process of modernisation invites teachers to abandon their reliance on mastery and instruction, and instead to become 'experts in uncertainty' – a stance and identity that, as Karin Filander has pointed out, is neither comfortable nor clear-cut (Filander, 2003, 194-203; see also Fenwick, 2003).

The fifth and final proposition concerns the relationship between learning and family. Previous sections of this book have considered the shifting nature of family relationships in Western societies, and some aspects of these changes have provoked considerable policy concern. While some policy responses appear to be trying to stand against a rip-tide of changing values and behaviour, it would be equally irresponsible to ignore them. Given the evidence that a child's family background will powerfully influence participation in learning during adulthood, it makes sense to devote resources to developing a supportive environment in the home. And here we run right up against the brute facts of contemporary Western societies. Let us leave aside the alleged 'problem' of lone parent households since, despite high volume media debate over this group, in the UK, for example, lone parent households are no larger a proportion of the whole than they were in the 1950s (Morgan, 1997, 8). Yet substantial and influential shifts are taking place, and policies for integrating learning in the family with education in the school must be based on recognition of these changing contexts.

By comparison with the family in the first half of the twentieth century, the household group today – like many other relationships – is a much looser and conditional set of arrangements As Giddens notes, family relationships are increasingly similar to relations of choice, such as friendship, in that they are based partly upon the outcomes of reflexive decision-making (Giddens, 1992). Equally, there is also some evidence that people are more inclined to treat friendship networks in family-like ways, as sources of social support and emotional sustenance in changing times (Pahl and Spencer, 1997). Average family sizes have become smaller, and adult participation in the labour market has expanded. Households with dependent children are much less likely to have one adult staying in the home for the bulk of the waking day. If there is more than one child in the household – and single child households are increasingly common – they may have different biological parents from one another. Grandparents and great-grandparents are around for longer, and the age at which mothers have their first child is rising.

Families are characterised by growing variety and complexity, and as with so many aspects of everyday existence, each individual's experiences of family life are becoming more different from those of other people. But public perceptions of the 'average family' still seem to be rooted in the 1950s. I have a leaflet on my desk, published by the government, urging me to help with my children's reading (quite right too!). On the front cover, there is a picture of a family. I know it is a family because it has photographs of two children and two parents. But this neat, compact, cosy image of the family is a symbolic representation of reality. It plays the same representational role as a road sign warning us that we are driving past a school or that a sharp bend lies ahead, but is much more loaded. Family learning will take place in a messy variety of contexts, some more complex than others.

There are also other challenges. Family learning initiatives at present involve mainly the children with their mothers, and are usually based on the assumption that the mother is teaching the child. While both these may well reflect the reality in most households, they do not tell the whole story. First, while mothers are far more likely, still, than fathers to take the primary responsibility for child care, and therefore might reasonably be the first focus for family learning policies, it is a mistake to assume that fathers have little or no influence over the ability to learn later in life. On the contrary, while the characteristics of parents are indeed 'key determinants of individual learning trajectories', there is no great difference between the significance of fathers and that of mothers. Sometimes one is the better indicator of the child's subsequent participation, sometimes the other, but the pattern is much the same in both cases (Gorard *et al*, 1999b, 43). Second, family learning is, and should be seen as, a two-way process, where children sometimes know more than their parents and grandparents. Information technology is a case in point, where what could be called 'inverse socialisation' – a child sharing information with a willing adult – can be an important means of modelling the behaviour – curiosity and readiness to learn – that the child will also need in order to continue learning throughout adult life. Age may bring wisdom, but in a fast-moving world that trades on knowledge, age may also bring ignorance. 'Continuous learning', asserts Tom Bentley, 'involves forgetting as well as remembering' (Bentley, 1998, 187).

The growing complexity of families, and the increasing recognition that knowledge is co-created and shared in multiple and diverse ways within them, can provide a platform for imaginative learning, rather than posing a barrier. A 'deficit model' of the 'problem family' which 'needs' to be taught how to learn is unlikely to achieve much more than cynicism and mutual suspicion. Some British educationalists have concluded that virtually any programme that seeks to support learning in families in deprived communities simply represents a new moral authoritarianism, an intrusive attempt to build social control through soft therapies (Ecclestone, 2004). A rather obvious question arises: why should anyone bother to control disadvantaged families in marginalised neighbourhoods? Rather more importantly, as Andrea Carlson and Linden West observe, family learning initiatives such as Sure Start can at their best form a kind of 'transitional space, allowing participants – often with constrained access to material or symbolic resources, even to the emotional resources that can come from a wide and lasting network of friends, workmates and kin – to take risks and build confidence in their own capacities (Carlson and West, 2005).

Widening participation

In humanising the learning society, widening participation in adult learning is central. If we leave lifelong learning to the tug and flow of market forces, the opportunities will drain towards those who are best educated already and the admirable goal of lifelong learning for all will remain elusive. But what does this mean in practice? Edwards distinguishes between 'three sets of interrelated discourses' in relation to participation (Edwards, 1997, 112). Institutional change, the first of these discourses, focuses on the need of providers to alter their structures and practices so as to enable different types of learner to benefit from their provision. System change, the second discourse, is somewhat more radical, concerned as it is with recasting the nature of provision; examples include the shift towards a credit-based system of learning, allowing learners to exercise a degree of choice and control over learning programmes. Lastly, Edwards identifies a discourse of culture and power, more radical still, but marginal and with little influence; from this perspective, all decisions about who takes part and in what are fundamentally political in nature. Edwards presents this third approach in largely Foucaultian terms, with power being diffused throughout social relations and behaviour. But whichever approach is taken, it is worth noticing that the discourse of wider participation assumes a higher level of (pent-up) demand than is currently satisfied.

Governments have, on the whole, preferred to treat 'wider participation' as synonymous with 'extending initial education'. In particular they have often focused on access to the higher education system. In many Western countries, the transition into higher education is virtually automatic for those who secure the appropriate qualifications. Has this in itself created a culture that favours continued learning, or has it on the contrary set an artificial academic 'gold standard', beyond which most people have little interest in pursuing their learning? There is some evidence that it has had the latter effect (Schuller and Field, 1999). As one rural development officer put it, during a group interview discussion of adult learning and vocational qualifications,

> I think there is still an attitude here that A Levels are really equivalent to getting a degree. If you get, particularly if you get a grammar education, and you get A Levels, that's nearly as far as you need to go. (Rural Development Focus Group, Dungannon, 1 July 1997)

However, this picture may be too negative. As a result of the expansion in higher education in the 1980s and 1990s, a number of European governments reduced their financial support for students. One result – largely unplanned – was that growing numbers of young people combined full-time education with part-time (occasionally full-time) work. In Denmark and the Netherlands, working students raised the employment rate in the early 1990s by between three and five per cent (Rubery and Smith, 1999, 18). Quite unintentionally, policies in these countries had created what was effectively a system of alternation between work and learning.

Planned integration of work-based learning with academic learning is less common. Yet if adult learning is to reach the majority of the population effectively, a new value must be placed on the work-based route. Work-based learning has grown considerably in importance as a method of upskilling the existing labour force. It has the confidence of trainers: in a survey of 800 members of the Institute of Personnel and Development in 1999, on-the-job training emerged with a higher rating than any other training approach. Coaching and mentoring – also work-based approaches – came close behind (Cannell, 1999, 35).

So far, the discussion has suggested that formal providing institutions are not the best places in which to teach the new curriculum. However, this is to underplay the value of that feature of providing institutions usually most heavily criticised by reforming politicians and others: their distance from daily life. As Alan Thomas argues, 'some segregation is necessary, for ... learning cannot take place without the freedom to make a mistake, and in many areas of daily life the margin for error without disastrous results is very limited' (Thomas, 1991, 134). It may well be that some distance is required in order to develop metacognitive abilities and strategies. Nevertheless, there remains a strong possibility of developing this distance within work-based learning, under certain conditions. Thus the Institute for Mechanical Engineers defines its mentoring programme as involving the 'wise counselling of a Trainee in a protected relationship which focuses on the Trainee's personal development of full potential from dependence and inexperience to maturity and independent professionalism' (Institute of Mechanical Engineers, 1998, 4).

But there are two major problems with this aspiration, laudable though it is. Firstly, in practice such protected relationships are often difficult, if not impossible, to create. Mentors and trainees are employed in a hierarchically structured context, and roles will overlap and cause tensions which will intrude into the 'protected relationship', just as they do between assessor and trainee in the examination of candidates for vocational qualifications (Field, 1995). Secondly, in principle the definition of 'maturity and independent professionalism' is loaded, and is based largely upon tacit and unstated assumptions of what these terms mean. This becomes somewhat more explicit later in the Institute's guidance to mentors, which urges them to help trainees become 'streetwise'. As is suggested below, the work-based route to lifelong learning is full of potential, provided that work itself is reformed.

Abandoning the idea of 'royal highways to learning' seems a vital part of the wider paradigm shift, away from structures of provision towards the concept of learning. However, this in turn requires – as already noted in the case of schooling – the development of more accurate ways of recognising and signalling achievement. Rather than identifying the institutional context and programme in which teaching has taken place, there is a need for qualifications that reflect the learning gain that has taken place. Yet qualifications are inherently a somewhat uncertain currency. Any system of credentials is essentially a language of signs, operating by its own rules, and regulated by an approved set of gatekeepers. Their function is to act as surrogates for, or signals of, certain qualities their bearer is deemed to possess; credentials do not in themselves make any direct contribution to these qualities – though they may do indirectly, for example by boosting confidence.

In practice, it seems that qualifications are generally used by employers and other agencies such as universities as 'screening' devices, rather than solely as signals of particular competences. Recent reforms, such as the national vocational qualifications framework in the UK, have sought to ensure that credentials give a more accurate and transparent record of their holder's abilities; in principle, they also allow for the recognition of prior experiential learning, and for the transfer of relevant skills from one job or sector to another. Such developments have had a significant impact in Norway and France, where a growing number of adults are entering higher education or advanced training on the basis of their assessed non-formal learning (Payne, 20005, 14; Pouget and Osborne, 2004). In the case of vocational qualifications reform in Britain, though, the changes have also had unintended consequences which, at least in the short term, have damaged the prospects of the new system. Thus a desire to test ability through observed performance of each specified skill (or 'element of competence' in the jargon of the UK's framework of National (or Scottish) Vocational Qualifications) led to a cumbersome system of written recording and verification which caused additional work for workplace supervisors without preventing apparently widespread abuse by unscrupulous training providers (Field, 1995; Field, 1996). Moreover, any change at all carries the risk of disrupting existing arrangements that are working perfectly well, or at least to the satisfaction of all concerned. Thus for at least five or six years after the new NVQ framework was established, survey evidence repeatedly showed that most British employers had a very low awareness of the new qualifications – and indeed, many had never heard of them (*Times Educational Supplement*, 11 December 1992).

Any further reform in the qualifications system brings the risks of further unreliability and uncertainty in the market place. Yet the alternative is precisely the congealed and rigid system criticised so lucidly by Bentley, Metthay, Riché-Magnier and others. The challenge is to develop systems of adult qualifications that are highly modularised, that accurately acknowledge what has been learned, and that allow for a comparison between informal learning and formalised expectations. In the UK, the work of Open College Networks (OCNs) during the 1980s and 1990s provides an example of an approach to qualifications that is highly modular and transparent, allowing for the accreditation of prior learning of various kinds and tolerating a wide variety of contexts and styles of assessment. This approach appears to be highly accessible to traditionally excluded groups (Davies, 1999), but still raises a number of questions. For one thing, in a labour market where trust in qualifications systems appears to be in decline, qualifications accredited by OCNs face an uncertain reception. For another, although OCNs frequently adopt a discourse of learner-centeredness, they have found themselves competing with other awarding bodies in a qualifications marketplace (Davies, 1999, 18). Yet any intervention by regulating bodies designed to manage this somewhat opaque market place are bound to expose the tensions between the need for qualifications to meet a national – and international – framework of standards on the one hand, and the flexibility demanded by a fast-moving labour market and a more open and fluid social system on the other. It is hard to escape the conclusion that high quality guidance plays a key role in helping learners to find a pathway through the tangled thickets of a complex marketplace of unitised and fast changing qualifications.

Nor is it at all clear that qualifications in themselves offer much of a solution to the problems of inclusion within a learning society. On the contrary, a policy focus on qualifications may produce yet sharper divisions between the educational haves and the educational have-nots, particularly if it is accompanied by a channelling of resources towards the upper ends of the educational scale. In most western societies, most public spending on post-18 education is dedicated to higher education, and barely anyone questions this differential pattern of distribution. In the UK, the government's decision to seek some contribution from students or their families towards the costs of their higher education was greeted with virtually unanimous outrage from the entire academic community, as well as from the main opposition parties and the devolved governments of Scotland and Wales. The lobby for literacy and numeracy is much more muted, despite good evidence that public investments in literacy education for adults produce disproportionately high returns (see eg. Ferrer *et al*, 2004, 26).

Moreover, there can be acute tensions between the needs of young people and the needs of adults. While the boundaries between adult life and youth are inevitably loose, in general young people require an opportunity to form a stable adult identity. Flexible qualifications and modular programmes, for example, may be highly accessible to some adult groups. But for the young, though, they may make it harder to establish a recognisable social and occupational identity (Colardyn and Durand, 1998, 246). Resolving such tensions, though, will be a necessary component of any learning society that is to endure.

Developing the workplace as a site of learning

At first sight, it may seem odd to allocate scarce space to yet another discussion of workplace learning. After all, it is not as though this is a neglected area. Policy makers appear to discuss little else, and there is a burgeoning academic literature on the topic, including a specialist *Journal of Workplace Learning*. There are two reasons for including it in this discussion, if only briefly. The first is that the workplace matters. It is still the single place where many adults spend the largest part of their waking day; it helps to create and recreate your sense of who you are; it is where people make and maintain the friendships and social practices that provide them with a variety of forms of support; and of course it provides the money that we can spend on other things. Work is also tightly associated with social class, and as we have seen class and occupation tend to be closely related to people's orientation towards and participation in learning. Second, much of the debate about workplace learning is unsatisfactory. It still focuses largely on formal education and training, to the exclusion of informal and self-directed learning. Moreover, one particular point of view is privileged: much of the debate is largely argued from what is taken to be the employers' perspective (whether it actually is the employers' perspective, or whether any such thing can exist with any coherence, is another matter). Other perspectives – those of consumers of goods and services, and of workers themselves – are heard much less frequently. Finally, the discussion of workplace learning tends to be an impoverished one, which concentrates on narrow skills acquisition by individuals rather than on the deep, rich and meaningful collective learning that is required to meet the longer term challenges of our shared future.

Much of this book has addressed the consequences of two combined and mutually reinforcing processes: social and cultural change on the one hand and economic and technological change on the other. Taken together, these two key dimensions of reflexive modernisation have significantly increased the need for a broad and expansive view of learning in relation to work. Peter Alheit, as was noted in Chapter Three, has shown in some detail that there has been a steady paradigm shift in the relations between work and learning since the 1970s, with the worker increasingly becoming an active subject who, 'independently and with growing levels of individual risk, must regulate their own vocational capabilities' (Alheit, 1994, 80-5). While the individualisation of everyday working life may carry negative consequences of the kind lamented so eloquently by Richard Sennett (1999, 2004), it is also a fact, to which workers are required to respond – and, since workers also behave reflexively, it follows that they also actively contribute to the general processes of individualisation through their own decisions and behaviour. Workers' choices are constrained choices of course, as to some extent are those of employers; while workers are clearly less powerful than employers, relatively speaking, some of the constraints are themselves the cumulative product of the reflexive behaviour of those concerned, both workers and employers. This raises the question of whether policy and public providers should seek to shape and influence workplace learning, and if so then in what directions.

There is a strong public good in respect of workplace learning which is not necessarily well served either by the individual subjective choices of workers (which anyway are constrained by external factors beyond their control), nor by the short term organisational interests of their employers. In circumstances of flexibility and turbulence in the employment relationship, then as Dubar has argued, workers may have a very limited interest in acquiring particular skills and abilities, which they will reasonably see as belonging to a set of tasks that they cannot afford to identify with over the longer term (Dubar, 2000). It has also been suggested that insecurity may discline workers to share their skills with others; where they expect to compete with others, workers will rationally defend their own employability by denying access to their resources of knowledge, information and skill (Maybe *et al*, 1998, 242). There is, then, a clear conflict in this particular case not only between workers and employers (particularly in the short term) but between workers and the wider community (over the longer term – with workers themselves of course belonging to the wider community).

If there is a public interest in workplace learning, then, what directions should we pursue? Part of the solution must be to develop individual capabilities for negotiating complex trajectories that Alheit associates with 'biographicity' (see below), among workers as among the community at large. However, the main issue that I wish to explore here is the need for breadth and generosity in what we define as a legitimate field for public intervention and provision. Particularly in new forms of work, workers are required to acquire a broad range of skills and understanding, much of it concerned not just with the immediate tasks on which they are ostensibly employed, but also with the nature of the organisation and its routines – 'the way we do things round here' – and even the demands and changes of the market place. One group of European researchers refers to this as 'work process knowledge', a form of knowledge much of which is tacit because it is embodied in everyday personal practices and social relationships. For work process knowledge to have value, it must be embedded organically in the culture and expectations of the workplace, usually in a taken-for-granted way (Boreham *et al*, 2002).

This recognition of context and culture is in marked contrast to the instrumentalism that dominates British policy thinking on vocational education and training. The UK is not alone in adopting a modernised form of behaviourism as the pedagogic basis for workplace learning. Competence-based approaches are widespread in the English-speaking world. Neither the theories nor practice of competence-based education and training find much place for context or culture. Rather, local and specific factors represent something of a threat to generic standards based training, along with its detailed lists of performative criteria for assessment (Hager and Smith, 2004, 34-8). Competence-based approaches of the kind developed in the UK also ignore the collective nature of much work process knowledge (Boreham, 2004), treating performance rather as a reflection of individual expertise.

Certainly, there is a strong case for developing a broad approach to workplace learning that encompasses the tacit and embedded skills and knowledge that workers create and acquire. As one group of European experts has argued, work process knowledge may be tacit but it is 'not elusive: it can be identified, analysed and expressed in ways that can serve as cognitive tools for performing work and generating further knowledge in the workplace' (Commission of the European Communities, 2003, 29). However, this requires a very different approach from that reflected in the instrumental and narrow thinking represented in the UK's National Vocational Qualifications scheme. Norwegian approaches to the documentation of informal learning, developed through a social partnership of unions and employers, have been premised upon a conscious decision to avoid the complex, time-consuming model offered by the UK's NVQ system (Payne, 2005, 20). The Norwegian approaches combine simplicity, cost-effectiveness and a high level of trust. There are thus viable alternatives to the narrow and individualistic models of the kind offered by NVQs in the UK.

Yet the Norwegian experiments draw attention to another feature of much existing workplace learning. Although initial evaluation reports suggest that the results have been largely successful, they also confirm that the Norwegian competence reform programme remains skewed towards certain sectors, usually those which already show high levels of commitment to training (Payne, 2005, 23-7). In so far as the Norwegian reforms include access to off-the-job education, in practice this has appealed least to those with the lowest levels of skills and qualifications, many of whom may have childhood memories of poor schools experiences (Payne, 2005, 29). Such inequalities reflect wider trends in the distribution of training and education within the workplace, as we saw in Chapter Three.

Can inequalities of access be overcome, or at least alleviated? One promising approach in the UK has been the involvement of trade unions in developing workplace learning. This has mirrored approaches found elsewhere, with trade unions taking an increasing interest in delivering learning opportunities, with some financial support from the Union Learning Fund and other sources, and assuming greater responsibility for influencing employer training strategies. Here the UK has lagged behind countries with a developed tradition of social partnership. Indeed, the Norwegian competence reform initiative began as a result of lobbying by trade unions, many of whose members were interested in establishing a legal right to paid educational leave (Payne, 2005, 7-11). Despite the weakness of the social partnership tradition in the UK, or perhaps because of it, the Union Learning Fund has had a marked impact on trade union behaviour, with emerging evidence that the Fund has helped to build longer term strategic capacity in some unions, particularly the larger ones (Shaw *et al*, 2002, 35).

The Fund also appears to have helped widen access, both directly through the involvement of such low-participation groups as shift workers and temporary or agency workers (Shaw *et al*, 2002, 48) and, indirectly, through the training of workplace union learning representatives (ULRs). The functions of ULRs are set out in the 2002 Employment Act. They include consulting with employers, negotiating with providers, and encouraging workers in matters relating to learning and training. Where the trade union is recognised by the employer, ULRs are entitled to statutory time off work to pursue these roles.

Trade union involvement is, of course, not a solution to all ills and inequalities. As the Norwegian example shows, a strong tradition of social partnership can coexist with continuing inequalities of access. Trade union membership has fallen in recent decades across much of the western world, and it tends to be heavily concentrated in the public sector and manufacturing industry. It is rare for part-time, contract and sub-contracted workers to belong to a trade union. And even union membership may no longer mean that much, at least in terms of active involvement in the union's collective affairs. So engaging unions in providing and negotiating over learning may further disadvantage some groups who are not part of the trade union movement. Yet trade unions are still potentially central players in the new workplace, as well as continuing to play a significant role in their public sector and industrial heartlands. In some cases, such as the British public sector union Unison, they have been highly successful in engaging with unskilled people or with those who have had poor experiences of education. Unions in turn may see lifelong learning as a tool for recruiting and retaining members. Where unions have significant bodies of membership, they clearly have a role to play in developing the learning workplace.

Investing in social capital

Our learning society is flawed by powerful tendencies, not simply towards the reproduction of existing inequalities but also towards the creation of new forms of exclusion. It is helping to erode established social relationships and to call into question widely held patterns of shared meaning. If all is in flux, if everything and everybody is ready for constant change, how can any social order hold together? Surely the learning society is doomed by its own internal contradictions to tear itself apart? Based as it is upon the principle of permanent instability and the search for individual solutions to the problems of risk and uncertainty, how can it be reconciled with any lasting idea of the common good?

Addressing precisely this problem, one eminent German adult education scholar has called for a rethink of politics in the light of the learning society. For Peter Alheit, the learning society

> ... represents a programme for civil publics that have to be further developed and newly shaped in institutions and enterprises, urban districts and associations, in trade unions and co-operatives. . . . The crucial legitimation for a *learning society* in this sense derives from the collapse of systemic integration and social integration in the advanced societies of Western Europe and North America, and in the transitional societies of Central and Eastern Europe. (Alheit, 1999, 80)

Perhaps this is somewhat apocalyptic. It is not that systemic and social integration are collapsing, but rather that their foundations are being questioned and are slowly changing: in a learning society, citizens are not only more highly individualised but are also ever more reflexive. But Alheit is undoubtedly right to urge that a learning society should seek to establish an ideological base for itself in the idea of an active and engaged citizenry, and not in notions of economic prosperity and growth alone.

How might this happen? Adult education in Western societies has its origins in the field of active citizenship. This was expressed with great eloquence in one of the landmarks of British adult education, the so-called '1919 Report', which was commissioned by the government to provide advice on its post-war policy:

> The adult education movement is inextricably woven with the whole of the organised life of the community. Whilst on the one hand it originates in a desire amongst individuals for adequate opportunities for self-expression and the cultivation of their personal powers and interests, it is, on the other hand, rooted in the

> social aspirations of the democratic movements of the country. In
> other words, it rests on the twin principles of personal development
> and social service ... In perhaps the greater majority of cases the
> dynamic character of adult education is due to its social motive.
> (Ministry of Reconstruction, 1919, section 330)

If this was conceivably the case in the unusual circumstances of
1919 – two years after the Bolshevik Revolution, one year after a
police strike, and at a time of unrest and mutiny in the armed forces
– it was a much more dubious proposition by the late 1920s. As left-
wing critics of the Workers' Educational Association were fond of
pointing out, much adult education was less of a social movement
than a social occasion (Lewis, 1993). Yet even if limited to an earnest
minority, the relationship between adult education and active
citizenship was real and of long standing. Can it be revived today?

Much adult learning takes place informally. It takes place through
interaction with our loved ones, or with friends, neighbours and
workmates. It takes place through membership of voluntary networks and organisations of various kinds, where individuals and
groups pursue the things that interest them, from golf to quilting to
parenting (Elsdon *et al,* 1995). It takes place through an engagement
in the public sphere, including the workplace which is itself a major
source of social capital. Survey evidence appears to confirm that the
boundaries separating informal learning and formal education are
porous, with a tendency for different types of learning to comple-
ment and even reinforce one another (Boudard and Morlaix, 2003,
521). But informal learning is still often undervalued and disregarded. How can we raise the status of this informal learning, extend its reach to those who are currently excluded from making the
most of it, and ensure that it is geared to the common good? And
how can it be broadened to meet the challenges of a complex knowledge society?

One possible answer lies in the learning capacities opened up by
new social movements. These movements are widely held to be inclusive, based as they are on struggles against hierarchy, secrecy, ex-
clusiveness and patriarchy (Seddon, 2004, 175-6). Their membership often includes a fairly high proportion of teachers and other
educationalists. Yet in many contemporary social movements, a
sizeable proportion of members appear to confine their 'activism' to
their cheque book (Maloney, 1999). Friends of the Earth (FoE) and
Greenpeace International are good examples of political activism in
a post-scarcity society. Rather than attending meetings and can-
vassing public opinion – 'tea, biscuits, claim-making or arguments

supposedly based on 'science", in the dismissive words of Green-peace's campaigns director – individual supporters pay a subscription which then funds Greenpeace officials to take direct action on their behalf (Rose, 1996, 51).

Maloney has described this as a process of sub-contracting political activity, leaving the job of influencing policy to paid professionals (Maloney, 1999, 114). Even so, as he also points out, many cheque-book citizens are active in more conventional face-to-face activity in grassroots organisations, including the local networks and activities associated with Greenpeace or FoE. Furthermore, joining these organisations may also generate an 'imaginary community' of 'like-minded people' (Maloney, 1999, 116). Drawing on survey data, Maloney shows that subscribers to FoE and Amnesty International are also likely to value highly the information function of member-ship, rating this as highly as the more obvious lobbying and cam-paigning activities. In both organisations, one of the most important reasons for joining was 'to keep me informed', and one of the most effective functions was 'trying to change British public opinion through information' (Maloney, 1999, 110-11). For their members, then, these movements are playing an actively educative as well as an oppositional role, both for themselves and for the wider public, despite their use of modern communications methods rather than traditional ones such as meetings and organised courses of study.

Thus we can still find abundant evidence of an association between adult learning and active citizenship. Nor is this confined to the learning that is undertaken by the mainly middle class members of the new social movements. One survey of access course students found that two-thirds had been active in voluntary organisations, a relatively high figure for adults with fairly low formal qualifications, leading to the conclusion that 'active participation in society in-creases an individual's perception of power and self-worth. This may help to overcome the residual aversion to education that is the legacy for so many who do not achieve well at school' (Benn, 1996, 173). But in general, active participation in the community is un-usual among adults with few qualifications. Poor work, low qualifi-cations and weak basic skills are often combined with highly loca-lised and dense forms of social capital, such as family members and immediate neighbours, who offer few resources to promote active embracing of lifelong learning.

Celebrating the informal learning that arises from civic engagement is not enough, then. It will not do firstly because networks and movements exclude as well as include: in so far as there is a public interest in investing in social capital, it does not lie in inadvertently recreating old-school-tie types of network and producing self-seeking forms of informal learning. Second, although all social capital represents resources that can be accessed for the common good, particular networks have unequal access to resources (Field, 2005). As noted in Chapter Four, in order to overcome structural inequalities, community development strategies need to tackle the creation of 'bridging ties' that enable the least advantaged to access resources from outside their own ethnic, neighbourhood and kinship networks (Li *et al*, 2003). Third, social capital is deeply gendered in nature, with men and women drawing on different types of network and tending to adopt different roles and strategies in their civic engagement (Campbell *et al*, 1999, 105-9, 156-7). This almost certainly means that a variety of approaches will need to be pursued if gender and class inequalities are not to be inadvertently reinforced.

The UK government's flirtation with lifelong learning under New Labour offers some policy lessons. In its early years, the government launched a number of programmes designed to engage non-participants with learning by supporting partnerships of providers with community-based and workplace organisations, largely led by the latter. In 1998, a series of Union Learning Funds were created across the UK to finance workplace-related learning, managed and led by trade unions. The results have been described as 'an important success story' (Forrester, 2004, 413). As well as supporting many local level activities, themselves usually undertaken in partnership with further education colleges and employers, the Funds raised the importance of adult learning within the trade union movement generally. The Trades Union Congress created its own regional networks of learning advisers, and several of the larger unions built their own networks of learning organisers, and many groups of workers elected local workplace learning representatives. According to the Trades Union Congress, in the first four years of the scheme some 14,000 members had taken part in at least one learning activity, and 4,500 learning representatives had undergone training. In general, work-related issues have tended to dominate much of the new activity, along with generic capacities such as literacy, English language skills, and information technologies. And the British trade union movement itself has taken considerable pride in its growing ability to engage workers in the skills agenda (Trades Union Congress, 2004). Yet an important minority element of active citizenship learning has also been supported under the ULF. What remains to be seen, as Forrester notes (2004, 419), is what this investment will contribute to the renewal of a trade union movement that has witnessed considerable erosion of membership levels and member engagement since the 1970s.

Similar lessons can be drawn from recent experiences in community based learning. Often designed as ways of 'engaging the disengaged', government-funded programmes of community-based learning are usually based on partnerships that concede at least some control and authority to community representatives and thereby create space for genuinely radical learning. Terri Seddon's account of partnership approaches to community based learning in South Australia depicts an uneasy alliance of local government, community groups and educational institutions that are slowly 'reconfiguring the social organisation of learning' (Seddon, 2004, 181). Similar experiences are reported in England, where the New Labour government's Adult and Community Learning Fund was managed at arm's length by two relatively independent bodies, and delivered at local level by partnerships of community and voluntary bodies along with education providers (Morrell *et al*, 2004). Seddon has drawn attention to the way in which even market-driven modernisation policies can create 'new learning spaces marked by different social relations of learning compared to the past' (Seddon, 2004, 182; see also Carlson and West, 2005). While these may often be by-products of the partnership process (or even unintended consequences, as described in Chapter One), the consequences are nonetheless real.

Yet there are limited to the new forms of learning citizenship. First, they are often very localised, and based on close existing social bonds rather than linking communities to social networks outside their own parochial horizons. Further, the new forms of civic engagement are based on cultural and political assumptions that need to be debated and not simply taken for granted because we admire the particular cause that they espouse. Like the self-help culture described in Chapter Two, the newer social movements may be quite short-lived, and are characterised by short term affiliations rather than lifetime loyalties. Elsewhere, as the Scottish cultural commentator Joyce McMillan has noted, 'politicians are facing the sad truth that if they can't get some well-loved celebrity to front their campaigns on health, safety, or the promotion of a decent, tolerant society, then they might as well forget it' (McMillan, 2005, 20). McMillan describes this as a 'dangerous game'. While I might endorse Bob Geldof's robust commitment to abolishing poverty, and chuckle quietly over Sean Connery's long-distance endorsement of Scottish independence, other possibilities are less endearing. One option is simple rejection: to denounce consumer culture as dumbing down, and build a pure alternative in isolation from the world of celebrity magazines and lifestyle gurus. But that is not the approach taken in this book. As McMillan suggests, 'as consumers of celebrity culture, we should perhaps be starting to ask ourselves more searching and sophisticated questions about which personalities we are encouraged to admire and trust, and why'.

If one aspect of the new educational order is rooted in locale, this is partly because immediate networks offer a counterweight to the forces of globalisation. But social relationships can and do also take root over distances of time and space, and education providers can play an important role in connecting local communities to other people in different parts of the world. New technologies are starting to play quite a spectacular role in bringing together communities of interest, for example, sports followers and family historians, as well as communities of practice, including groups of professionals, across barriers of space and time that were previously seldom, if at all, passable. Moreover, it is precisely the most global of corporations that have sought to promote versions of corporate responsibility and citizenship; while part of this is simply a public relations ploy, the corporate citizenship movement has unlocked resources for local initiatives, some of them very much connected with lifelong learning and social capital, such as GrandMet's sponsorship of open learning centres in post-apartheid South Africa, and even encouraged some real changes in corporate behaviour (GrandMet, 1998).

While business leaders justify their activities primarily in terms of the financial bottom line, the 1980s and 1990s witnessed the emergence in senior positions of managers who shared many of the values of their peers in the wider community (Phillips, 1987, 137-9). Some had been associated with the hippy movement, like Richard Branson of the Virgin conglomerate; some, like the group who founded the Virago publishing house, were 1960s feminists; some, like Anita Roddick of the Body Shop, were active environmental campaigners. It is easy to be cynical about business leaders who declare a commitment to 'corporate citizenship', not least because the number of businesses involved in any particular practical activity is relatively small, and even these may not give a great deal of thought to the matter. According to one British estimate, in 1995 only 30 or 40 firms had any systematic policy on relations with the voluntary sector (Commission on the Future of the Voluntary Sector, 1996, 61).

But the corporate citizenship movement is based on a number of powerful forces, including self-interest and mutual advantage, in addition to more or less sincerely held ethical values. In a recent review of the corporate citizenship movement, Chris Marsden and Jörg Andriof suggest that one key factor is corporate concern over the 'reputation market place', which may be particularly significant for multinational concerns; moreover, they note that reputational damage can have serious consequences not only externally, among potential customers and suppliers, but also internally, in terms of staff morale, recruitment and turnover (Marsden and Andriof, 1998). Marina Micari has similarly drawn attention to the way in which the idealistic aspirations and language of corporate citizenship can also be found in advertising campaigns which seek to portray the corporation – and its product line – as serving to combat poverty, racism or ill-health (Micari, 2004, 219). So there is much to cause us to doubt the efficacy of corporate citizenship as a vehicle for educational and social progress, particularly where good civic discourse is deployed in order to mask oppressive behaviour. Yet, in advanced capitalist societies there is really little alternative: we have to seek to civilise the corporates, and this must mean working with and within the corporates rather than simply boycotting their more obnoxious products and proclaiming our own purity.

But we can go further. Between individual and nation stand a variety of organisations and relationships – family, community, company, voluntary bodies, trades unions, governmental institutions, and not least education providers – within which everyday experience is shaped and carried out. Many of these organisations show remarkably low levels of trust and involvement of their own employees; even those major institutions that underpin public systems of life-long learning are likely to fail to generate the kind of collective intelligence and expansive learning that can be produced through open dialogue (Avis, 2002). Without a democratisation of these intermediary institutions, the learning society will continue to generate ever greater inequity and exclusion, and become ever more unstable. As Peter Alheit remarks, to say this is not to indulge in a major ideologically driven project of radical transformation, but without an inclusive democratisation the learning society will be unable to deliver its own promise of greater autonomy, fulfilment and at least a modicum of security (Alheit, 1999, 78).

Pursuing the search for meaning

But is a secure identity a feasible goal? Not all of our environment is turbulent, and not everything around us is changing. All the same, many of the old coordinates of everyday life that have long been accepted as fixed and given have become looser and more mobile. For Richard Sennett, the new capitalism has simultaneously eroded social capital and individual character. 'The short time frame of modern institutions', he writes, 'limits the ripening of informal trust', which depends largely upon long association (Sennett, 1999, 24-5). Flexibility and instability have 'created a conflict between character and experience, the experience of disjointed time threatening the ability of people to form their characters into sustained narratives' (Sennett, 1999, 31). In a perceptive article, Jim Crowther has recently explored the implications of Sennett's recent work for lifelong learning (Crowther, 2004). Yet despite the undoubted insights of his critique, Sennett's approach is flawed by a nostalgic and romantic view of industrial labour and its virtue. Like many from the political left, he views capitalism – that great abstraction – as responsible for the situation in which we find ourselves. Capitalism, however, requires active agents in order to succeed; and the high-value global capitalism of today particularly requires enthusiastic consumers, and not simply willing workers. In respect of work, if my argument in this book is right, Sennett is probably exaggerating the extent of change; in respect of consumption, where it is not great abstractions but living men and women who are pushing ahead the decisive changes, I believe that he has understated the extent of change. But we can agree that the core values of Western society are changing, partly as a result of the learning society.

Take what Giddens calls 'life politics'. For Giddens, life politics is the politics of choices, of struggles over self-realisation, which can be expressed entirely independently of any particular grouping or organisation, however loose. As he notes, this 'presumes (a certain level of) emancipation, in both . . . emancipation from the fixities of tradition and from conditions of hierarchical domination' (Giddens, 1991, 214). Taking what is more or less an anarchist perspective, Theodore Roszak has neatly exemplified Giddens's point: 'We live in a time when the very private experience of having a personal identity to discover, a personal destiny to fulfil, has become a subversive political force of major proportions' (Roszak, 1981, 23). Individuals' values, oriented towards post-materialist goals such as self-actualisation, form a powerful ethical framework within which they make sense of and direct their own learning. The question is not whether education and development are based on ethics, but how best to combine radical reflexivity and individualism with the need for social integration and continuity.

The learning society clearly places considerable and varied strains on people, and educational interventions are already responding to this. One recent definition of career counselling, for instance, spoke of

> ... a continuum of intervention processes which range from facilitating self and occupational awareness, exploration of possibilities and the learning of career planning skills, to stress reduction or anger management, issues of indecisiveness, and work-adjustment issues that require a fusion of career and personal counselling. (Herr, 1997, 81)

But this is dealing with symptoms. Underlying these is the challenge of developing what Peter Alheit has called the competence of 'biographicity', which he defines as the capacity 'to attach modern stocks of knowledge to biographical resources of meaning and, with this knowledge, to associate oneself afresh' (Alheit, 1992, 206-7). We should not underestimate the difficulties of following this course, not least because the integration of emotional competences and biographical (self-)knowledge into the curriculum can disempower as well as empower. In her study of women who had undertaken care courses, Beverley Skeggs found that the 'emphasis on feelings and natural dispositions makes it difficult for the women to take up positions of resistance, for what comes to be at stake is their sense of self, their feelings' (Skeggs, 1997, 69). It is precisely at this point that the capacity of lifelong learning to legitimate failure becomes most telling, and most disabling.

Yet a commitment to values remains integral to the humanisation of lifelong learning. In part, the new ethical concern is fuelled by the concerns of individual learners, the most vocal of whom – as we have seen – frequently espouse post-materialist values (Inglehart, 1990). Many are also part of or influenced by the ideas of such new social movements as feminism, environmentalism, and the human rights and global solidarity movements. Some have even argued that these new social movements, rooted in post-materialist values, are functioning inherently as 'learning movements'.

For Claus Offe, the emergence of new social movements in the 1960s and 1970s represented a positive response to the 'learning blockages' that were being experienced in mainstream politics, helping to 'increase the learning capacity of political systems by diminishing their degree of 'blindness' or unawareness of foreseeable and often catastrophic consequences' (Offe, 1985, 295). An example might be the way in which environmentalist movements challenged the technocratic assumptions of 'big science', for example by campaigning against genetic technology or nuclear energy. For Offe, this would represent an area where the combined forces of capital and state are only able to learn when placed under pressure from outside challengers. Viewed with the benefit of hindsight, Offe's perspective looks both over-optimistic – the new social movements had lost momentum in the early 1990s – and a touch too Hegelian – social movements can also foster a wilful ignorance, as radical right and fundamentalist movements have tended to do, and as parts of the environmentalist movement have done in their blanket hostility to all science and their reification of values and spontaneity.

But in a sense Offe is right: the new social movements do tend to be learning movements. Even fundamentalist movements are largely concerned with authenticity, albeit a somewhat selective form of authenticity. The new social movements characteristically have a particularly strong and developed sense of their own subjective identity, and will resist what they regard as external labelling of any kind. Emerging as they did from the student movements of the 1960s, several of the new social movements have also evolved a distinctive critique of knowledge – indeed, one of their mutual characteristics tended to be a practical integration of expert knowledge and personal values (Hornstein, 1984, 152-3). Not that social movements always get it right. For the new movements as for everyone else, knowledge is often provisional, fragmentary or partial – as, spectacularly, during the Greenpeace campaign over the disposal of the Brent Spar oil platform in 1995.

There are many such examples of an attempt to integrate personal values such as autonomy and authenticity with the fast-moving map of expert knowledge. For the postmodernist there is no question of integrating these diverse elements, as the status of expert knowledge is inherently suspect. If postmodernist arguments hold sway, all we are left with is endless difference, articulated through a multitude of discourse, each of which is anchored in subjectivity and no more valid than any other. I suggested at the opening of the chapter that postmodernism is little more than a consumer revolt, directed by the knowing against the idea of knowledge. In the context of the learning society, which has an apparent excess of information and expertise, such intellectual bohemianism may be inevitable; it is also, in my view, pernicious, suggesting as it does that since all knowledge is relative, inequalities of access and control do not matter. Was Ken Saro-Wiwa right to warn of environmental degradation caused by oil companies in Nigeria, or was he simply pursuing one story which was no better and no worse that the discourse of his executioners (see also Hobsbawm, 1997, 351-66)? It seems to me both appropriate and heartening that the twentieth century closed with massive street demonstrations outside the World Trade Organisation in Seattle, motivated by anger over the WTO's failure to tackle the downside of globalisation such as Third World debt levels and environmental degradation. It was also downright disheartening that the Seattle demonstrators did not articulate a plausible set of answers. If they were at least posing some of the right questions, many were too easily tempted into physical violence and blind fury.

The pursuit of continuous innovation and permanent learning is, in the learning society that exists at present, also the apparently endless pursuit of ever higher rates of growth and ever more dangerous assaults upon an already fragile environment, and at the cost of ever greater division between knowledge-rich and knowledge-poor. Yet alternative movements, whose critique is rooted in the findings of environmental science and a commitment to human rights, are likely to be discredited if all they offer in exchange is mysticism and direct action. An ever more greedy global capitalism needs rational, humanistic and knowledgeable critics as a prerequisite for human survival. Is the learning society amenable to change? The alternative, as Riccardo Petrella puts it, is 'a future associated with one of the greatest wastes of creativity and knowledge ever organised on a global scale' (Petrella, 1997, 32). Petrella also points out that the dominance of the market economy is not complete. Alongside the anonymous multinational corporations and global consumers – and, we might add, among them – there are 'pockets of resistance' which ask us to re-examine some of the fundamental assumptions on which our current policies and strategies appear to be based. Such a re-examination would, I hope, place lifelong training and education at the service of a global development strategy that is economically efficient, socially equitable, ecologically sustainable and politically democratic.

Note on primary sources

Some of the material used in this book was first collected in the course of other studies. In Chapters Three and Four, I have plundered the interviews and focus groups conducted as part of a study of Divergence between Initial and Continuing Education in Scotland and Northern Ireland, funded by the Economic and Social Research Council as part of its Learning Society Programme. I particularly wish to acknowledge the contribution made by Lynda Spence (fellow researcher) and Tom Schuller (co-director), as well as Frank Coffield who led the Learning Society Programme. A brief report on the methods used for this study is given in Schuller and Field (1999), and the findings are presented in greater detail in Field (2005). In addition, five additional semi-structured interviews were conducted specifically for this volume. The questions of agency, identity and workplace change that I examine in Chapters Two and Three are currently under examination in the Learning Lives project, also funded by ESRC, this time under its Teaching and Learning Research Programme (www.learninglives.org), with fieldwork conducted on a longitudinal basis between 2004 and 2008.

References

Abercrombie, N. and Urry, J. (1983) *Capital, Labour and the Middle Classes*, Allen and Unwin, London

Adick, C. (1992) Modern Education in 'Non-Western' Societies in the Light of the World Systems Approach in Comparative Education, *International Review of Education*, 38, 3, 241-55

Adult Education Committee of the Ministry of Reconstruction (1919) *Final Report*, His Majesty's Stationery Office, London

Aldcroft, D. H. (1992) *Education, Training and Economic Performance, 1944 to 1990*, Manchester University Press

Aldridge, F. and Tuckett, A. (2005) *Better New This Time?*, National Institute of Adult Continuing Education, Leicester

Alheit, P. (1992) The Biographical Approach to Adult Education, pp. 186-221 in W. Mader (ed.), *Adult Education in the Federal Republic of Germany: scholarly approaches and professional practice*, University of British Columbia, Vancouver

Alheit, P. (1994) *Zivile Kultur: Verlust und Wiederaneignung der Moderne*, Campus Verlag, Frankfurt-am-Main

Alheit, P. (1999) On a contradictory way to the 'Learning Society': a critical approach, *Studies in the Education of Adults*, 31, 1, 66-82

Anderton, B., Riley, R. and Young, G. (1999) *The New Deal for Young People: first year analysis of implications for the macroeconomy, Research and Development* Report ESR33, Employment Service, Sheffield

Argyris, C. and Schön, D. (1978) *Organizational Learning: a theory of action perspective*, Addison-Wesley, Reading

Armistead, C. (1994) *The Future of Services Management*, Kogan Page, London

Arriva plc (2004) *Annual Report and Accounts 2003*, Arriva plc, Sunderland

Arthur, M. B., Inkson, K. and Pringle, J. K. (1999) *The New Careers: individual action and economic change*, Sage, London

Atkinson, J. (1999) *The New Deal for Unemployed Young People: a summary of progress*, Institute for Employment Studies, Brighton

Avis, J. (2002) Social Capital, Collective Intelligence and Expansive Learning: thinking through the connections, *British Journal of Educational Studies*, 50, 3, 308-26

Axmacher, D. (1989) Widerstand gegen Erwachsenenbildung als historischer und theoretische Kategorie, *Zeitschrift für Sozialisationsforschung und Erziehungssoziologie*, 9, 1, 23-40

Bagnall, R. (2005) Dealing with Difference by Creating Dependency? A critique of the dependency thesis in lifelong learning and adult education, pp. 13-20 in P. Coare, P. Armstrong, M. Boice and L. Morrice (eds) *Diversity and Difference in Lifelong Learning*, Standing Conference on University Teaching and Research in the Education of Adults, University of Sussex, Brighton

Ball, C. (1991) *Learning Pays: the role of post-compulsory education and training*, Royal Society of Arts, London

Bandura, A. (1994) Self-efficacy, pp. 78-81 in V.S. Ramachaudran (ed.), *Encyclopedia of Human Behavior*, vol. 4, Academic Press, New York

Banks, S. (1993) Accrediting Prior Learning for a Professional Qualification, *Adults Learning*, 5, 2, 39-41

Baptiste, I. (1999) Beyond Lifelong Learning: a call to civically responsible change, *International Journal of Lifelong Education*, 18, 2, 94-102

Barnett, R. (1990) *The Idea of Higher Education*, Open University Press, Buckingham

Barrett, W. (1979) *The Illusion of Technique: a search for meaning in a technological civilization*, Anchor Doubleday, New York

Bauman, Z. (1998) *Work, Consumerism and the New Poor*, Open University Press, Buckingham

Baynham, M. (1996) Humour as an Interpersonal Resource in Adult Numeracy Classes, *Language and Education*, 10, 2/3, 187-200

Beck, U. (1992) *Risk Society*, Sage, London

Beck, U. (1996) Risk Society and the Provident State, pp. 27-43 in B. Szerszynski, S. Lash and B. Wynne (eds) *Risk, Environment and Modernity: towards a new ecology*, Sage, London

Beck, U. (1997) *Was ist Globalisierung?* Suhrkamp Verlag, Frankfurt-am-Main

Beck, U. and Beck-Gernsheim, E. (1994) Individualisierung in modernen Gesellschaften – Perspektiven und Kontroversen einer subjektorientierten Soziologie, pp. 10-39 in U. Beck and E. Beck-Gernsheim (eds) *Riskante Freiheiten*, Suhrkamp Verlag, Frankfurt-am-Main

Beck, U. and Sopp, P. (1997) Individualisierung und Integration – eine Problemskizze, pp. 9-19 in U. Back and P. Sopp (eds.) *Individualisierung und Integration: Neue Konfliktlinien und neuer Integrationsmodus*, Leske and Budrich, Opladen

Beckett, D. and Hager, P. (2002) *Life, Work and Learning: Practice in postmodernity*, Routledge, London

Beinart, S. and Smith, P. (1998) *National Adult Learning Survey 1997*, Department for Education and Employment, Sheffield

Bélanger, P. (1999) The Threat and the Promise of a 'Reflexive' Society: the new policy environment of adult learning, *Adult Education and Development*, 52, 179-95

Bell, D. (1973) *The Coming of Post-Industrial Society*, Basic Books, New York

Benn, R. (1996) Access for adults to higher education: targeting or self-selection? *Journal of Access Studies*, 11, 2, 165-76

Bentley, T. (1998) *Learning Beyond the Classroom: Education for a changing world*, Routledge/DEMOS, London

Biesta, G. (2004) Against Learning: Reclaiming a language for education in an age of learning, *Nordisk Pedagogik*, 24, 70-82

Black, P. (2004) *The Beauty Industry: gender, culture, pleasure*, RoutledgeFalmer, London

Blaug, M. (1985) Where are we now in the economics of education? *Economics of Education Review*, 4, 1, 17-28

Blaxter, L. and Tight, M. (1994) Juggling with time: how adults manage their time for lifelong education, *Studies in the Education of Adults*, 26, 2, 162-79

Blaxter, L., Hughes, C. and Tight, M. (1996) Living lifelong education: the experiences of some working class women, *Adults Learning*, 7, 7, 169-71

Blaxter, L., Hughes, C. and Tight, M. (1997) Education, Work and Adult Life: how adults relate their learning to their work, family and social lives, pp. 135-47 in P. Sutherland (ed.), *Adult Learning: a reader*, Kogan Page, London.

Boreham, N. (2004) A Theory of Collective Competence: Challenging the neo-liberal individualisation of performance at work, *British Journal of Educational Studies*, 52, 1, 5-17

Boreham, N., Fischer, M. and Samurçay, R. (eds.) (2002) *Work Process Knowledge*, Routledge, London

Borg, C. and Mayo, P. (2005) The EU Memorandum on lifelong learning. Old wine in new bottles? *Globalisation, Societies and Education*, 3, 2, 257-78

Boshier, R. (1998) Edgar Faure after 25 Years: down but not out, pp. 3-20 in J. Holford, P. Jarvis and C. Griffin (eds) *International Perspectives on Lifelong Learning*, Kogan Page, London

Boudard, E. and Morlaix, S. (2003) Accumuler le capital social tout au long de la vie: quels facteurs prédictifs de la participation à la formation permanente? *Revue Internationale de l'Education*, 49, 5, 509-24

Bounds, A. (1999) Survey – World's Most Respected Companies, *Financial Times*, 7 December 1999

Bourdieu, P. (1984) *Distinction: A social critique of the judgement of taste*, Routledge, London

Bourgeois, E., Duke, C., Guyot, J.-L. and Merrill, B. (1999) *The Adult University*, Open University Press, Buckingham

Box, D. and Waples, J. (2005) Fighting Fit, *Sunday Times* (Business Focus), 3 April 2005, 5

Boyle, M., Findlay, A., Lelievre, E. and Paddison, R. (1996) World cities and the limits to global control: a case study of executive search firms in Europe's leading cities, *International Journal of Urban and Regional Research*, 20, 3, 498-517

Braverman, H. (1974) *Labor and Monopoly Capital: the degradation of work in the twentieth century*, Monthly Review Press, New York

Brockett, R.G. and Hiemstra, R. (1991) *Self-Direction in Adult Learnng: perspectives on theory, research and practice*, Routledge, London

Brockmann, A. (1999) Fitneßtraining im Kampfanzug, *Die Tageszeitung*, 22 April 1999

Brödel, R. (1997) Einführung: Erwachsenenbildung in der gesellschaftlichen Moderne, pp. 9-49, in R. Brödel (ed.), *Erwachsenenbildung in der gesellschaftlichen Moderne*, Opladen

Brödel, R. (1998) Lebenslanges Lernen – lebensbegleitende Bildung, pp. 1-32 in R. Brödel (ed.), *Lebenslanges Lernen – lebensbegleitende Bildung*, Luchterhand, Neuwied

Bryson, A., Knight, G. and White, M. (2000) *New Deal for Young People: national survey of participants: Stage 1*, Research and Development Report ESR44, Employment Service, Sheffield

Buechtemann, C.F. and Soloff, D.J. (1994) Education, Training and the Economy, *Industrial Relations Journal*, 25, 3, 234-46

Burgoyne, J. (1999) Designs of the Times, *People Management*, 3 June 1999, 39-44

Bynner, J. and Parsons, S. (1998) *Use it or Lose it? The impact of time out of work on literacy and numeracy skills*, Basic Skills Agency, London

Byrne, D. (1999) *Social Exclusion*, Open University Press, Buckingham

Cable, V. (1995) The Diminished Nation-State: a study in the loss of economic power, *Daedalus*, 124, 2, 25-53

Cadbury Schweppes (1999) *Managing for Value: Annual Report 1998*, Cadbury Schweppes plc, London

Campaign for Learning (1998) *Attitudes to Learning '98: MORI state of the nation survey*, Campaign for Learning, London

Campbell, C., Wood, R. and Kelly, M. (1999) *Social Capital and Health*, Health Education Authority, London

Campbell, M., Sanderson, I., and Walton, F. (1998) *Local Responses to Long-term Unemployment*, Joseph Rowntree Foundation, York

Candy, P., Crebert, G. and O'Leary, J. (1994) *Developing Lifelong Learners through Undergraduate Education*, National Board of Employment, Education and Training, Canberra

Cannell, M. (1999) Tradition before technology, *People Management*, 8 April 1999, 35

Cannell, M., Ashton, D., Powell, M. and Sung, J. (1999), Ahead of the field, *People Management*, 22 April 1999, 48-9

Carlson, A. and West, L. (2005) Border Country: Therapy, learning and research and the challenge of Sure Start, pp. 37-45 in P. Coare, P. Armstrong, M. Boice and L. Morrice (eds.) *Diversity and Difference in Lifelong Learning, Standing Conference on University Teaching and Research in the Education of Adults*, University of Sussex, Brighton

Castells, M. (1989) *The Informational City: information technology, economic restructuring and the urban-regional process*, Blackwell, Oxford

Castells, M. (1998) *End of Millennium*, Blackwell, Oxford

Centre européenne pour la développement de la formation professionelle (2003) *Lifelong Learning: citizens' views*, Office for Official Publications, Luxembourg

Chaney, D. (1998) The New Materialism? The challenge of consumption, *Work, Employment and Society*, 12, 2, 533-44

Chappell, C., Rhodes, C., Solomon, N., Tennant, M. and Yates, L. (2003) *Reconstructing the Lifelong Learner: Pedagogy and identity in individual, social and organisational change*, Routledge, London

Cherfas, J. (1992) Two weeks to save the planet, *New Scientist*, 29 February 1992

Chittenden, M. (1998) Modern face of mnemonics ends memory man's unforgettable run, *Sunday Times*, 22 November 1998

Clark, A. (2003) EC investigation into Ryanair, *Guardian*, 23 September 2003, Travel Supplement, 5

Clark, A. (2005) Ryanair's latest cut on costs: staff banned from charging phones, *Guardian*, 23 April 2005, 3

Cloonan, M. (2004) A Capital Project? The New Deal for Musicians in Scotland, *Studies in the Education of Adults*, 36, 1, 40-56

Cochinaux, P. and de Woot, P. (1995) *Moving Towards a Learning Society*, Conseil des Recteurs Européens/European Roundtable of Employers, Geneva/Brussels

Coffield, F. (1999) Introduction: lifelong learning as a new form of social control? pp. 1-12 in F. Coffield (ed.) *Why's the Beer Always Stronger up North? Studies of lifelong learning in Europe*, Policy Press, Bristol

Colardyn, D. and Durand, M. (1998), Recognising Skills and Qualifications, pp. 241-7 in D. Neef (ed.) *The Knowledge Economy*, Butterworth Heinemann, Boston

Collin, A. and Watts, A.G. (1996) The death and transfiguration of career – and of career guidance? *British Journal of Guidance and Counselling*, 12, 3, 385-98

Collins, M. (1998) Critical Perspectives and New Beginnings: reforming the discourse on lifelong learning, pp. 44-55 in J. Holford, P. Jarvis and C. Griffin (eds) *International Perspectives on Lifelong Learning*, Kogan Page, London

Commission of the European Communities (1994) *Competitiveness, Employment, Growth*, Office for Official Publications, Luxembourg

Commission of the European Communities (1995) *Teaching and Learning: towards the learning society*, Office for Official Publications, Luxembourg

Commission of the European Communities (1996a) *Living and Working in the Information Society: People First*, Office for Official Publications, Luxembourg

Commission of the European Communities (1996b) *Europeans and their Attitudes to Education and Training: Eurobarometer Summary*, Office for Official Publications, Luxembourg

Commission of the European Communities (1997) *The 1998 Employment Guidelines: Council Resolution of 15 December 1997*, Office for Official Publications, Luxembourg

Commission of the European Communities (1998a) *Social Action Programme 1998-2000*, Directorate General for Employment, Industrial Relations and Social Affairs, Brussels

Commission of the European Communities (1998b) *Learning for Active Citizenship*, Directorate General for Education, Training and Youth, Brussels

Commission of the European Communities (1999) *The 1999 Employment Guidelines: Council resolution of 22 February 1999*, Directorate-General for Employment, Industrial Relations and Social Affairs, Brussels

Commission of the European Communities (2000) *Commission Staff Working Paper. A Memorandum on Lifelong Learning*, European Commission, Brussels

Commission of the European Communities (2003) *Commission Staff Working Paper. Building the Knowledge Society: social and human capital interactions*, European Commission, Brussels

Commission on the Future of the Voluntary Sector (1996) *Meeting the Challenge of Change: voluntary action into the 21st century*, National Council for Voluntary Organisations, London

Creaton, S. (2005) Ryanair issues redundancy notices to pilots over training, *Irish Times*, 11 August 2005, 1

Cropley, A. J. (1979), Lifelong Education: issues and questions, in A. J. Cropley (ed.) *Lifelong Learning: a stocktaking*, Unesco Institute for Education, Hamburg, 8-27

Cross, K. P. (1981) *Adults as Learners*, Jossey-Bass, San Francisco

Crowther, J. (2004) 'In and against' lifelong learning: flexibility and the corrosion of character, *International Journal of Lifelong Education*, 23, 2, 125-36

Dahrendorf, R. (1999) Whatever happened to liberty? *New Statesman*, 6 September 1999, 25-7

Daneshku, S. (1998) Fitness firms speed ahead but some may have to peak, *Financial Times*, 27 August 1998

Dasgupta, P. amd Sertageldin, I., editors (1999) *Social Capital: a multifaceted perspective*, World Bank, Washington

Dave, R. H. (1977) *Lifelong Learning and School Curriculum*, Unesco Institute for Education, Hamburg

Davies, P. (1999) A New Learning Culture? Possibilities and contradictions in accreditation, *Studies in the Education of Adults*, 31, 1, 10-20

Delors, J. (1996) *The Treasure Within: Report to UNESCO of the International Commission on Education for the Twenty-first Century*, UNESCO, Paris

Dempsey, A. (1999) Talk it out, *Irish Times*, 25 August 1999, 10

Dennison, S.R. (1984) *Choice in Education*, Institute of Economic Affairs, London

Department of Education and Science (1973) *Adult Education: a plan for development*, Her Majesty's Stationery Office, London

Department of Education and Science (1998) *Adult Education in an Era of Lifelong Learning*, Stationery Office, Dublin

DfEE (1995) *Lifetime Learning: a consultation document*, Department for Education and Employment/Scottish Office/Welsh Office, Sheffield

DfEE (1997) *Learning and Working Together for the Future: a consultation document*, Department for Education and Employment, Sheffield

DfEE (1998a) *The Learning Age: a renaissance for a new Britain*, Department for Education and Employment, Sheffield

DfEE (1998b) *60,000 start their New Deal*, Department for Education and Employment Press Release 328/98, website www.nds.coi.gov.uk/coi/coipress.ns

DfEE (1999a) *Delivering Skills for All: second report of the National Skills Task Force*, Department for Education and Employment, Sheffield

DfEE (1999b) *Learning to Succeed: a new framework for post-16 learning*, Department for Education and Employment, Sheffield

DfEE (1999c) *Labour Market and Skill Trends 1998/1999*, Department for Education and Employment, Sheffield

DfEE (2000) *Tackling the Adult Skills Gap: upskilling adults and the role of workplace training: third report of the National Skills Task Force*, Department for Education and Employment, Sheffield

Dixon, S. (2003) Migration within Britain for job reasons, *Labour Market Trends*, 111, 4, 191-200

Dohmen, G. (1996) *Lifelong Learning: guidelines for a modern education policy*, Bundesministerium für Bildung, Wissenschaft und Forschung, Bonn. (English version of the original, *Das lebenslange Lernen. Leitlinien einer modernen Bildungpolitik*, which appeared simultaneously)

Dohmen, G. (1998) *Zur Zukunft der Weiterbildung in Europa: Lebenslanges Lernen für Alle in veränderten Lernumwelten*, Bundesministerium für Bildung, Wissenschaft und Forschung, Bonn

Dore, R. (1997) Reflections on the Diploma Disease Twenty Years Later, *Assessment in Education*, 4, 1, 189-206

Dubar, C. (2000) *La crise des identities: L'interpretation d'une mutation*, Presses Universitaires de France, Paris

Dulewicz, V. and Higgs, M. (1998) Soul researching, *People Management*, 1 October 1998, 42-45

Dumazadier, J. (1995) Aides à l'autoformation: un fait social d'aujourd'hui, *Education Permanente*, 122, 243-56

Ecclestone, K. (2004) Learning or Therapy? The demoralisation of education, *British Journal of Educational Studies*, 52, 2, 112-37

Eden, D. and Kinnar, J. (1991) Modeling Galatea: boosting self-efficacy to increase volunteering, *Journal of Applied Psychology*, 6, 6, 770-80

Edwards, R. (1995) Behind the Banner: whither the learning society? *Adults Learning*, 6, 6,187-9

Edwards, R. (1997) *Changing Places: flexibility, lifelong learning and a learning society*, Routledge, London

Edwards, R., Ranson, S. and Strain, M. (2002) Reflexivity: Towards a theory of lifelong learning, *International Journal of Lifelong Education*, 21, 6, 525-36

Elger, T. (1991) Task Flexibility and the Intensification of Labour in UK Manufacturing in the 1980s, pp. 46-66 in A. Pollert (ed.), *Farewell to Flexibility?*, Blackwell, Oxford

Elsdon, K. T., Reynolds, J. and Stewart, S. (1995) *Voluntary Organisations – citizenship, learning and change*, National Institute for Adult Continuing Education, Leicester

Emler, N. and McNamara, S. (1996) The Social Contact Patterns of Young People: effects of participation in the social institutions of family, education and work, in H. Helve and J. Bynner (eds) *Youth and Life Management: research perspectives*, Yliopistpaino, Helsinki

Eraut, M. (2000) Non-formal learning, implicit learning and tacit knowledge in professional work, pp 12- 31 in F. Coffield (ed.) *The Necessity of Informal Learning*, Policy Press, Bristol

Evans, T. and Nation, D. (1996) Educational Futures: globalisation, educational technology and lifelong learning, pp. 162-76 in T. Evans and D. Nation (eds)

Opening Education: policies and practices from open and distance education, Routledge, London

Fairbrother, P. (1991) In a State of Change: flexibility in the civil service, pp. 69-83 in A. Pollert (ed.), *Farewell to Flexibility?* Blackwell, Oxford

Fairclough, N. (1999) Global Capitalism and Critical Awareness of Language, *Language Awareness,* 8, 2, 71-83

Faure, E. (1972) *Learning to Be: the world of education today and tomorrow,* UNESCO, Paris

Fejes, A. (2005) New Wine in Old Skins: Changing patterns in the governing of the adult learner in Sweden, *International Journal of Lifelong Education,* 24, 1, 71-86

Felstead, A., Fuller, A., Unwin, L., Ashton, D., Butler, P., Lee, T. and Walters, S. (2004) Exposing Learning at Work: Results from a recent survey, *Work, Employment and Society Conference,* University of Manchester, 1-3 September 2004

Felstead, A., Gallie, D. and Green, F. (2002) *Work Skills in Britain, 1986-2001,* Department for Education and Skills, Nottingham

Felstead, A., Jewson, N. and Walters, S. (2005) *Changing Places of Work,* Palgrave Macmillan, Basingstoke

Fenwick, T. (2003) Flexibility and Individualisation in Adult Education Work: the case of portfolio educators, *Journal of Education and Work,* 16, 2, 165-84

Fenwick, T. (2004) What Happens to the Girls? Gender, work and learning in Canada's 'new economy', *Gender and Education,* 16, 2, 169-85

Ferrer, A., Green, D.A. and Riddell, W.C. (2004) *The Effect of Literacy on Immigrant Earnings,* Statistics Canada/Human Resources and Skills Development Canada, Ottawa

Feutrie, M. and Verdier, É. (1993) Entreprises et formations qualifiantes: une construction sociale inachevée, *Sociologie du travail,* 35, 4, 469-91

Field, J. (1979) British Historians and the Concept of the Labor Aristocracy, *Radical History Review,* 19, 61-85

Field, J. (1988) What Workers, What Leave? Changing patterns of employment and the prospects for paid educational leave, pp. 63-75 in F. Molyneux, G. Low and G. Fowler (eds) *Learning for Life: politics and progress in recurrent education,* Croom Helm, Beckenham

Field, J. (1991) Out of the Adult Hut: institutionalisation, individuality and new values in the education of adults, pp. 128-41 in P. Raggatt and L. Unwin (eds) *Change and Intervention: vocational education and training,* Falmer, London

Field, J. (1992) *Learning through Labour: Training, education and the state, 1890-1939,* Leeds Studies in Continuing Education, University of Leeds

Field, J. (1995) Reality-Testing in the Workplace: are NVQs employer-led? pp. 28-43 in P. Hodkinson and M. Issitt (eds.) *The Challenge of Competence: professionalism through vocational education and training,* Cassell, London

Field, J. (1996) Vocational Education and Training, in R. Fieldhouse (ed.), *A History of Modern British Adult Education,* National Institute for Adult Continuing Education, Leicester

Field, J. (1998) *European Dimensions: education, training and the European Union,* Jessica Kingsley, London

Field, J. (2001) The role of risk and contingency in adults' descriptions of participation in education and training, *Journal of Adult and Continuing Education*, 7, 1, 75-92

Field, J. (2005) *Social Capital and Lifelong Learning*, Policy Press, Bristol

Field, J., Lovell, T. and Weller, P. (1991) *Research Quality in Continuing Education: a study of citation patterns*, Research Papers in Continuing Education, University of Warwick

Field, J. and Schuller, T. (1999) Researching the Learning Society, *Studies in the Education of Adults*, 31, 1, 1-10

Field, J. and Spence, L. (2000) Social Capital and Informal Learning, pp. 32-42 , F. Coffield (ed.), *The Necessity of Informal Learning*, Policy Press, Bristol

Fieldhouse, R. (1997) *Adult Education History: why rake up the past?* Sixteenth Albert Mansbridge Memorial Lecture, University of Leeds

Filander, K (2003) Vocabularies of Change: Analysing talk on change and agency in development work, Roskilde University Press, Roskilde

Filander, K. (1998) Is There any Space for Agency? A study of changing agent identity and ethos in the public sector, pp. 121-42 in H. S. Olesen (ed.), *Adult Education and the Labour Market IV*, European Society for Research in the Education of Adults, Roskilde

Fitzgerald, R., Taylor, R. and La Valle, I. (2003) *National Adult Learning Survey (NALS) 2002*, Department for Education and Skills, Nottingham

Florida, R. (1995) Toward the Learning Region, *Futures*, 27, 5, 527-36

Forrester, K. (2004) 'The Quiet Revolution?' Trade union learning and renewal strategies, *Work, Employment and Society*, 18, 2, 413-20

Forster, N. and Whipp, R. (1995) Future of European human resource management: a contingent approach, *European Management Journal*, 13, 4, 434-42

Foucault, M. (1989) *The Birth of the Clinic: an archaeology of medical perception*, Routledge, London

Frankfurter Allgemeine Zeitung (2005) *Trübe Jahresbilanz am Arbeitsmarkt*, FAZ, 5 January 2005, 11

Friedenthal-Haase, M. (1998) Orientierung und Reorientierung: Kategorien und Aufgaben lebensbegleitender Bildung, pp. 60-72 in R. Brödel (ed.), *Lebenslanges Lernen – lebensbegleitende Bildung*, Luchterhand, Neuwied

Front Row (1999) *Front Row*, BBC Radio 4, 6 September 1999

Fryer, R.H. (1998) *Learning for the Twenty-first Century: First Report of the National Advisory Group for Continuing Education and Lifelong Learning*, Department for Education and Employment, Sheffield

Fryer, R.H. (1999) *Creating Learning Cultures: next steps in achieving the Learning Age, Second Report of the National Advisory Group for Continuing Education and Lifelong Learning*, Department for Education and Employment, Sheffield

Fuller, A., Ashton, D., Felstead, A., Unwin, L., Walters, S. and Quinn, M. (2003) *The Impact of Informal Learning at Work in Business Productivity*, Department of Trade and Industry, London

Füller, C. (1998) Daimler-Uni startet im August, *Die Tageszeitung*, 8 December 1998, 13

Furedi, F. (1997) *Culture of Fear: risk-taking and the morality of low expectation*, Cassell, London

Further Education Funding Council (1999) *Bilston Community College Inspection Report*, FEFC, Coventry

Gallie, D. and White, M. (1993) *Employee Commitment and the Skills Revolution*, Policy Studies Institute, London

Gallie, D. (1996) Skill, Gender and the Quality of Employment, pp. 133-59 in R. Crompton, D. Gallie and K. Purcell (eds.) *Changing Forms of Employment: organisations, skills and gender*, Routledge, London

Gardiner, K. (1997) *Bridges from benefit to work: a review*, Joseph Rowntree Foundation, York

Garvin, D.A. (1993) Building a Learning Organisation, *Harvard Business Review*, 51, 78-90

Gaskell, T. (2005) Basil Bernstein's Theory of Pedagogic Transmission: pedagogy, curriculum and aging, Ph D Thesis, University of Dundee

Geddes, M. (1997) *Partnership Against Poverty and Exclusion? Local regeneration strategies and excluded communities in the UK*, Policy Press, Bristol

Giddens, A. (1990) *Consequences of Modernity*, Polity, Cambridge

Giddens, A. (1991) *Modernity and Self-Identity: self and society in the late modern age*, Polity, Cambridge

Giddens, A. (1992) *The Transformation of Intimacy*, Polity, Cambridge

Giddens, A. (1994) *Beyond Left and Right: the future of radical politics*, Polity, Cambridge

Giddens, A. (1998) *The Third Way: The renewal of social democracy*, Polity, Cambridge

Giere, U. and Piet, M. (1997) *Adult Learning in a World at Risk: emerging policies and strategies*, UNESCO Institute for Education, Hamburg

Gilleard, C. (1996) Consumption and Identity in Later Life: toward a cultural gerontology, *Aging and Society*, 16, 3, 489-98

Gorard, S., Rees, G. and Fevre, R. (1999a) Two dimensions of time: the changing social context of lifelong learning, *Studies in the Education of Adults*, 31, 1, 35-48

Gorard, S., Rees, G. and Fevre, R. (1999b) Patterns of Participation in Lifelong Learning: do families make a difference? *British Educational Research Journal*, 25, 4, 517-32

Gordon, J. (1999) Approaches to transparency of vocational qualifications in the EU, *European Journal of Education*, 34, 2, 203-17

Gorz, A. (1994) *Capitalism, Socialism, Ecology*, Verso, London

Goudevert, D. (1993) Welche Zukunft hat die Arbeit? *Die Welt*, 22 April 1993, 12

Grand Metropolitan (1997) *Report on Corporate Citizenship*, Grand Metropolitan, London

Granovetter, M. (1973) The strength of weak ties, *American Journal of Sociology*, 78, 1360-80

Green, F. and Gallie, D. (2002), *High Skills and High Anxiety: Skills, hard work and mental well-being*, SKOPE Research Paper no. 27, SKOPE, Oxford/Coventry

Greenhalgh, C. and Mavrotas, G. (1996) Job Training, New Technology and Labour Turnover, *British Journal of Industrial Relations*, 34, 1, 131-50

Griffiths, J. (1999) UK's biggest car plant now 400 acres of pure paradox, *Financial Times*, 20 December 1999, 6

Group of Eight (1999) *Köln Charter: aims and ambitions for lifelong learning, 18 June 1999*, Group of Eight, Cologne

Gustavsson, B. (1995) Lifelong Learning Reconsidered, pp. 89-110 in M. Klasson, J. Manninen, S. Tøsse and B. Wahlgren (eds) *Social Change and Adult Education Research*, Linköping University, Linköping

Habermas, J. (1985) *Die neue Unübersichtlichkeit*, Suhrkamp Verlag, Frankfurt-am-Main

Hager, P. and Smith, E. (2004) The Inescapability of Significant Contextual Learning on Work Performance, *London Review of Education*, 2, 1, 33-46

Hague, D. (1991) *Beyond Universities: A new republic of the intellect*, Institute of Economic Affairs, London

Hake, B. J. (1998) Lifelong Learning and the European Union: a critique from a 'risk society' perspective, pp. 32-43 in J. Holford, P. Jarvis and C. Griffin (eds) *International Perspectives on Lifelong Learning*, Kogan Page, London

Hall, P. (1999) Social Capital in Britain, *British Journal of Political Science*, 29, 3, 417-61

Halman, L. (1996) Individualism in Individualised Society? Results from the European Values Surveys, *International Journal of Comparative Sociology*, 37, 3/4, 195-214

Hancock, P. and Tyler, M (2004) 'MOT Your Life': Critical management studies and the management of everyday life, *Human Relations*, 57, 5, 619-45

Harley, B. (1999) The Myth of Empowerment: work organisation, hierarchy and employee autonomy in contemporary Australian workplaces, *Work, Employment and Society*, 13, 1, 41-66

Hasluck, C. (2000) *The New Deal for Young People, Two Years On*, Research and Development Report ESR41, Employment Service, Sheffield

HEBS (1997) *Strategic plan for 1997 to 2002*, Health Education Board for Scotland, Edinburgh

Hedoux, J. (1982) Des publics et des non-publics de la formation d'adultes: l'accès à l'Action Collective de Formation de Sallaumines-Noyelles-sous-Lens, *Revue française de la sociologie*, 23, 253-74

Heenan, D. (2002) 'It won't Change the World but it Turned My Life Around': participants' views on the Personal Advisor Scheme in the New Deal for Disabled People, *Disability and Society*, 17, 4, 383-402

Heinz, W. (1999) Lifelong learning: learning for life? Some cross-national observations, pp.13-20, in F. Coffield (ed.) *Why's the Beer Always Stronger up North? Studies of lifelong learning in Europe*, Policy Press, Bristol

Henderson, J. (1999) Fit for the job. *Scotsman* (recruitment supplement), 16 April 1999, 1

Henry, I.P. (1999) Social Inclusion and the Leisure Society, *New Political Economy*, 4, 2, 283-88

Herr, E. L. (1997) Career Counselling: a process in process, *British Journal of Guidance and Counselling*, 25, 1, 81-93

Hills, J. (1998) *Income and Wealth: the latest evidence*, Joseph Rowntree Charitable Trust, York

Hobsbawm, E. (1997) *On History*, Abacus, London

187

Hoffritz, J. (1997) *Immer auf den Punkt, Wirtschaftswoche*, 16 January 1997, 64-5

Hornstein, W. (1984) Neue soziale Bewegung und Pädagogik, *Zeitschrift für Pädagogik*, 30, 2, 147-67

House of Commons Education and Skills Committee (2005) *UK e-University: Third Report of Session 2004-05*, Stationery Office, London

Hülsberg, W. (1988) *The German Greens: a social and political profile*, Verso, London

Husén, T. (1974) *The Learning Society*, Methuen, London

Hyland, T. and Johnson, S. (1998) Of Cabbages and Key Skills: exploding the myth of core transferable skills in post-school education, *Journal of Further and Higher Education*, 22, 2, 163-72

Hyman, R. (1991) Plus ça change? The theory of production and the production of theory, pp. 259-83 in A. Pollert (ed.), *Farewell to Flexibility?* Blackwell, Oxford

Industrial Relations Services (1999) The Young Ones: the annual IRS survey, *Employee Development Bulletin*, 114, June 1999, 5-16

Information Society Forum (1996) *Networks for People and their Communities: first annual report to the European Commission from the Information Society Forum*, CORDIS, Luxembourg

Inglehart, R. (1990) *Culture Shift in Advanced Industrial Societies*, Princeton University Press, Princeton

Institute of Mechanical Engineers (1998) *A Guide to Mentoring: the mentored professional development scheme*, Institute of Mechanical Engineers, Bury St. Edmunds

Istance, D. (2003) Schooling and Lifelong Learning: insights from OECD analyses, *European Journal of Education*, 38, 1, 85-98

Jansen, T. and Klaassen, C. (1994) Some Reflections on Individualisation, Identity and Socialisation in (Post)Modernity, pp. 61-80 in P. Jarvis and F. Pöggeler (eds) *Developments in the Education of Adults in Europe*, Peter Lang, Frankfurt-am-Main

Jansen, T. and Veen, R. van der (1992) Reflexive modernity, self-reflective biographies: adult education in the light of the risk society, *International Journal of Lifelong Education*, 11, 4, 275-86

Jansen, T., Finger, M. and Wildemeersch, D. (1998) Lifelong Learning for Social Responsibility: exploring the significance of aesthetic reflexivity for adult education, pp. 81-91 in J. Holford, P. Jarvis and C. Griffin (eds) *International Perspectives on Lifelong Learning*, Kogan Page, London

Jarvis, P. (1992) *Paradoxes of Learning: on becoming an individual in society*, Jossey-Bass, San Francisco

Jarvis, P. (2000) The Corporate University, in J. Field and M. Leicester (eds) *Lifelong Learning: education across the lifespan*, Falmer, London

Jarvis, P., Holford, J. and Griffin, C. (1998) *The Theory and Practice of Learning*, Kogan Page, London

Jenoptik (2004) *Annual Report 2003*, Jenoptik AG, Jena

Johnston, R. (1999) Adult Learning for Citizenship: towards a reconstruction of the social purpose tradition, *International Journal of Lifelong Education*, 18, 3, 175-90

Jones, A.M. and Hendry, C. (1994) The Learning Organisation: adult learning and organizational transformation, *British Journal of Management*, 5, 2, 153-62

Jones, H.C. (2005) Lifelong Learning in the European Union: whither the Lisbon Strategy?, *European Journal of Education*, 40, 3, 247-60

Kade, J. and Seitter, W. (1998), Bildung – Risiko – Genuß. Dimensionen und Ambivalenzen legenslangen Lernen in der Moderne, pp. 51-59 in R. Brödel (ed.) *Lebenslanges Lernen – lebensbegleitende Bildung*, Luchterhand, Neuwied

Keep, E. and Mayhew, H. (1999) Towards the Knowledge-driven Economy, *Renewal*, 7, 4, 50-9

Kennedy, H. (1997) *Learning Works: widening participation in further education*, Further Education Funding Council, Coventry

Kluge, N., Hippchen, G. and Fischinger, E. (1999) *Körper und Schönheit als soziale Leitbilder: Ergebnisse einer Repräsentativerhebung in West- und Ostdeutschland*, Peter Lang Verlag, Frankfurt-am-Main

Knights, D. and McCabe, D. (2003) *Organisation and Innovation: guru schemes and American dreams*, Open University Press, Maidenhead

Knoll, J. (1998) 'Lebenslanges Lernen' und internationale Bildungspolitik – Zur Genese eines Begriffs und dessen nationale Operationalisierungen, pp. 35-50 in R. Brödel (ed.), *Lebenslanges Lernen – lebensbegleitende Bildung*, Luchterhand, Neuwied

Knowles, M. (1983) Andragogy: an emerging technology for adult learning, pp. 53-69 in M. Tight (ed) *Adult Learning and Education*, Croom Helm, Beckenham

Kramlinger, T. (1992) Training's Role in a Learning Organisation, *Training*, July 1992, 46-51

La Valle, I. and Finch, S. (1999) *Pathways in Adult Learning: summary*, Department for Education and Employment, Sheffield

Lankshear, C., Gee, J.P., Knobel, M. and Searle, C. (1997) *Changing Literacies*, Open University Press, Buckingham

Lasch, C. (1980) *The Culture of Narcissism*, Abacus, London

Latrive, F. (1997) CD-Rom avec frontières, *Libération*, 4 April, I-II

Lave, J. and Wenger, E. (1991) *Situated Learning*, Cambridge University Press, Cambridge

Law, M. (1998) Market-oriented Policies and the Learning Society: the case of New Zealand, pp. 168-79 in J. Holford, P. Jarvis and C. Griffin (eds) *International Perspectives on Lifelong Learning*, Kogan Page, London

Lewis, R. (1993) *Leaders and Teachers: adult education and the challenge of labour in South Wales, 1906-1940*, University of Wales Press, Cardiff

Li, Y., Savage, M. and Pickles, A. (2003) Social capital and social exclusion in England and Wales (1972-1999), *British Journal of Sociology*, 54, 4, 497-526

Lichterman, P. (1992) Self-help reading as a thin culture, *Media, Culture and Society*, 14, 3, 421-47

R.M. Lindley and R.A. Wilson (eds.) (1998), *Review of the Economy and Employment 1997/98*, Institute for Employment Research, Coventry

Livingstone, D. W. (1999) Lifelong Learning and Underemployment in the Knowledge Society: a North American perspective, *Comparative Education*, 35, 2, 163-86

Livingstone, S.M. and Lunt, P. (1991) Expert and Lay Participation in Television Debates: an analysis of audience discussion programmes, *European Journal of Communication*, 6, 1, 9-35

Long, E. (2003) *Book Clubs: Women and the uses of reading in everyday life*, University of Chicago Press, Chicago

Longworth, N. (1999) *Making Lifelong Learning Work: learning cities for a learning century*, Kogan Page, London

Lundvall, B.-Å. and Johnson, B. (1994) The Learning Economy, *Journal of Industry Studies*, 1, 2, 23-42

MacEarlean, N. (1999) See our shrink – or you're fired, *Observer* (Business Supplement), 20 June 1999

McGivney, V. and Sims, D. (1986) *Adult Education and the Challenge of Unemployment*, Open University Press, Milton Keynes

McGivney, V. (1991) *Education's for Other People*, National Institute for Adult and Continuing Education, Leicester

McGovern, P., Hope-Hailey, V. and Stiles, P. (1998) The Managerial Career after Downsizing: case studies from the 'leading edge', *Work, Employment and Society*, 12, 2, 457-77

McGrath, M. (1991) *Multi-Disciplinary Teamwork: community mental handicap teams*, Avebury, Aldershot

McLeod, D.M. and Perse, E. (1994) Direct and Indirect Effects of Socioeconomic Status on Public Affairs Knowledge, *Journalism Quarterly*, 71, 2, 433-42

McMillan, J. (2005) Trusting in the Stars is a Dangerous Game, *The Scotsman*, 2 April 2005, 20

Maloney, W. (1999) Contracting out the Participation Function: social capital and cheque-book participation, 108-19, in J.W. van Deth, M. Maraffi, K. Newton and P. F. Whiteley (eds) *Social Capital and European Democracy*, Routledge, London

Marginson, S. (1995) The Decline in the Standing of Educational Credentials in Australia, *Australian Journal of Education*, 39, 1, 67-76

Marsden, C. and Andriof, J. (1998) Understanding Corporate Citizenship and How to Influence It, *Journal of Citizenship Studies*, 2, 2, 329-52

Marsden, D. (1994) The integration of European labour markets, in D. Marsden (ed.), *European Integration and the European Labour Market*, Supplement 1/94 to Social Europe

Marshall, T. H. (1992) *Citizenship and Social Class*, Pluto Press, London

Martin, L. (1999) The Right Stuff – human capital formation in small and medium-sized enterprises, Ph. D. Thesis, University of Warwick

Maskell, P., Skelinen, H., Hannibalsson, I., Malmberg, A. and Vatne, E. (1998) *Competitiveness, Localised Learning and Regional Development: specialisation and prosperity in small open economies*, Routledge, London

Matthews, J.J. and Candy, P.C. (1999) New dimensions in the dynamics of learning and knowledge, 47-64 in D. Boud and J. Garrick (eds) *Understanding Learning at Work*, Routledge, London

Maybe, C., Salaman, G. and Storey, J. (1998) Human Resource Management: a strategic introduction, Blackwell, Oxford

Merrill, B. (1999) *Gender, Change and Identity: mature women students in universities*, Ashgate, Aldershot

Merrill, B. and Collins, T. (1999) European Universities: how accessible are they for adults? Paper presented to Annual Conference of the Universities Association for Continuing Education, University of Cambridge, April 1999

Mhaolrunaigh, S. and Clifford, C. (1997) The Preparation of Teachers for Shared Learning Environments, *Nurse Education Today*, 17, 1-4

Micari, M. (2004) From Science to Citizenship: an analysis of twentieth-century trends in corporate rhetoric on employee education, *Studies in the Education of Adults*, 36, 2, 206-21

Miller, R. (1997) Economic Flexibility and Social Cohesion, *OECD Observer*, 207, 24-27

Miller, R. and Stewart, J. (1999) Opened University, *People Management*, 17 June 1999, 42-6

Ministry of Culture, Education and Science (1998) *'Life-long Learning': the National Action Programme of the Netherlands*, Ministry of Culture, Education and Science, Zoetermeer

Ministry of Reconstruction (1919) *Final Report of the Committee on Adult Education*, His Majesty's Stationery Office, London

Morgan, D. H. (1997) Socialization and the family: change and diversity, pp. 4-29, B. Cosin and M. Hales (eds) *Families, Education and Social Differences*, Routledge, London

Morrell, J., Chowdhury, R. and Savage, B. (2004) *Progression from Adult and Community Learning*, Department for Education and Skills Research Report 546, Nottingham

Murphy, M. (2001) A Challenge to Change, *Adults Learning*, 12, 7, 20-22

Murray, C. (1990) *The Emerging British Underclass*, Institute for Economic Affairs, London

Nadler, L. (1984) *The Handbook of Human Resource Development*, Wiley, New York

Naidoo, V. and Schutte, C. (1999) Virtual Institutions on the African Continent, 89 – 124 in G. M. Farrell (ed) *The Development of Virtual Education: a global perspective*, Commonwealth of Learning, Vancouver

NACETT (1998) *Fast Forward for Skills*, National Advisory Council for Education and Training Targets, London

Nickson, D., Warhurst, C. and Dutton, E. (2004) Aesthetic Labour and the Policy-Making Agenda: time for a reqappraisal of skills?, SKOPE Research Paper no. 48, SKOPE, Oxford/Coventry

Nickson, D., Warhurst, C., Witz, A. and Cullen, A.M. (1998) Aesthetic Labour in the Service Economy: an overlooked development, Paper presented to Third International Labour Market Conference, Robert Gordon University, Aberdeen, June 1998

Nolan, P. (1999) Director's Report, pp. 4-5, *Annual Report 1998-1999*, Workers' Educational Association, Belfast

Nonaka, I. and Takeuchi, H. (1995) *The Knowledge-creating Company: how Japanese companies create the dynamics of innovation*, Oxford University Press, Oxford

Northern Ireland Audit Office (1995) *Community Economic Regeneration Scheme and Community Regeneration and Improvement Special Scheme*, Northern Ireland Office, Belfast

Northern Ireland Audit Office (1996) *Department of the Environment: control of Belfast Action Teams expenditure*, Northern Ireland Office, Belfast

Nuissl, E. (1988) Dreizehn Jahre Bildungsurlaub, *Volkshochschulen im Westen*, 40, 5, 246-8

OECD (1973) *Recurrent Education: a strategy for lifelong learning*, Organisation for Economic Co-operation and Development, Paris

OECD (1991) *Reviews of National Policies for Education: Ireland*, Organisation for Economic Co-operation and Development, Paris

OECD (1994) *OECD Jobs Study*, Organisation for Economic Co-operation and Development, Paris

OECD (1996) *Lifelong Learning for All: Meeting of the Education Committee at Ministerial Level, 16/17 January 1996*, Organisation for Economic Co-operation and Development, Paris

OECD (1997a) *Literacy Skills for the Knowledge Society: further results of the international adult literacy survey*, Organisation for Economic Co-operation and Development, Paris

OECD (1997b) *What Works in Innovation in Education: combatting exclusion through adult learning*, Organisation for Economic Co-operation and Development, Paris

OECD (1999) *Overcoming Exclusion through Adult Learning*, Organisation for Economic Co-operation and Development, Paris

Offe, C. (1985) *Contradictions of the Welfare State*, Verso, London

Octoby, B. (1990) Rover Learning Business – something out of nothing, ESRC Seminar on Researching Lifelong Learning, Department of Management Learning, University of Lancaster, 10 December 1999

Okumoto, K. (2004) Lifelong Learning Policy in England and Japan: A comparative analysis, Ph D Thesis, University of London, Institute of Education

Pahl, R. and Spencer, L. (1997) The politics of friendship, *Renewal*, 5, 3/4, 100-107

Payne, J. (2005) *What Progress is Norway Making with Lifelong Learning? A study of the Norwegian competence reform*, SKOPE Research Paper no. 55, SKOPE, Oxford/Coventry

Petrella, R. (1997) The Snares of the Market Economy for Future Training Policy: beyond the heralding there is a need for denunciation, *Adult Education and Development*, 48, 19-33

Phillips, A. (1987) *Divided Loyalities: dilemmas of sex and class*, Virago, London

Poell, R., Tijmensen, L. and Van der Krogt, F. (1997) Can Learning Projects Help to Develop a Learning Organisation? *Lifelong Learning in Europe*, 2, 2, 67-75

Pouget, M. and Osborne, M. (2004) Accreditation or validation of prior experiential learning: knowledge and savoirs in France – a different perspective? *Studies in Continuing Education*, 26, 1, 45-66

Prusack, L. (1998) Introduction to Series – Why Knowledge, Why Now? pp. ix-x, in D. Neef (ed.), *The Knowledge Economy*, Butterworth-Heinemann, Boston

Purcell, K. (1998) Flexibility in the Labour Market, pp. 69 – 89 in R.M. Lindley and R.A. Wilson (eds) *Review of the Economy and Employment 1997/8*, Institute for Employment Research, Coventry

Purcell, K. and Hogarth, T. (1999) *Graduate Opportunities, Social Class and Age*, Council for Industry and Higher Education, London

Putnam, R. D. (2000) *Bowling Alone: The collapse and revival of American community*, Simon and Schuster, New York

Raggatt, P. and Williams, S. (1999) *Governments, Markets and Vocational Qualifications: an anatomy of policy*, Falmer, Lewes

Ramsay, H. (1996) Managing Sceptically: a critique of organisational fashion, pp. 155-72 in S.R. Clegg and G. Palmer (eds) *The Politics of Management Knowledge*, Sage, London

Rees, G. and Thomas, M. (1994) Inward Investment, Labour Market Adjustment and Skills Development: recent experiences in South Wales, *Local Economy*, 9, 1, 48-61

Reich, R. (1993) *The Work of Nations: preparing ourselves for twentyfirst-century capitalism*, Simon and Schuster, London

Reich, R. (1997) *Locked in the Cabinet*, Random House, New York

Revans, R. (1982) *The Origin and Growth of Action Learning*, Chartwell Bratt, Bromley

Reynolds, D. (1995) Why are the Asians so good at Learning? *Demos Quarterly*, 6, 35-6

Reynolds, J. (1998) Retailing, pp. 37-43 in R.M. Lindley and R.A. Wilson (eds) *Review of the Economy and Employment 1997/98*, Institute for Employment Research, Coventry

Rhodes, R.A.W. (1996) The New Governance: governing without government, *Political Studies*, 44, 4, 652-67

Riché-Magnier, M. and Metthey, J. (1995) Société de l'information: 'new deal' liberal ou nouveau modèle de société? *Revue du marché commun et de l'Union Européenne*, 390, 417-22

Ritzer, G. (1998) *The McDonaldisation Thesis*, Sage, London

Ritzer, G. (2000) *The McDonaldisation of Society*, Pine Forge Press, Thousand Oaks

Rosanvallon, P. (1995) *La nouvelle question sociale: repenser l'État-providence*, Editions du Seuil, Paris

Rose, C. (1996) The future of environmental campaigning, *Journal of the Royal Society of Arts*, 144, 5467, 49-55

Rosenfeld, S. A. (2002) *Just Clusters: Economic development strategies that reach more people and places*, Regional Technology Strategies Inc., Carrboro, North Carolina

Roszak, T. (1981) *Person/Planet*, Granada, London

Rothery, B. (1995) *ISO 14000 and ISO 9000*, Gower, Aldershot

Rover Group (1998) *Success through People*, Rover Group plc, Birmingham

Rubenson, K. (1992) Human Resource Development: a historical perspective, pp. 3-30 in L.E. Burton (ed.), *Developing Resourceful Humans: adult education within the economic context*, Routledge, London

Rubenson, K. (1999) Adult education and training: the poor cousin. An analysis of OECD reviews of national policies for education, *Scottish Journal of Adult and Continuing Education*, 5, 2, 5-32

Rubery, J. and Smith, M. (1999) *The Future European Labour Supply*, Official for Official Publications of the European Communities, Luxembourg

Salisbury, J. and Murcott, A. (1992) Pleasing the Students: teachers' orientation to classroom life in adult education, *Sociological Review*, 40, 3, 561-75

Sandvik, H. (1999) Health Information and Interaction on the Internet: a survey of female urinary incontinence, *British Medical Journal*, 319, July 1999, 29-32

Sarangi, S. (1996) Vocationally Speaking: (further) educational construction of 'workplace identities', *Language and Education*, 10, 2/3, 201-18

Sargant, N., Field, J., Francis, H., Schuller, T. and Tuckett, A. (1997) *The Learning Divide: a study of participation in adult learning in the United Kingdom*, National Institute of Adult Continuing Education, Leicester

Savage, M. (2000) *Class Analysis and Social Transformation*, Open University Press, Buckingham

Scarbrough, H. (1999) System error, *People Management*, 8 April 1999, 68-74

Schemmann, M. (2002), Reflexive Modernisation in Adult Education Research: the example of Anthony Giddens' theoretical approach, pp. 64-80 in A. Bron and M. Schemmann (eds) *Social Science Theories in Adult Education Research*, Lit Verlag, Münster

Schrank, R.C. (1994) Changing the Way People Learn, *Applied Learning Technologies in Europe*, 07, 4-7

Schuller, T. and Field, J. (1999) Is there divergence between initial and continuing education in Scotland and Northern Ireland? *Scottish Journal of Adult Continuing Education*, 5, 2, 61-76.

Schuller, T., Preston, J., Hammond, C., Brassett-Grundy, A. and Bynner, J. (2004), *The Benefits of Learning: the impact of education on health, family life and social capital*, RoutledgeFalmer, London

Schwartz, B. (1985) Re-assessing Braverman: socialisation and dispossession in the history of technology, pp. 189-205 in L. Levidow and B. Young (eds) *Science, Technology and the Labour Process: Marxist studies*, vol. 2, Free Association Books, London

Scott, P. (1995) *The Meanings of Mass Higher Education*, Open University Press, Buckingham

Searle-Chatterjee, M. (1999) Occupation, biography and new social movements, *Sociological Review*, 47, 2, 258-79

Seddon, T. (2004) Rethinking Civic Formation: towards a learning citizen? *London Review of Education*, 2, 3, 171-86

Select Committee on Education and Employment (1999) *Eighth Report: Access for All? A survey of post-16 participation*, House of Commons, London. http://www.publications.parliament.uk/pa/cm199899/cmselect/cmeduemp/57

Sennett, R. (1998) *The Corrosion of Character: the personal consequences of work in the new capitalism*, W.W. Norton, New York

Sennett, R. (2004) *Respect: The formation of character in an age of inequality*, Penguin, London

Shaw, N., Armistead, C., Rodger, J. and Hopwood, V. (2002) *Evaluation of the Union Learning Fund Year 4*, Department for Education and Skills Research Report 378, Nottingham

Sheehy, G. (1976) *Passages: predictable crises of adult life*, Dutton, New York

Sheehy, G. (1996) *New Passages*, Harper Collins, London

Skeggs, B. (1997) *Formations of Class and Gender: Becoming respectable*, Sage, London

Skills and Enterprise Network (1996) Managing Careers in the 21st Century, *Skills and Enterprise Briefing*, 4, August 1996, 3-5

Smidt, L.T. (1999) Use of Information Technology in Adult Education, 44-53, in Arne Carlsen (ed.), *Grundtvig and Europe*, Grunbak, Copenhagen

Smith, J. and Spurling, A. (1999) *Lifelong Learning: riding the tiger*, Cassell, London

Snape, D., Bell, A. and Jones, A. (2004) *Pathways in Adult Learning Survey* (PALS) 2003, Department for Education and Skills, Nottingham

Social Exclusion Unit (2000) *Report of Policy Action Team 16: Learning Lessons*, Cabinet Office, London

Sotarauta, M. (2005) *Resilient City Regions – Mission Impossible? Tales from Finland and beyond about how to build self-renewal capacity*, Observatory PASCAL, Melbourne/Stirling

Stauber, B. and Walther, A. (1998) Lebenslanges Lernen – ein offenes Konzept zwischen normativen Überschuss und der Verdeckung sozialer Ungleichheit, in A. Walther and B. Stauber (eds) *Lifelong Learning in Europe: options for the integration of living, learning*, Neuling Verlag, Tübingen

Strain, M. (2000) Schools in a Learning Society: New purposes and modalities of learning in late modern society, *Educational Management and Administration*, 28, 3, 281-98

Strathdee, R. (2005) *Social Exclusion and the Remaking of Social Networks*, Ashgate, Aldershot

Streumer, J. N., van der Klink, M. and van de Brink, K. (1999) The future of HRD, *International Journal of Lifelong Education*, 18, 4, 259-74

Suoranta, J. and Lehtimäki, H. (2004) *Children in the Information Society: The case of Finland*, Peter Lang, New York

Suoranta, J. and Tomperi, T. (2002) From Gothenburg to Everywhere: Bonfires of revolutionary learning, *Review of Education, Pedagogy and Cultural Studies*, 24, 29-47

Sweeney, K., Morgan, B. and Donnelly, D. (1998) *Adult Literacy in Northern Ireland, Statistics and Research Agency*, Belfast

Tavistock Institute (1999) *A Review of Thirty New Deal Partnerships*, Research and Development Report ESR 32, Employment Service, Sheffield

Taylor, R. (2005) Lifelong Learning and the Labour Governments 1997-2004, *Oxford Review of Education*, 31, 1, 101-18

Thomas, J. E., Takamichi, V. and Suichi, S. (1997) New Lifelong Learning Law in Japan: promise or threat?, *International Journal of Lifelong Education*, 16, 2, 132-40

Thomas, N. and Paterson, I. (1998) *Web Site Assessment: research report,* National Museum of Science and Industry, London. http://www.nmsi.ac.uk/eval/rep. htm

Thomas, R. and Dunkerley, D. (1999) Careering Downwards? Middle managers' experiences in the downsized organisation, *British Journal of Management,* 10, 2, 157-69

Thompson, P. (1989) *The Nature of Work: an introduction to debates on the labour process,* Macmillan, London

Thurow, L. (1994) New game, new rules, new strategies, *Journal of the Royal Society of Arts,* 142, 50-53

Tight, M. (1998a) Bridging the 'learning divide': the nature and politics of participation, *Studies in the Education of Adults,* 30, 2, 110-19

Tight, M. (1998b) Education, Education, Education! The vision of lifelong learning in the Kennedy, Dearing and Fryer reports, *Oxford Review of Education,* 24, 4, 473-85.

Tight, M. (1995) *Education, work and adult life: a literature review,* Research Papers in Education, 10, 3, 383-400

Toffler, A. (1970) *Future Shock,* Random House, New York

Tomlinson, A. (1986) Playing away from home: leisure, disadvantage and issues of income and access, pp. 53-54 in P. Golding (ed) *Excluding the Poor,* Child Poverty Action Group, London

Trades Union Congress (2004) Only One in Four Non-union Workers get Regular Training, Press Release 18 May 2004, Accessed on 31 May 2005 at www.learning services.org.uk/national/learning-3706-f0.cfm

Trivellato, P. (1996) Japan as a Learning Society: an overall view by a European sociologist, pp. 185-206 in F. Coffield (ed) *A National Strategy for Lifelong Learning,* Economic and Social Research Council/University of Newcastle, Newcastle

Tuckett, A. and Sargant, N. (1999) *Marking Time: the NIACE survey on adult participation in learning 1999,* National Institute of Adult Continuing Education, Leicester

Tuijnman, A. (2003) Measuring Lifelong Learning in the New Economy, *Compare,* 33, 4, 471-82

Tuomisto, J. (1998) Demands and Possibilities for Lifelong Learning in a Market-oriented Society: a Finnish perspective on public policy and reality, pp 155-67 in J. Holford, P. Jarvis and C. Griffin (eds) *International Perspectives on Lifelong Learning,* Kogan Page, London

Tyers, C. and Sinclair, A. (2004) *Tracking Learning Outcomes: Evaluation of the impact of Ufi,* Department for Education and Skills Research Report 569, Nottingham

UK Coal plc (2004) *Annual Report and Accounts 2003,* UK Coal plc, Doncaster

UNESCO Institute for Education (2004) Synthesis Report: Recommitting to adult education and learning, *Adult Education and Development,* 61, 125-48

United Kingdom Central Council (1992) *The Scope of Professional Practice,* UKCC, London

Unwin, L. (1996) Employer-led Realities: apprenticeship past and present, *Journal of Vocational Education and Training,* 48, 1, 57-69

Unwin, L. (1999) 'Flower Arranging's Off but Floristry is On': lifelong learning and adult education in further education colleges, pp. 69 – 85 in A. Green and N. Lucas (eds) *FE and Lifelong Learning: Realigning the sector for the twenty-first century*, Institute of Education, London

Unwin, L. and Wellington, J. (1995) Reconstructing the Work-based Route: lessons from the Modern Apprenticeship, *Journal of Vocational Education and Training*, 47, 6, 337-52

Usher, R. and Bryant, I. (1989) *Adult Education as Theory, Practice and Research: the captive triangle*, Routledge, London

van den Toren, J.P. (1999) Employability: how to organise the individualisation of the labour market, Paper presented to Fourth International Labour Market Conference, Robert Gordon University, Aberdeen, October 1999

van der Kamp (1997) The Netherlands: impacts of a new policy environment, in P. Bélanger and S. Valdavielso (eds) *The Emergence of Learning Societies: who participates in adult learning?* Pergamon, Oxford

Vaughan, L. (1999) When the drugs won't work, *Financial Times*, 17 June 1999

Vehviläinen, S. (2001) Evaluative Advice in Educational Counseling: the use of disagreement in the 'Stepwise Entry' to advice, *Research on Language and Social Interaction*, 34, 3, 371-98

Vester, M. (1997) Soziale Milieus und Individualisierung. Mentalitäten und Konfliktlinien im historischen Wandel, pp. 99-123 in U. Back and P. Sopp (eds.) *Individualisierung und Integration: Neue Konfliktlinien und neuer Integrationsmodus*, Leske and Budrich, Opladen

Vision Consultancy Group (1999) *Opportunities in Streaming Media*, http://www.visionconsult.com

Walsh, J. (1996) Multinational management strategy and human resource decision making in the single European market, *Journal of Management Studies*, 35, 5, 633-48

Ward, M. E. (1999) Club members relax over a couple of pints and an investment portfolio, *Irish Times*, 27 August 1999, Business supplement 2, 3

Waterman, R.H., Waterman, J.A. and Collard, B.A. (1996) Toward a career-resilient workforce, pp. 207-220, in P. Raggatt, R. Edwards and N. Small (eds) *The Learning Society: challenges and trends*, Routledge, London

Weiss, L. (1997) Globalization and the Myth of the Powerless State, *New Left Review*, 225, 3-27

Werner, H. (1994) Economic change, the labour market and migration in the single European market, in D. Marsden (ed) *European Integration and the European Labour Market*, Supplement 1/94 to Social Europe.

West, L. (1996) *Beyond Fragments: adults, motivation and higher education: a biographical analysis*, Taylor and Francis, London

West, L. (1998) Intimate Cultures of Lifelong Learning: on gender and managing change, pp. 555-83 in P. Alheit and E. Kammler (eds) *Lifelong Learning and its Impact on Social and Regional Development*, Donat Verlag, Bremen

West Belfast Economic Forum (1994) *Response to Consultative Document, Making Belfast Work: Strategy Proposals*, Belfast, WBEF

West Midlands Regional TECs (1999) *West Midlands Region: household survey 1998*, West Midlands Regional Training and Enterprise Councils, Birmingham

Westat, K. K., and Creighton, S. (2000) *Participation in Adult Education in the United States: 1998-99*, US Department for Education, Washington.

Wilcox, D. (1998) The European Dimension, *CivicNet Chautauqua*, http://www.civicnet.org/civicnet

Wilkinson, D. (2003) *New Deal for People Aged 25 and Over: A synthesis report*, Department of Work and Pensions, Sheffield

Williams, S. and Raggatt, P. (1998) Contexualising Public Policy in Vocational Education and Training: the origins of competence-based vocational qualifications policy in the UK, *Journal of Education and Work*, 11, 3, 275-92

Wilson, J. (1999) Larry's Legacy, *Continental*, October 1999, 50-52

Wilterdink, N. (1993) The European Ideal: an examination of European and national identity, *Archives européennes de sociologie*, 34, 119-36

Wright, S. (2001) Activating the Unemployed: the street-level implementation of UK policy, pp. 235-50 in J. Clasen (ed.) *What Future for Social Security?* Kluwer Law International, Dordrecht

Wright, T. G. R. (1996) *Bradford Mechanics' Institute in the Nineteenth Century*, M. Phil. Thesis, University of Leeds

World Bank (1995) *Global Economic Prospects and the Developing Countries*, World Bank, Washington

Wu, M.-L. (2000) *Auf dem Weg zur Lerngesellschaft: Eine vergleichende Studie über Deutschland und Taiwan in den 90er Jahren*, Verlag Dr Köster, Berlin

Yeaxlee, B. (1921) *An Educated Nation*, Oxford University Press, London

Young, M. (1998) *The Curriculum of the Future: from the 'new sociology of education' to a critical theory of learning*, Falmer, London

Ziehe, T. (1998) Die Modernisierung der Lernkultur, pp. 124-32 in A. Walther and B. Stauber (eds.) *Lifelong Learning in Europe: options for the integration of living, learning*, Neuling Verlag, Tübingen

Index

children 19, 21, 65, 149, 153-4, 160
citizenship 12-3, 16, 28, 31, 54, 66-7, 165-7, 169
  see also corporate citizenship, social capital
class 107, 125-7, 160
Cleese, J. 65
Clinton, B. 79
Cloonan, M. 123, 139
Coaching 106
Coffield, F. 45, 76, 131
communications skills 85, 88, 100
community based learning 147, 166, 169
community development 36, 40, 76
community, imaginary 67, 167
competitiveness 11, 16-7
compulsion 25, 86, 97, 107, 122, 130-6
confidence 114, 146
Connery, S. 169
constructivism 23
  see also meaning
consumerism 4, 55, 82, 86-7, 111-2, 119, 122
consumption 54, 172
continuing professional development 86, 132
corporate citizenship 170-1
corporate universities 32, 91-2
corruption – *see* fraud
counselling 59, 66, 72, 173; *see also therapy*
creativity 39, 152-3, 155
'credentialism' 96
crime 103, 114, 122
Cross, K.P. 149
Crowther, J. 80, 107, 172
cultural capital 62
cynicism 95, 100, 111

Dahrendorf, R. 35
Daimler-Benz 91
Davies, P. 159
de-industrialisation 81, 87
delayering 94-5
Delors, J. 11, 16
Denmark 19, 101, 131, 157
deskilling 80, 88, 117
Dickens, C. 125
disability 123, 138
disaffection 134, 150
Dohmen, G. 12, 35
Dore, R. 117
Dubar, C. 80, 82, 84, 106-7, 121, 161-2
Dumazadier, J. 45, 77
Dumbing down 76, 119-20
Durkheim, E. 69

Easyjet 93
Ecclestone, K. 155
Economic and Social Research Council 46, 176
Edwards, R. 22, 76, 130, 156
emancipation 18, 26, 59 112, 130, 142
'emotional labour' – *see* affective skills
emotional competence 152, 173
employability 103-4, 106-7, 121
Encarta 64
enlightenment 22, 142
entertainment 65, 68, 75
environment, environmentalism 43, 62, 66, 70, 136, 141, 148, 166, 173-4
equality 113
ethnicity 19, 42, 129-30, 138, 141, 168
e-University 148

European Commission 11-2, 15-6, 25, 26, 30, 41, 46, 82, 84, 93, 98, 100-2, 105, 120, 150, 152-3, 163
European Structural Funds 42, 133-4, 139
European Union 9, 12, 16, 30, 42, 103, 111, 129, 133-4, 137
European Year of Lifelong Learning 11, 35
everyday life 72
experiential learning 99-100, 109-10
expertise, expert knowledge 20, 24, 69-70, 76, 174

failure 115, 121, 124-5, 143, 149, 173
family 19, 21, 63-5, 76, 121, 141, 153-6, 167
fashion 58-63, 72, 75, 85-6, 87, 145, 152
Faure, E. 13, 149
Felstead, A. 76, 81, 82, 88, 95, 96, 106
feminism 80, 114, 141, 173
Fenwick, T. 58, 59, 80, 83, 128, 153
Filander, K. 76, 153
Finland 12, 49, 50, 101, 117-8
first aid 133
First World War 47
fitness 55-8, 60, 62, 106
'flat organisation' 94
flexibility 84-5, 87, 88, 92, 95-100, 103, 104-5, 111, 118-9, 138-9, 141, 153, 161, 172
Fordism 89, 118, 129
Forrester, K. 147, 168
France 13, 14, 64, 84, 99, 139-40, 153, 158
fraud 36-7, 148
Freire, P. 113